SOCIAL MEDIA FOR SENIORS MADE EASY

Connecting You to Friends & Family

By James Bernstein

Copyright © 2021 by James Bernstein. All rights reserved.

All rights reserved. This book or any portion thereof
may not be reproduced or used in any manner whatsoever
without the express written permission of the publisher
except for the use of brief quotations in a book review.

Printed in the United States of America

Bernstein, James
Social Media for Seniors Made Easy
Part of the Computers for Seniors series

For more information on reproducing sections of this book or sales of this book,
go to **madeeasybookseries.com**

Contents

Introduction 6

Chapter 1 – Social Media Overview 7
    What is Social Media? 7
    Getting Yourself Online Using your Computer or Smartphone 7
    Web Browsers 12

Chapter 2 – Facebook 16
    Facebook Overview 16
    Signing Up for an Account 16
    The Facebook Interface 19
    Editing Your Profile 24
    Inviting Friends (Friend Requests) 28
    Sending Messages 32
    Creating Posts 34
    Joining Groups and Following Others 38
    Games 43
    Facebook Marketplace 46
    Account Settings & Security 54
    Facebook Mobile App 60
    Deleting Your Account 63

Chapter 3 – Instagram 65
    Instagram Overview 65
    Signing Up for an Account 65
    Installing and using the Instagram App 73
    Sharing Photos and Videos 78

Adding a Profile Picture 81

Following Others and Follow Requests 83

Liking and Commenting on Posts 90

Instagram Feed and Search 94

Reels 96

Notification Settings 99

Chapter 4 – Twitter 103

The Twitter Interface 103

Signing Up for an Account 106

Installing the Smartphone App 110

Profile Settings 111

Composing Tweets 113

Hashtags 116

Following Others 117

Liking, Commenting and Sharing Tweets 121

Notifications 123

Chapter 5 – Pinterest 127

Pinterest Overview 127

Signing Up for an Account 128

Editing Your Profile 131

Creating Pins 134

Creating Boards 143

Sharing Pins and Boards 150

Chapter 6 – YouTube 153

YouTube Overview 153

Signing Up for an Account 153

Searching for Videos.. 157

Watching Videos 159

Liking, Commenting, Subscribing and Sharing 166

Creating a Channel for Your Videos 171

Uploading Videos 177

YouTube Studio 182

Chapter 7 - WhatsApp 186

WhatsApp Overview... 186

Installing and Configuring the Mobile App 186

Sending Text and Voice Messages 193

Making Voice and Video Calls 200

Using WhatsApp on Your Computer 202

Settings.. 208

Chapter 8 - Staying Safe Online 211

Email Scams.. 211

Phone Scams 212

Website Popups 213

Fake Antivirus Software 214

File Encryption Scams (Ransomware) 215

Fake Websites 215

Secure vs. Unsecure Websites 216

Providing Personal Information 221

Browser Toolbars 224

What's Next? 226

About the Author 229

Introduction

You might have noticed that people like to stay in touch with each other online using their computers and smartphones more than in person. And like it or not, if you insist on only communicating the old fashioned way then you might find yourself talking to yourself rather than your friends and family!

Many people don't like to learn new things which makes a lot of sense but sometimes it's best to just "bite the bullet" and dive in and try to become familiar with new technology so you can join the rest of the world and see all of the things that the internet has to offer.

The best way to do this is to sign up for some social media accounts to get in touch with friends from your past and stay in touch with your family, and maybe even make some new friends at the same time. You would be surprised how easy it is to get in touch with people you have lost contact with over the years.

Not all social media platforms are for communicating with friends and family but are rather used to express your ideas, advertise your goods and services or even find a new job. You can join as many of these services as you like and if you realize you don't like a particular platform, you can just delete your account. For the most part, all social media platforms are free to use even though you might be prompted to sign up for some sort of "premium service" which you can usually just say no to.

The goal of this book is to get you familiar with the most commonly used social media accounts that are used by more "mature" users and to show you how to sign up for these accounts. I will also be going over how to do things such as create your profile, post pictures and videos, perform online chats, search for other people and so on.

As with all my books, I make the content as easy as possible to follow so users at any skill level can easily follow along. I will also include screenshot images to help you visualize what the content of the book is describing. One thing you might find useful is to follow along with your accounts while reading to make things easier to understand.

So on that note, let's start sharing our lives with our loved ones!

Chapter 1 – Social Media Overview

As you may or may not realize, the internet and social media have changed the way we do things from sending birthday wishes to running a large scale business. It's gotten to the point where without it, many people wouldn't know what to do with themselves and many companies would lose a large percentage of their profits.

If you are reading this book then obviously you are ready to take the social media plunge or if you have already gotten your feet wet, you are looking to fine tune your skills to make yourself a more proficient social media user.

What is Social Media?
The term social media refers to using technology such as websites and applications to enable you to share content such as photos and videos, connect with people and maybe even influence people to buy something you might be selling or to support a particular cause you might believe in.

Social Media is a powerful tool and can be used for good and can also be used by people looking to cause harm or steal information or money. With that being said, you need to be very careful when using whichever platforms you choose to use to avoid becoming a potential victim. But if you keep things simple and take basic precautions, you should be just fine and not run into any real trouble.

What you can do with social media will depend on what platform you decide you want to use. For example, Facebook will let you start a page for your business while LinkedIn will only let you post your profile with relevant job experiences and your resume. And if you are only looking to post pictures of your grandkids or projects around the house then Instagram might be all you need.

Once you read through the various chapters in this book you should have a good idea of which types of accounts you wish to use and also how to use them since they all vary quite a bit. Or you might even decide that you don't want to use any type of social media!

Getting Yourself Online Using your Computer or Smartphone
The first step in using social media is being to get on the internet since all the platforms require an internet connection to use. There are many ways to get online, and you can use devices such as your desktop PC, laptop, tablet or

Chapter 1 – Social Media Overview

smartphone. Once you sign up for your account, you can then access it from any of these devices and all of the information will be identical so you don't need to worry about your laptop not having the same information and your phone for example. You can even access your accounts from other people's devices and everything will be current as well.

When using social media on a computer, you will most likely access your accounts using your web browser. All computers come with web browsers, so it doesn't matter if you are using a Windows PC or a Mac, even though there are different web browsers available to both types of computers. By the way, a web browser is the software that connects your computer to the internet and lets you view web pages. Google Chrome, Firefox, Microsoft Edge and Safari are all examples of web browsers.

To access a particular social media website, you can type in the name in the browser search box and click on the result you want (figure 1.1). Or you can type in the actual address of the site in the address bar such as **www.facebook.com** (figure 1.2).

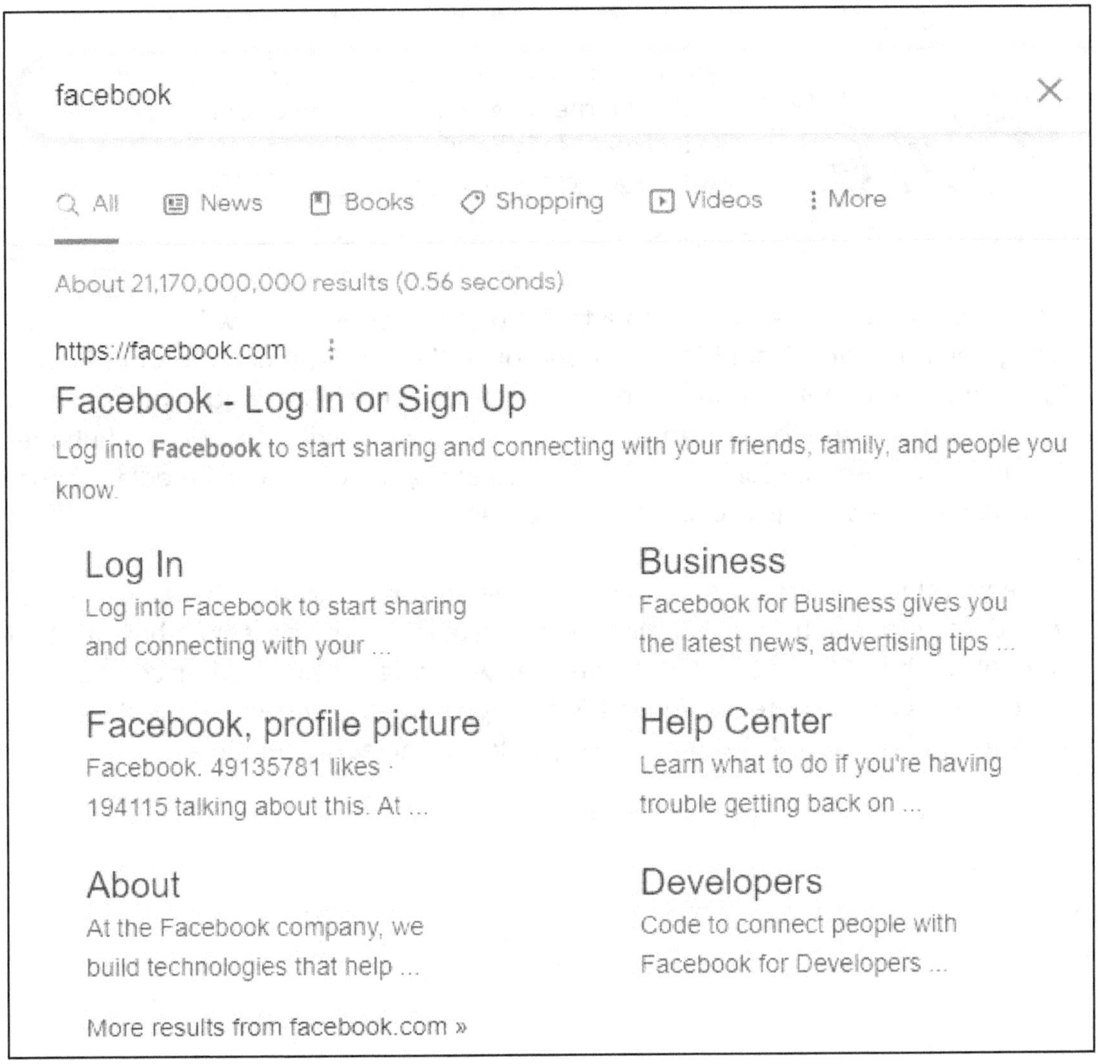

Chapter 1 – Social Media Overview

facebook ✕

🔍 All　📰 News　📘 Books　🛍 Shopping　▶ Videos　⋮ More

About 21,170,000,000 results (0.56 seconds)

https://facebook.com ⋮
Facebook - Log In or Sign Up
Log into **Facebook** to start sharing and connecting with your friends, family, and people you know.

Log In
Log into Facebook to start sharing and connecting with your ...

Business
Facebook for Business gives you the latest news, advertising tips ...

Facebook, profile picture
Facebook. 49135781 likes · 194115 talking about this. At ...

Help Center
Learn what to do if you're having trouble getting back on ...

About
At the Facebook company, we build technologies that help ...

Developers
Code to connect people with Facebook for Developers ...

More results from facebook.com »

Figure 1.1

Figure 1.2

Chapter 1 – Social Media Overview

If you want to learn more about web browsers and how to use the internet in general, then check out my book titled **The Internet Made Easy**
https://www.amazon.com/dp/1074973836

When accessing your accounts on a tablet or smartphone, you will most likely be using apps that you install for each platform. You can still use the built in web browser on your tablet or phone, but the apps do a much better job and are easier to use. All you need to do is go to the Play Store (Android) or App Store (iPhones and iPads) and search for the app that goes along with the social media account you wish to use such as Facebook or Instagram.

Once you find the app you need, simply search for it and then install it like you would any other app that you might have installed in the past. Just be sure that the app is the right one and not one that was created by another company or developer. As you can see in figure 1.3, the app name is *Twitter* and the developer who created the app is *Twitter, Inc.* so you know the app is legitimate.

Chapter 1 – Social Media Overview

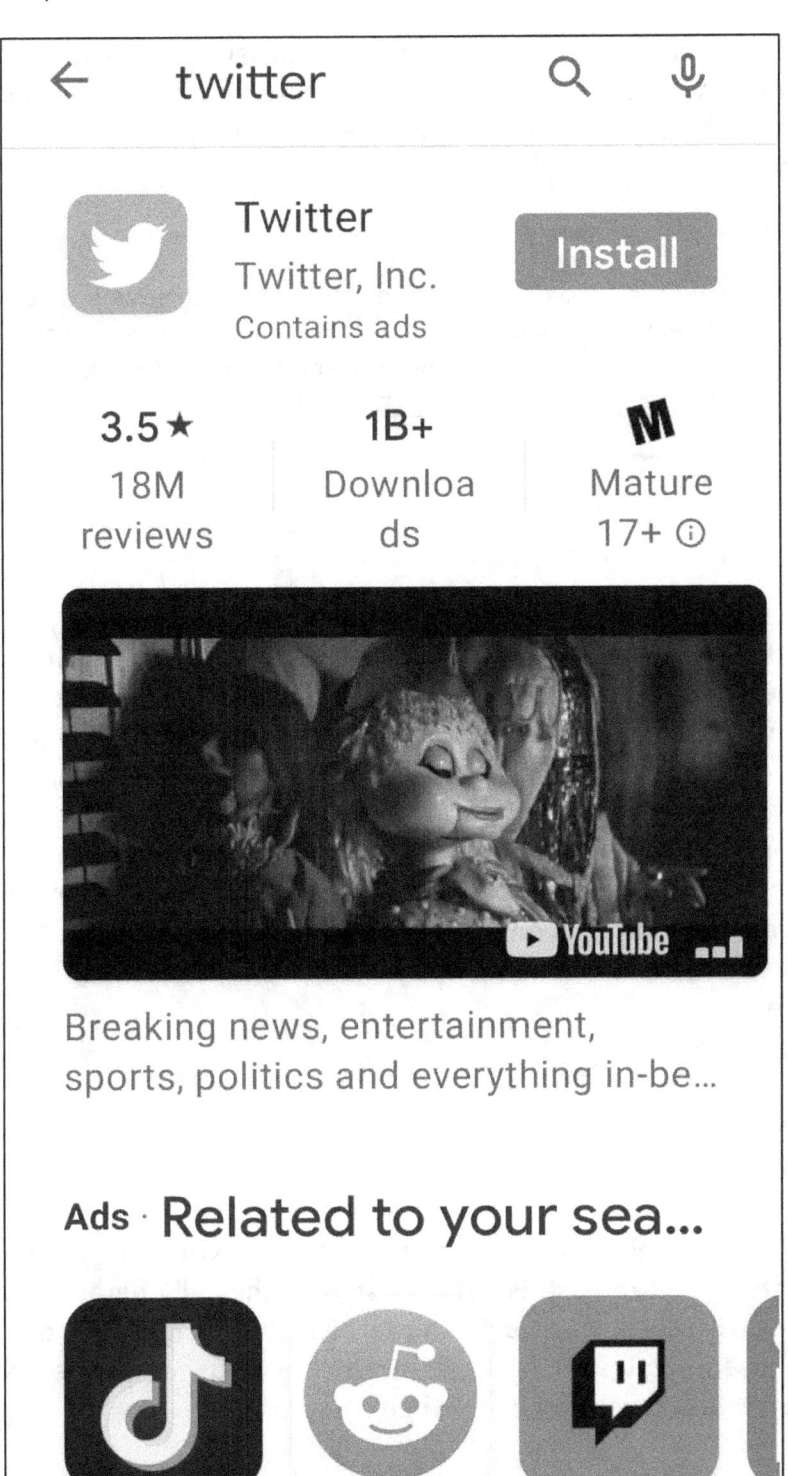

Figure 1.3

Chapter 1 – Social Media Overview

Once you tap on Install and finish the process, you would either sign in with your username and password and everything will be there where you left it. I will be going over how to sign up for social media accounts when I get into the chapters on each type of platform.

If you have an Android based smartphone or tablet and want to improve your skills to help you master your device, then check out my book titled **Android Smartphones Made Easy**. https://www.amazon.com/dp/1086026837

Web Browsers

Like I mentioned in the last section, web browsers are software installed on your computer or mobile device that are used to display the text and images from websites. Most computers and other devices come with one or more already installed, but you can install others and use more than one at a time. For example, Windows computers will come preinstalled with the Edge web browser and Apple computers (and iPhones) will come preinstalled with the Safari web browser. When reading this information, keep in mind that the process for various tasks will vary between browsers and it's impossible to show every process for every browser. Here is a listing of the more commonly used web browsers:

- Google Chrome
- Microsoft Edge
- Opera
- Safari
- Mozilla Firefox

You can install more than one web browser on your computer so you can try them out and find the one that you like best. For the most part, they all operate in a similar fashion, but they will vary in ways such as how the menu items are laid out, how bookmarks are used, and also how they perform. Plus, they are all customizable to some degree so you can tweak them to your liking.

Chapter 1 – Social Media Overview

 Different web browsers will perform differently depending on what you are using them on. For example, Google Chrome might perform better on an Android smartphone compared to an iPhone since Google makes the Android operating system.

Figure 1.4 shows an example of the Microsoft Edge web browser that comes installed with Windows. As you can see, there are a lot of components that make up a web browser, but that doesn't mean you should be intimidated by them.

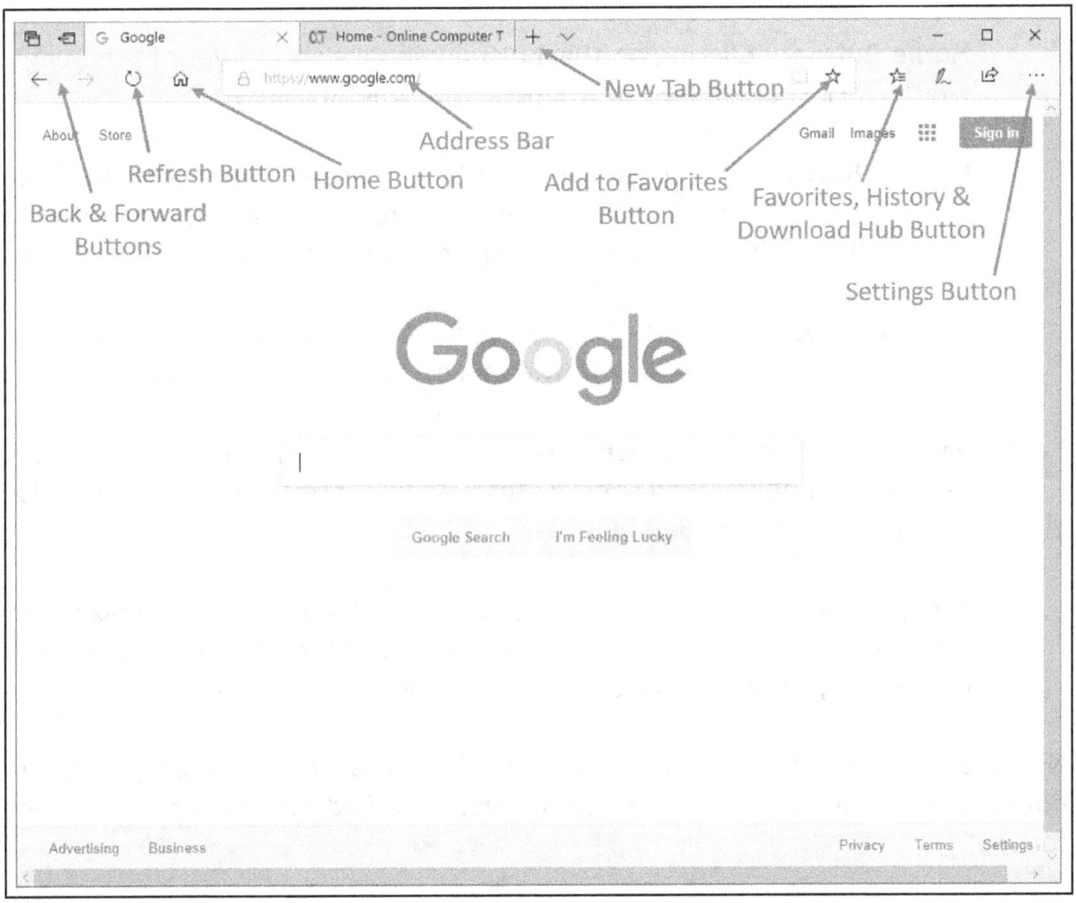

Figure 1.4

Now I will go over each of the main areas of a typical web browser. Keep in mind that they can vary a bit from browser to browser.

Chapter 1 – Social Media Overview

- **Address Bar** – This is where you type the website addresses you want to go to if you prefer to do that rather than do a search for the site.

- **New Tab Button** – All modern browsers allow you to have multiple website pages open within one web browser session. Simply click the new tab button and it will open up another page that you can use to browse to another site while leaving your other pages open.

- **Add to Favorites Button** – Use this button to add websites that you are on to your favorites so you can easily find them later and go back to them. Favorites are also known as bookmarks.

- **Home Button** – Clicking on this button will take you to your home page, which can be customized to whatever you want it to be.

- **Refresh Button** – If you want to reload the web page you are on to check for updates or in case it doesn't seem to be responding, you can press this button. (F5 on the keyboard will do the same thing if you use Windows.)

- **Back & Forward Buttons** – You can cycle backward and forwards through all the pages you have been to within a certain tab with these buttons.

- **Favorites, History & Download** – If you go here, you can view your favorites or bookmarked sites, go through your browsing history, and also look at your downloaded files.

- **Settings Button** – This is where you can configure and customize your browser to suit your needs. You can also do things like set your default home page, clear your history, and check out your saved passwords.

Now that you can see the main components of a typical web browser, you can try out some other browsers to see how they work and find the one that works best for you.

I like to stick with one web browser because once you start having it save things (like your information, bookmarks, and passwords) it will make things more complicated when switching back and forth between other browsers since one will most likely have information stored that another won't.

Chapter 1 – Social Media Overview

To install another web browser simply go to the website for that browser, download the installation file, and install it like you would any other program on your computer. For mobile devices, you can go to the App Store or Play Store and install a new browser from there.

Once you find the browser you want to stick with, then it's a good idea to make it your default browser on your computer or mobile device. How to do that is beyond the scope of this book and varies between operating systems, so you might want to get some help with the process. The reason you want to do this is because if you click on a link within an email, for example, your computer will use its default web browser to open the website, so you want to make sure it's using the right browser. Another option is to uninstall the browsers you don't want so you only have one.

Chapter 2 – Facebook

Out of all the social media platforms, Facebook is probably the most popular and widely used (depending on who you ask). Although it's not as popular with the really young crowd as it is with us older folks, it still has plenty of members to keep it going. As of this writing, Facebook has almost 3 billion monthly users. Yes, billion with a B.

Facebook Overview
Facebook started back in February of 2004 in Cambridge MA and became available to the public in September of 2006. It was originally called TheFacebook and was created by Mark Zuckerberg and Dmy Lin and some other fellow Harvard University students. It was originally limited to Harvard students only and gradually made its way to other universities across the United States and Canada and was then made available to anyone over 13 with an email address.

Facebook has many features but the main area that most people use is called the News Feed. This section shows you posts made by your friends and any pages or groups you follow. You will also find things like a news section with all the latest news stories, various videos you can watch and also a marketplace where you can buy and sell used items from and to other Facebook members.

Facebook is not only for individual users but also for people who want to form a group for some type of cause etc. and also for businesses to create pages to display their goods and services. Many musical groups also use Facebook to list tour dates and new albums. So you can see there is much more to Facebook than finding your old high school friends! But once you do find your long lost friends you can have online chats with them to catch up on things.

Signing Up for an Account
The first thing you need to do before logging on to Facebook is create an account which is easy to do and also free. Simply go to the Facebook website (facebook.com) on your computer or download the Facebook app on your smartphone or tablet and sign up with your email address and a secure password.

Once you click on *Create new account* you will be prompted to enter some details such as your name, email address or phone number, birthdate and so on.

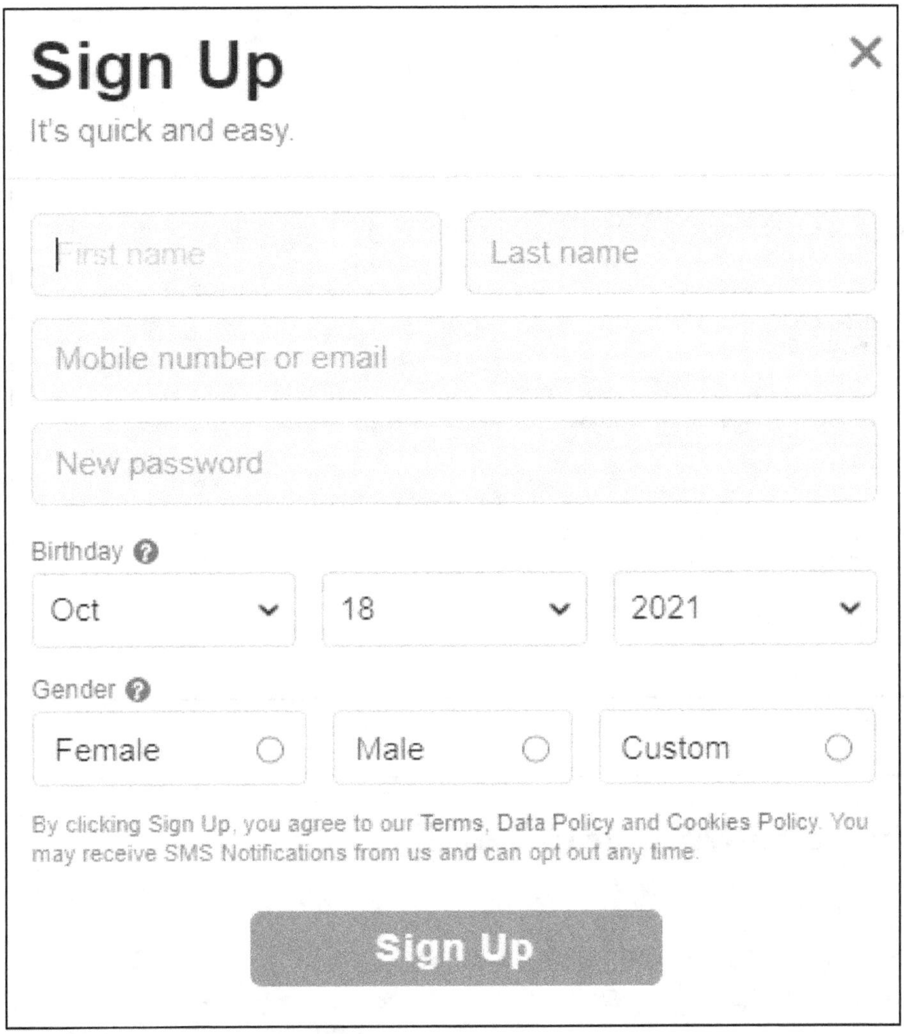

Chapter 2 – Facebook

Sign Up
It's quick and easy.

[First name] [Last name]

[Mobile number or email]

[New password]

Birthday ❓

[Oct ▼] [18 ▼] [2021 ▼]

Gender ❓

Female ○   Male ○   Custom ○

By clicking Sign Up, you agree to our Terms, Data Policy and Cookies Policy. You may receive SMS Notifications from us and can opt out any time.

Sign Up

Figure 2.1

Facebook uses your age to make sure that you can see age appropriate content but that doesn't mean you need to be completely truthful when entering this information if you don't want to be. I'm sure many users say they are older than they are rather than younger for this step.

Once you click on *Sign Up,* you will receive an email (figure 2.2) to the email address that you used to sign up with. It will include a confirmation code that you will need to enter into the box that you will be presented with on the next screen (figure 2.3).

Chapter 2 – Facebook

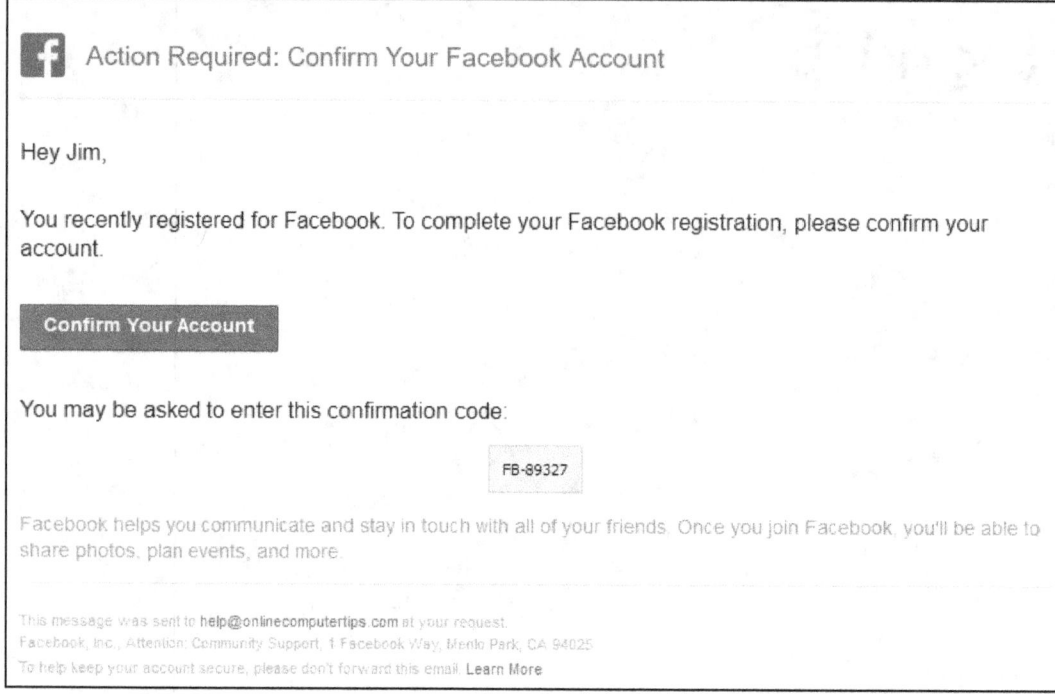

Figure 2.2

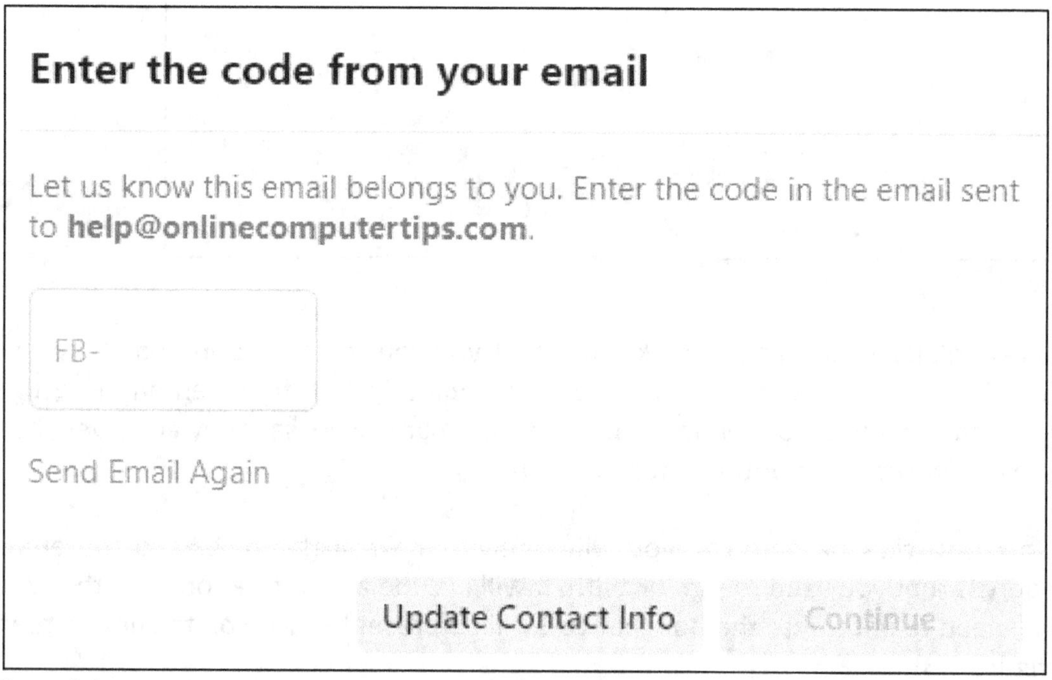

Figure 2.3

After you enter the confirmation code you will be logged into your new account and see the main Facebook page.

Chapter 2 – Facebook

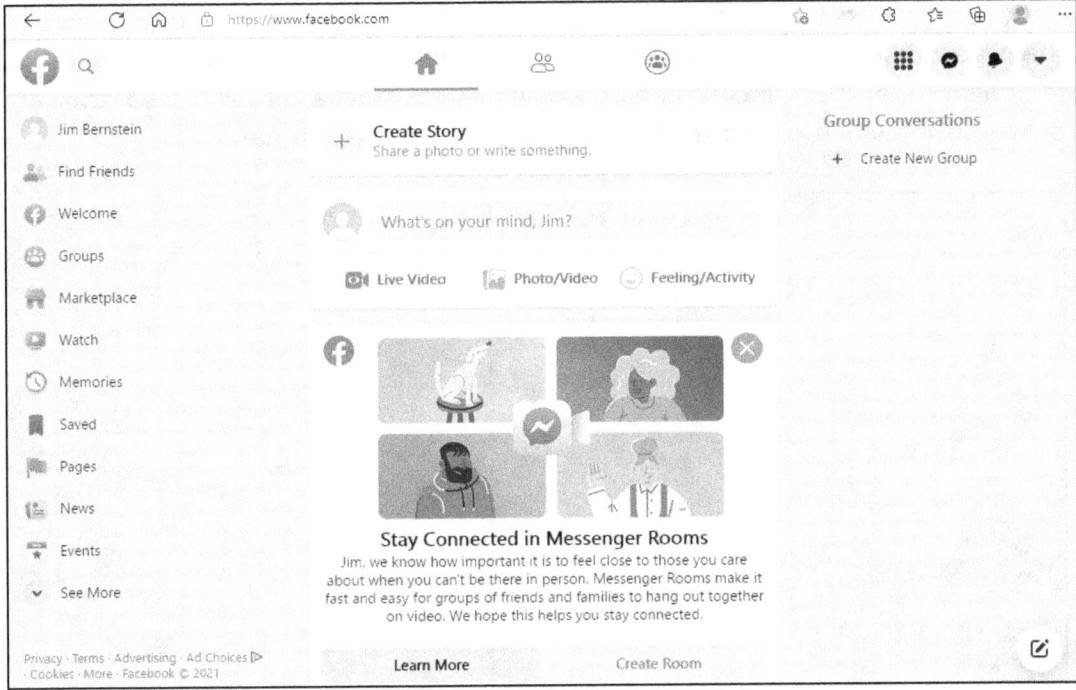

Figure 2.4

The Facebook Interface

Now that you are logged in to your new Facebook account, you might be wondering what you are even looking at and may even be a bit overwhelmed. Don't worry because you most likely will not even use a large majority of the functions that you see on your page.

The Facebook interface is broken down into sections or groups and what you see here will vary depending on things such as your friend's activities, groups you follow, things you have searched for on Facebook and so on.

I had mentioned the News Feed at the beginning of the chapter, and this can be seen in the center of the page in figure 2.4. This is where you will see content from your friends, people and groups you follow as well as other things you might not be interested in such as advertisements.

At the left side of the page in figure 2.4, you will see many different items such as a place to watch videos, search for friends, see weather reports, view other pages you might have for your business, read the news and much more. I would take some time and poke around here just to get an idea of what types of things you can access from the many choices in this section.

Chapter 2 – Facebook

Until you connect with other people such as friends and family, the right side of the page will seem a little bare. Once you accumulate some friends, they will start to appear here, and you can then do things such as start a chat and see if they are online or not which is indicated by a green dot next to their name.

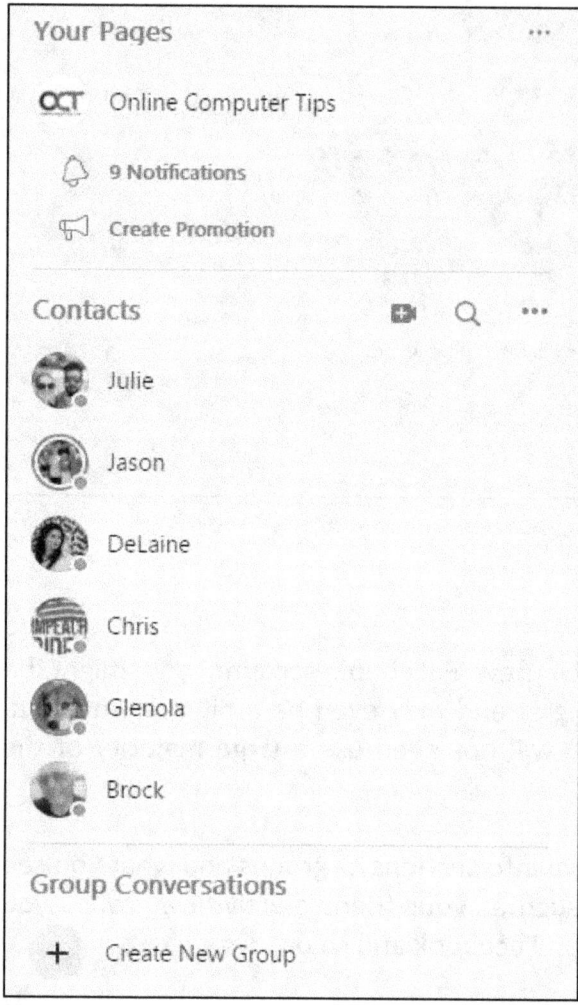
Figure 2.5

At the top of the page, you will see various icons that represent different types of categories. The icons that you have may vary depending on what features of Facebook you use or have used.

Figure 2.6

Chapter 2 – Facebook

It's always a good idea to know how to get back to your main home page which is what you see when you log in because if you are clicking around certain areas, you might find it difficult to get back to where you started from. Clicking on the *Home* icon will take you back to where you started from.

The *Pages* icon is used to take you to any extra Facebook pages that you have created for things like a special group or a business page. If you don't have any additional pages, then you won't see this icon here.

The *Watch* icon will take you to the Facebook video feed where you can watch various videos. At first the content will be random but as you spend more time on certain types of videos such as funny dog clips for example, Facebook will start putting more of those types of videos in the Watch section.

You will probably have a *Groups* section where you can create and join groups that you might be interested in. Facebook will use your location to try and find groups that are local to you.

At the top right of the page, you will see a circle with 9 boxes inside. This is the Facebook Menu, and you will see various items here such as a place to create a new post (discussed later), start a new chat room, create a new page and so on.

Chapter 2 – Facebook

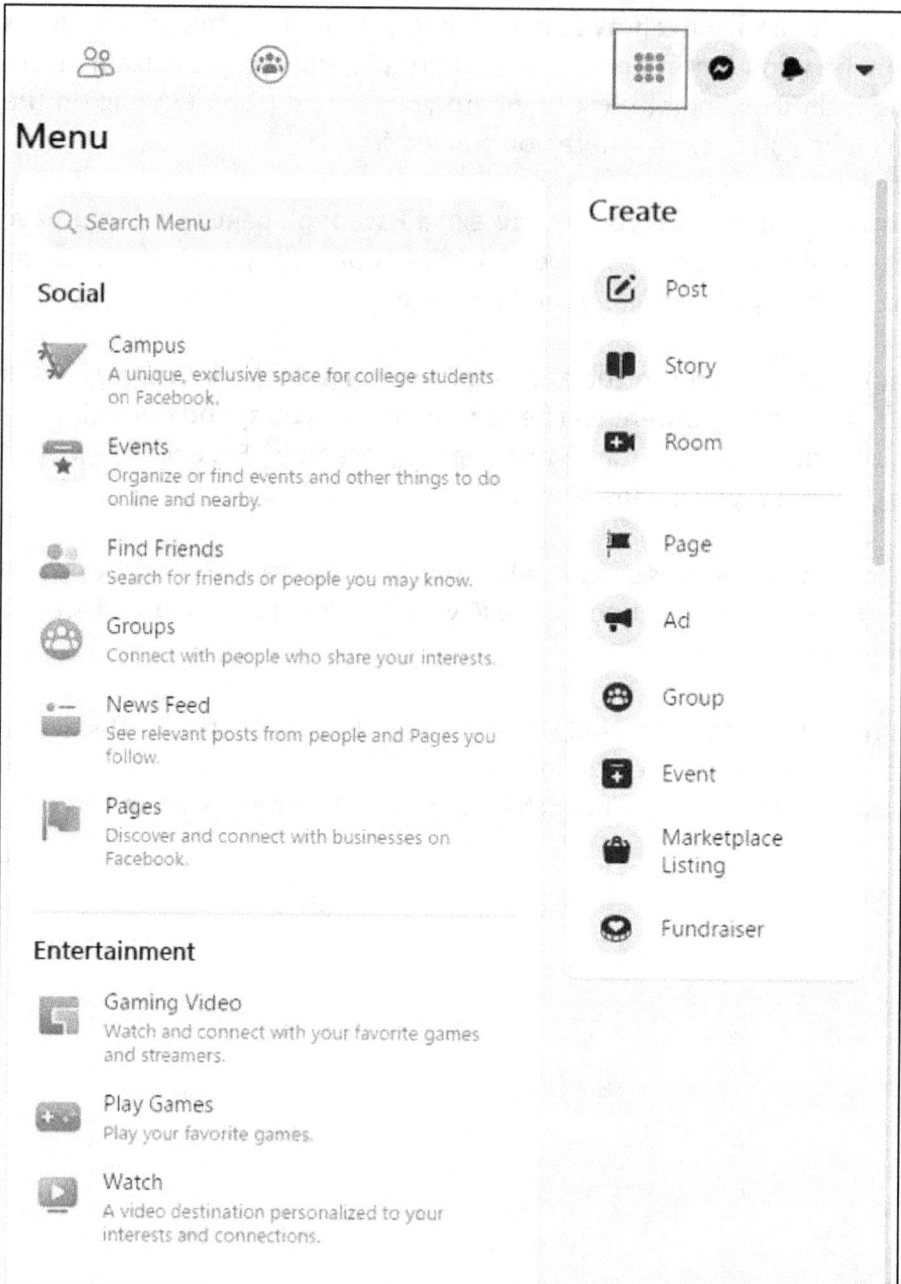

Figure 2.7

The icon next to that is the *Messenger* feature and I will be discussing this later in the chapter.

Next to that, you have your Notifications (bell icon), and here is where you will be alerted about things such as a new post from a friend, new friend requests, notifications on your additional pages and so on. When you log in you will see a number on the icon letting you know how many new notifications you have.

Figure 2.8

At the top right of the page, you will see a down arrow icon and when you click on that, you will have options to adjust your settings (discussed later chapter), get help, change accessibility options such as enable dark mode and keyboard shortcuts, and log out of your account.

You can also click where it says *See your profile* to make changes there. This will be discussed in the next section.

Chapter 2 – Facebook

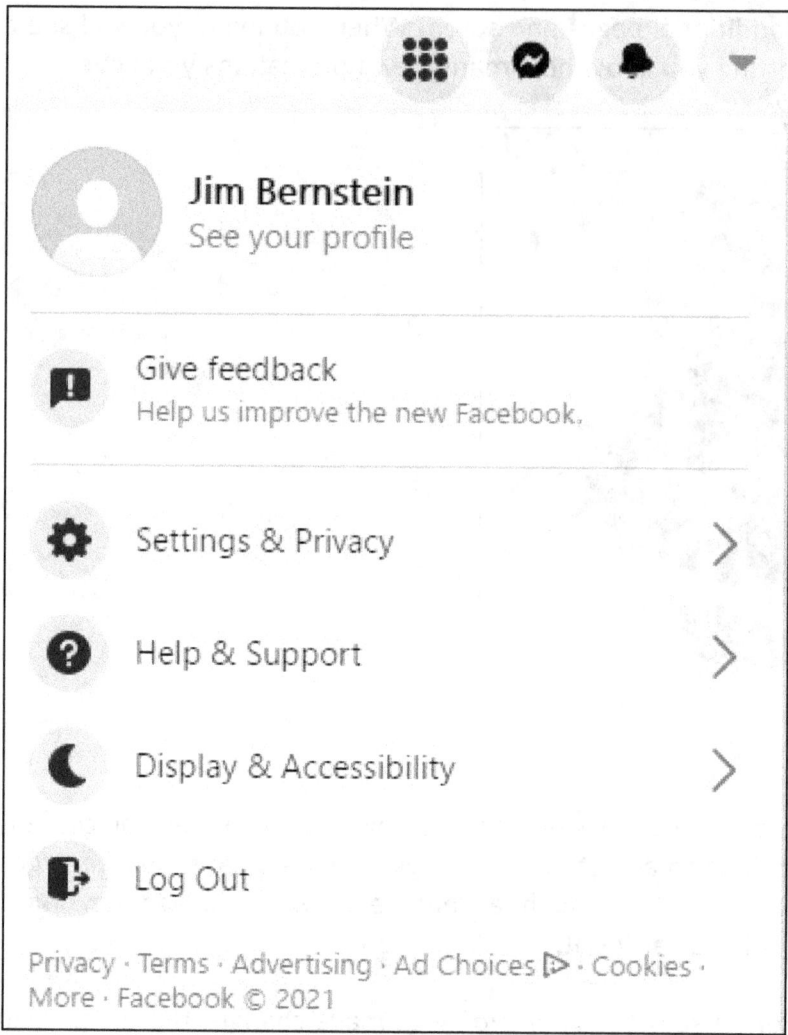

Figure 2.9

Editing Your Profile

Most people like to personalize their profile and add things like a picture of themselves, where they work, where they live, where they went to school, if they are in a relationship or not, and so on.

To get to these settings simply, click the down arrow as seen in figure 2.9 and then click where it says *See your profile*.

To add information about yourself you can go to the *About* section and then click on the type of information you wish to add.

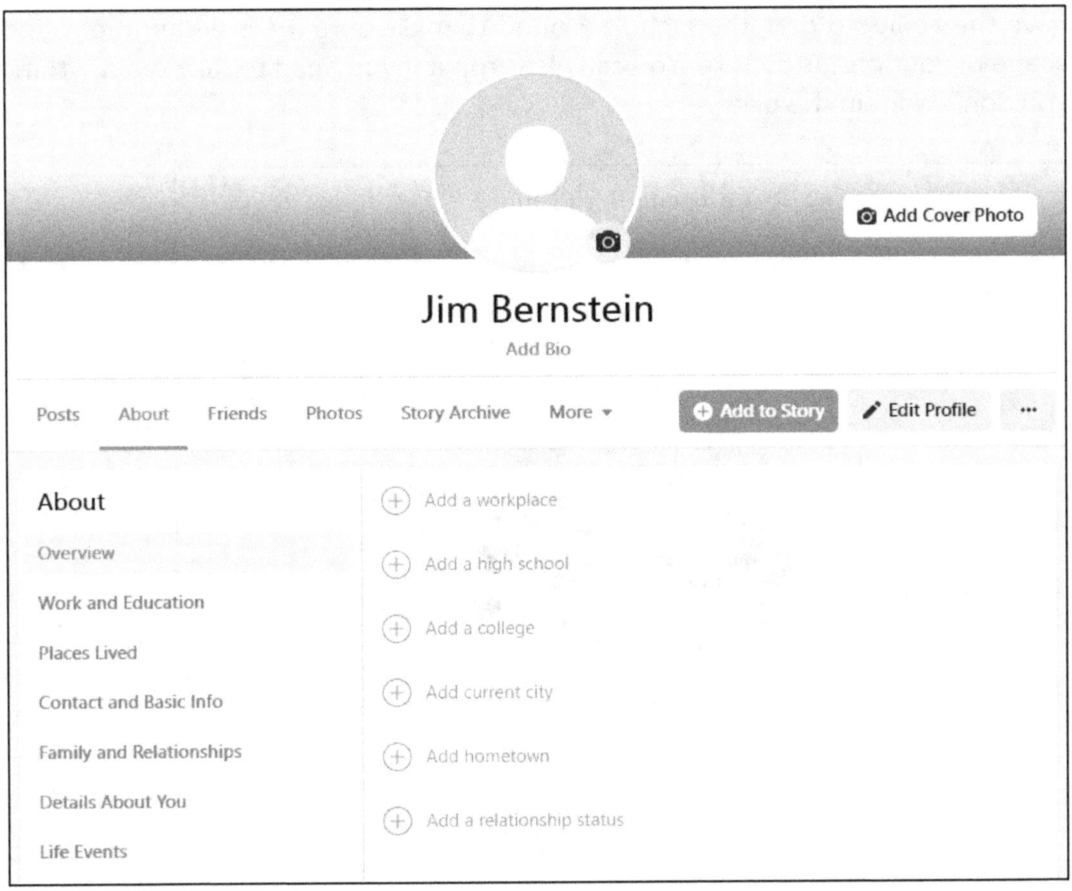
Add Cover Photo
Jim Bernstein
Add Bio
Posts
About
Friends
Photos
Story Archive
More
Add to Story
Edit Profile
About
Overview
Work and Education
Places Lived
Contact and Basic Info
Family and Relationships
Details About You
Life Events
Add a workplace
Add a high school
Add a college
Add current city
Add hometown
Add a relationship status

Figure 2.10

To add a photo, click on the camera icon next to the silhouette above your name and you will then need to browse your computer to find the photo you wish to use.

You will also have a choice to use just a photo or add a custom frame around your picture. To upload a photo, you have on your computer, click on the *Upload Photo* button.

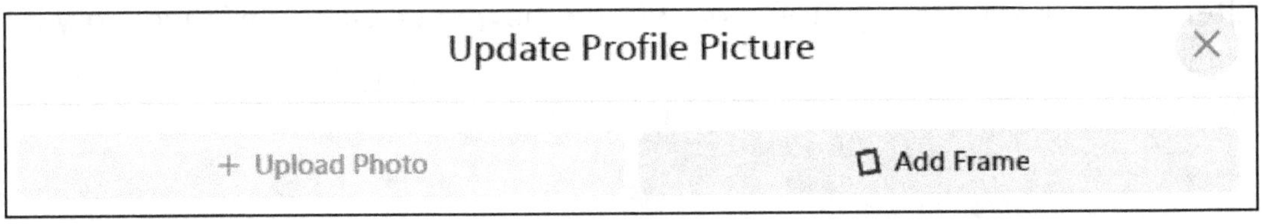
Update Profile Picture
+ Upload Photo
Add Frame

Figure 2.11

You will need to know how to browse to the folder on your computer where you have the picture saved and then select it and click the *Open* button. Then you will have the ability to drag the picture around to make sure it fits within the round shape of your profile picture. You can also crop it if you need to take out anything you don't want in the picture.

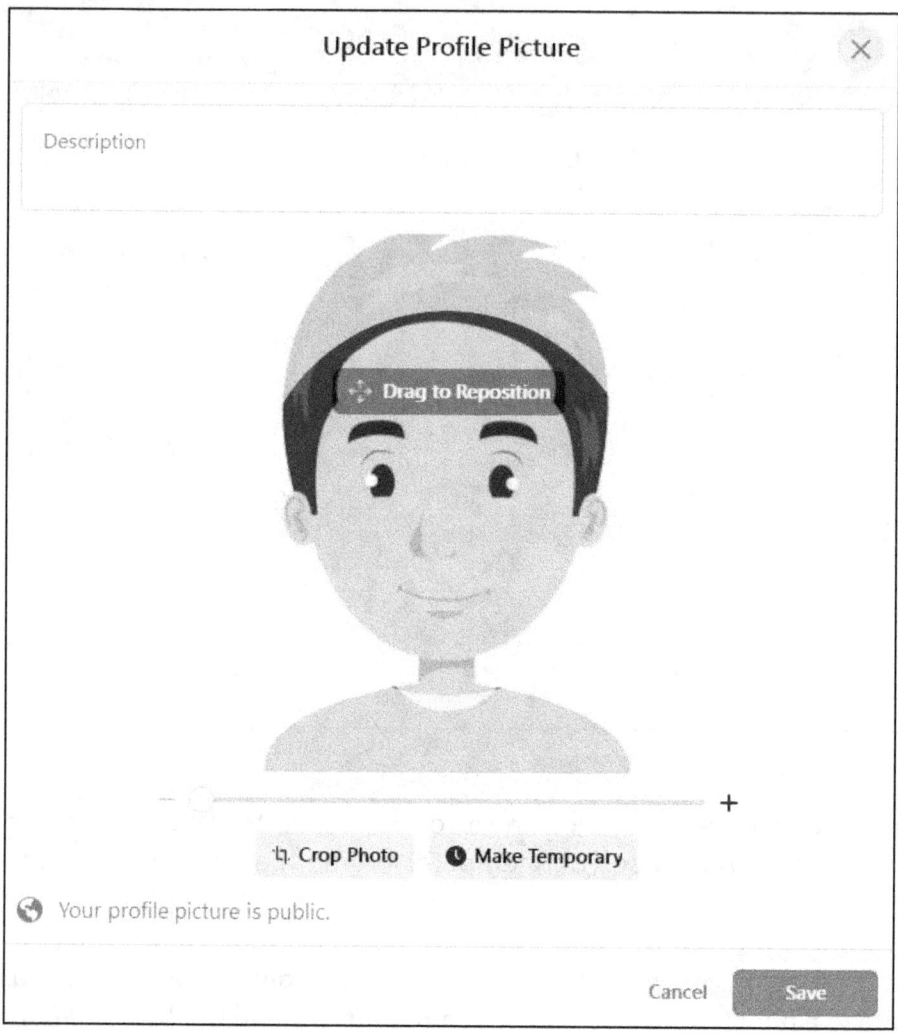

Figure 2.12

After you click the *Save* button, you will see how your picture will look in your profile.

Chapter 2 – Facebook

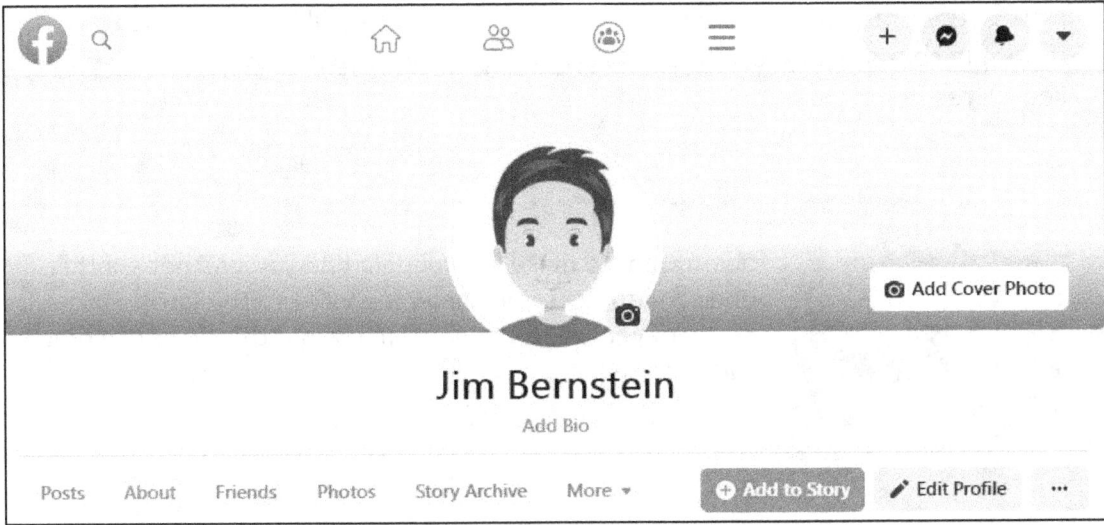
Figure 2.13

You can also add a cover photo which will be displayed behind your profile picture by clicking on the *Add Cover Photo* button. Just be sure to choose a picture that is in landscape format so it will fit across the page.

Figure 2.14

Now every time you make a post, your profile picture will be seen next to it. And if people search for your name looking for you, your picture will show up in the search results.

If you want to make sure people find you and not another person with the same name, then it is a good idea to use a photo of yourself for your profile rather than your dog or a cartoon like I have used.

Inviting Friends (Friend Requests)
Once you complete your profile, you might want to start looking for friends and relatives so you can "friend" them to make them part of your Facebook account. Once they are your friends, you will be able to see their posts to see what they are up to and send them messages etc.

To find your friends, you can click on the search box at the top left of the screen and type in their name. I will be looking for Todd Simms so I will click *on Search for Todd Simms.*

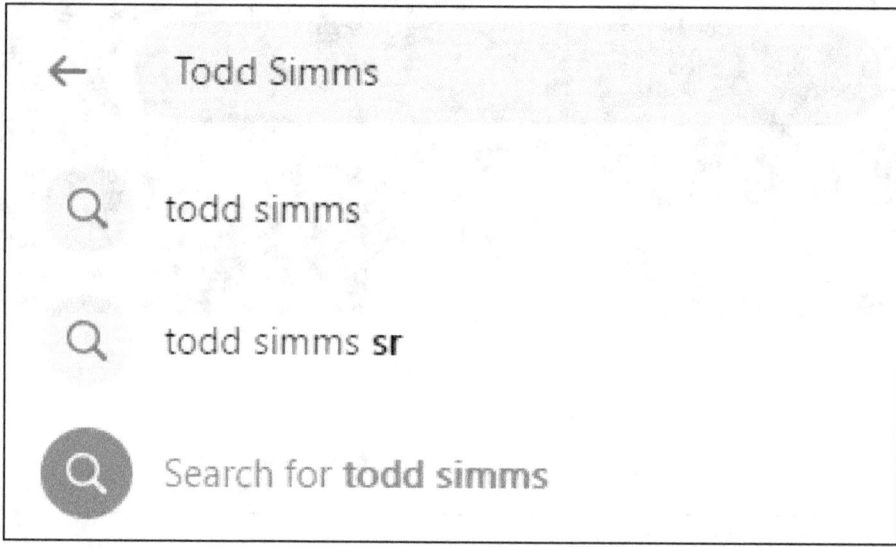

Figure 2.15

Then I can click on the *People* category since I am looking for a person. If it's a common name I might get way more results than I care to sort through. If that is

Chapter 2 – Facebook

the case, I can use some of the options below the People section such as adding a city or workplace, assuming I know this information. If this person is a friend of one of my other Facebook friends, then I can turn on the *Friends of Friends* option.

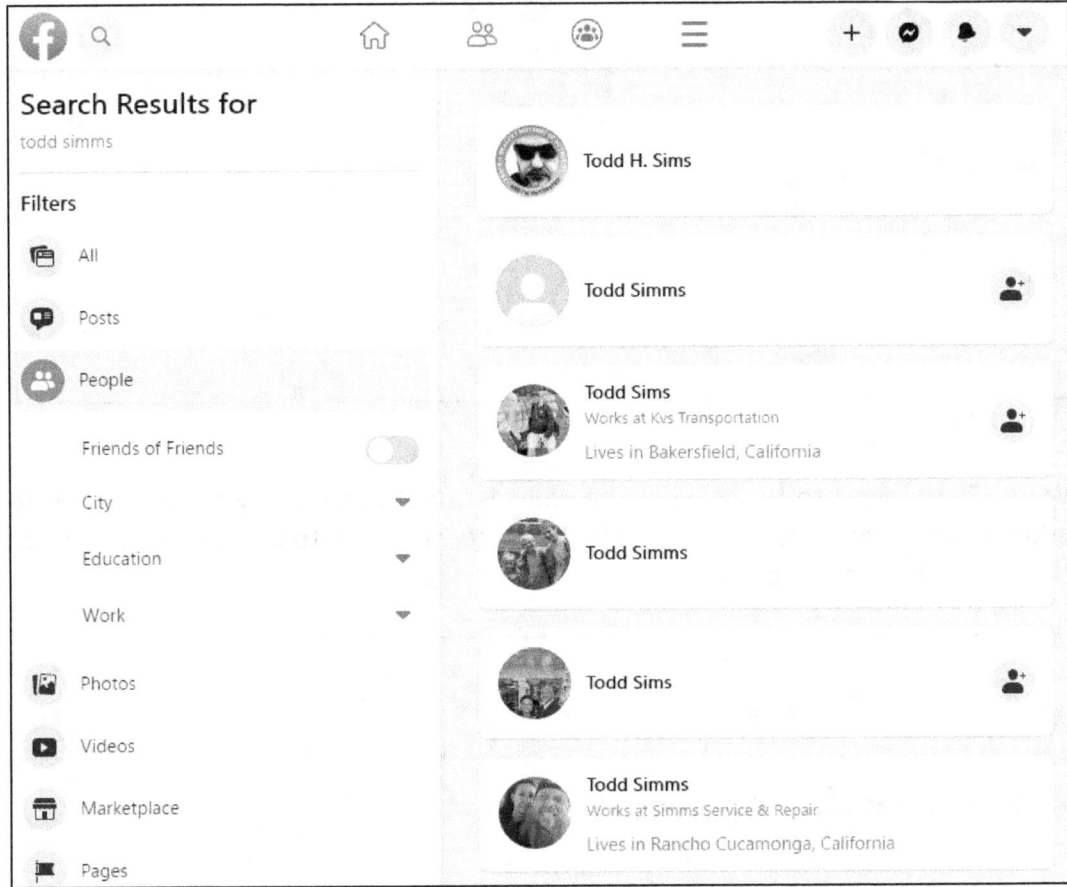

Figure 2.16

For this friend, I entered his location under city and now he shows up in my search and is actually the only Todd Simms in Bellingham, WA.

To send a friend request I can click on the silhouette icon with the **+** sign to the right of his name.

Chapter 2 – Facebook

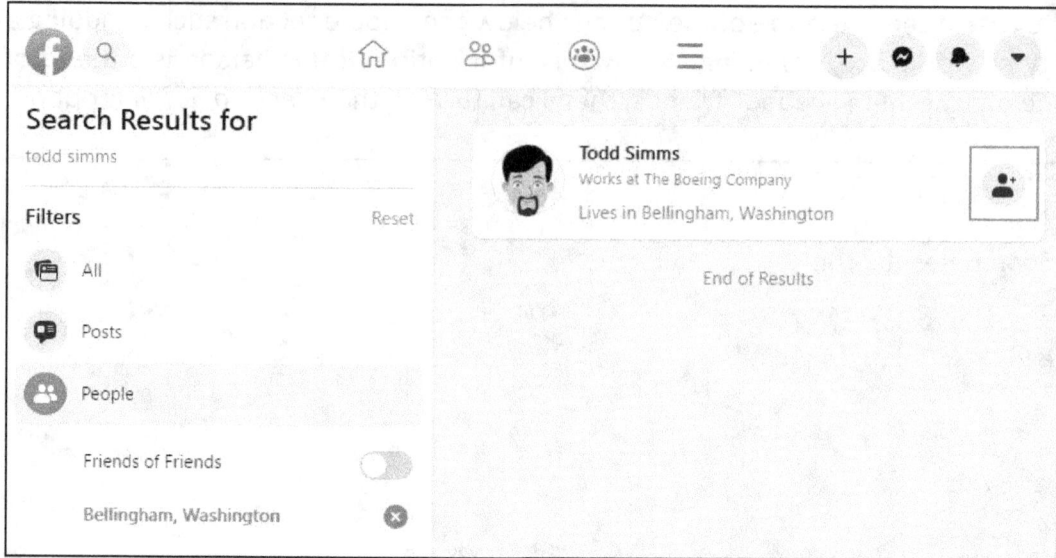

Figure 2.17

When Todd logs into his account, he will see a notification saying that I wish to add him as a friend. He can then click the *Confirm* button to accept my request or the *Delete* button to deny it.

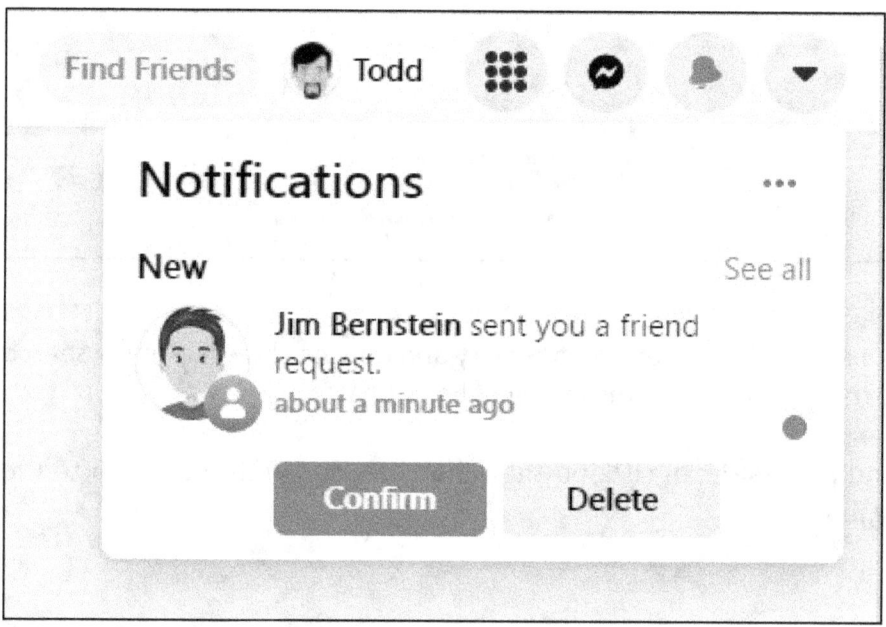

Figure 2.18

Once he accepts my request, I will then get a notification telling me the good news. I will also receive an email telling me the same information.

Chapter 2 – Facebook

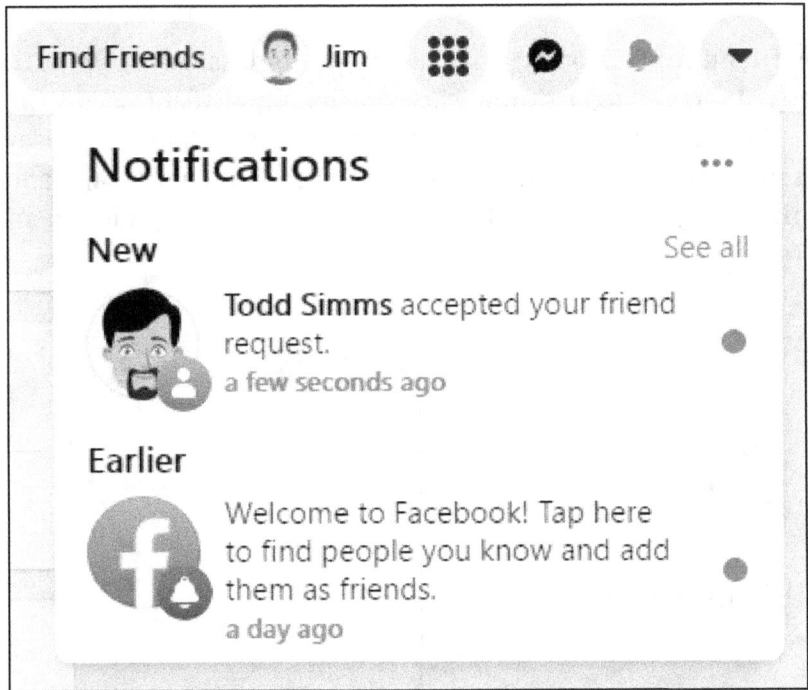

Figure 2.19

Todd will now show up in my contacts on the right side of the page.

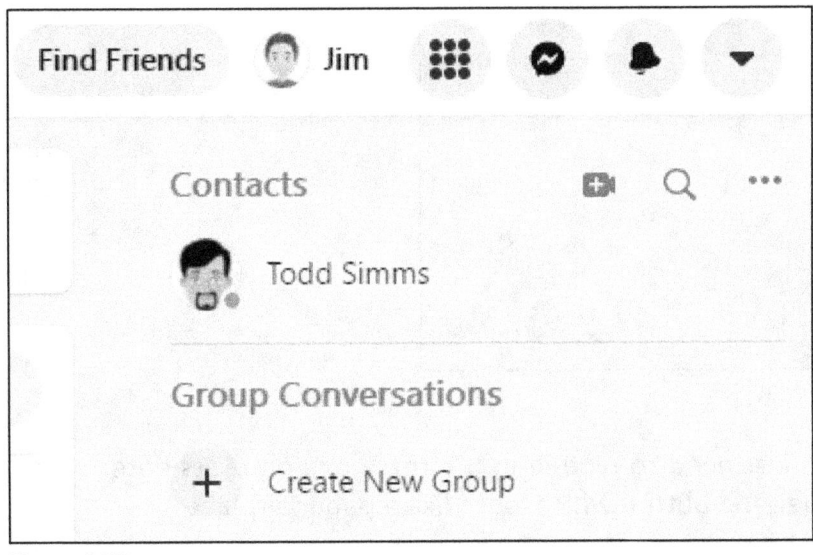

Figure 2.20

Chapter 2 – Facebook

Sending Messages

Now that Todd is my friend on Facebook, I can send him a message if I want to start up a chat with him. To do so, I simply click on his name to bring up the Facebook messenger. If he is logged into his Facebook account (online), it will say Active Now under his name. Even if he is not active, I can send him a message and he will see it next time he logs on. He should also get an email telling him I sent him a message.

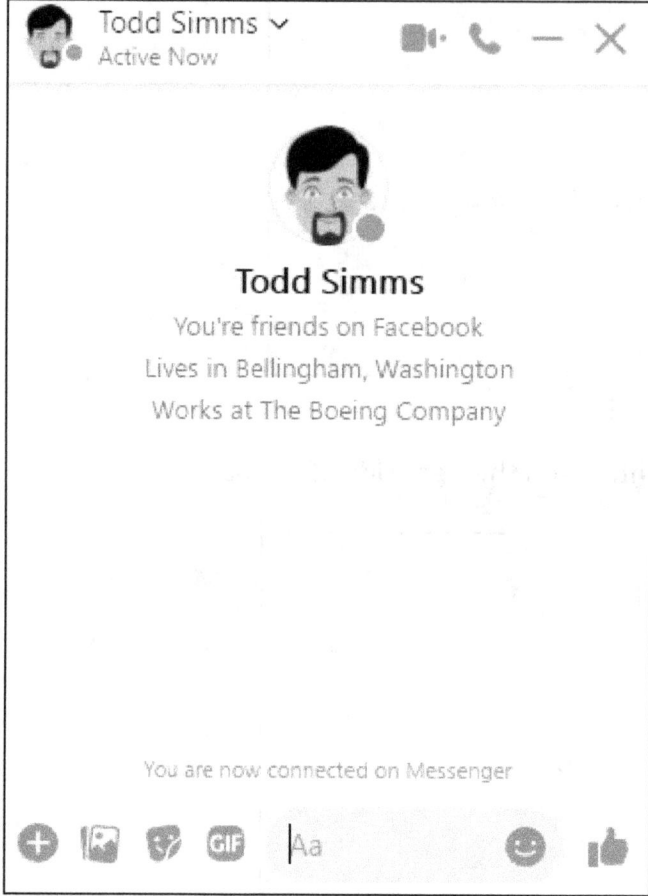

Figure 2.21

To send a message I just need to type in in the text box and press enter on my keyboard or press the send button which looks like a paper airplane.

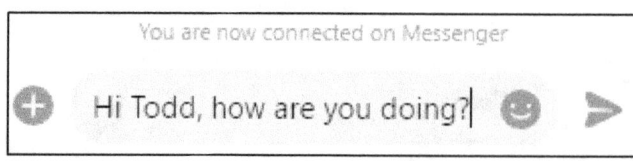

Figure 2.22

Chapter 2 – Facebook

Then Todd can reply, and we can have a back and forth conversation.

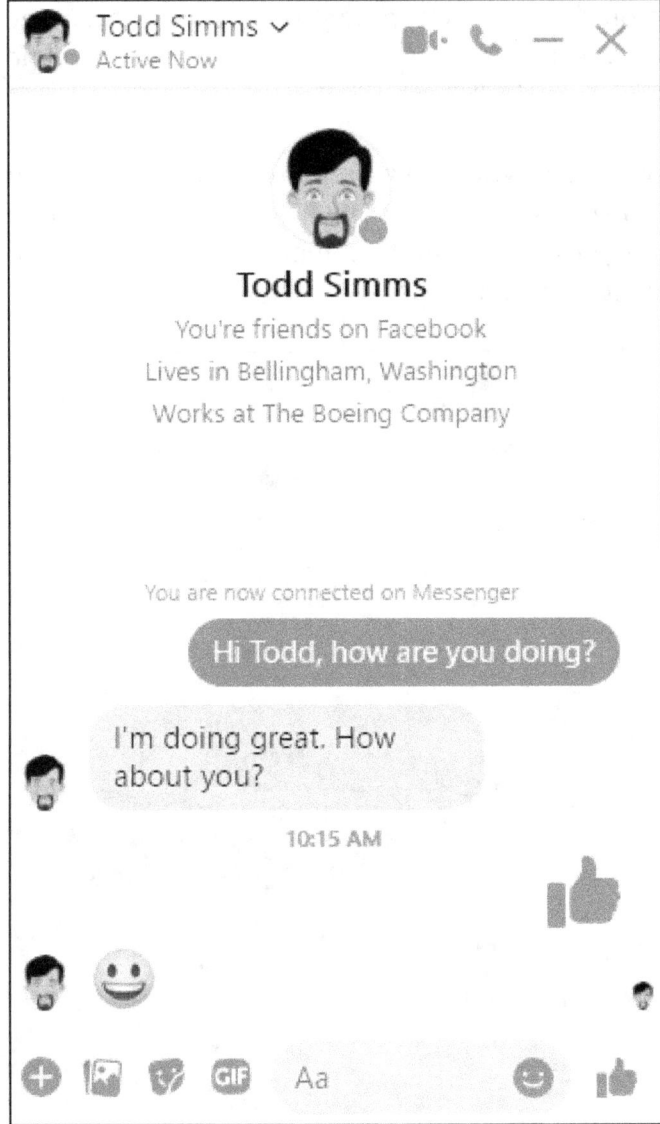

Figure 2.23

The icons\buttons at the bottom of figure 2.23 can be used to insert items such as pictures, photos, stickers, animated images, emojis etc. The thumbs up icon is used to add a like to your conversation to show the person you are talking to that you like what they said.

The icons at the top of the messenger window can be used to start a video chat or voice call with the other person. Just keep in mind that you will need a webcam

Chapter 2 – Facebook

on your computer to use the video chat feature. If you are going to do this with your smartphone then you will be able to use it's built in camera. If you close out the message window by clicking on the X at the top right hand corner, then you will be able to go back to your conversation later by clicking on your friend's name once again.

If you click on the down arrow next to your friend's name in the messenger window, you will have many other options as to what you can do with your chat. This section can come in handy if you need to mute someone who is being too chatty or block someone that might be getting rude.

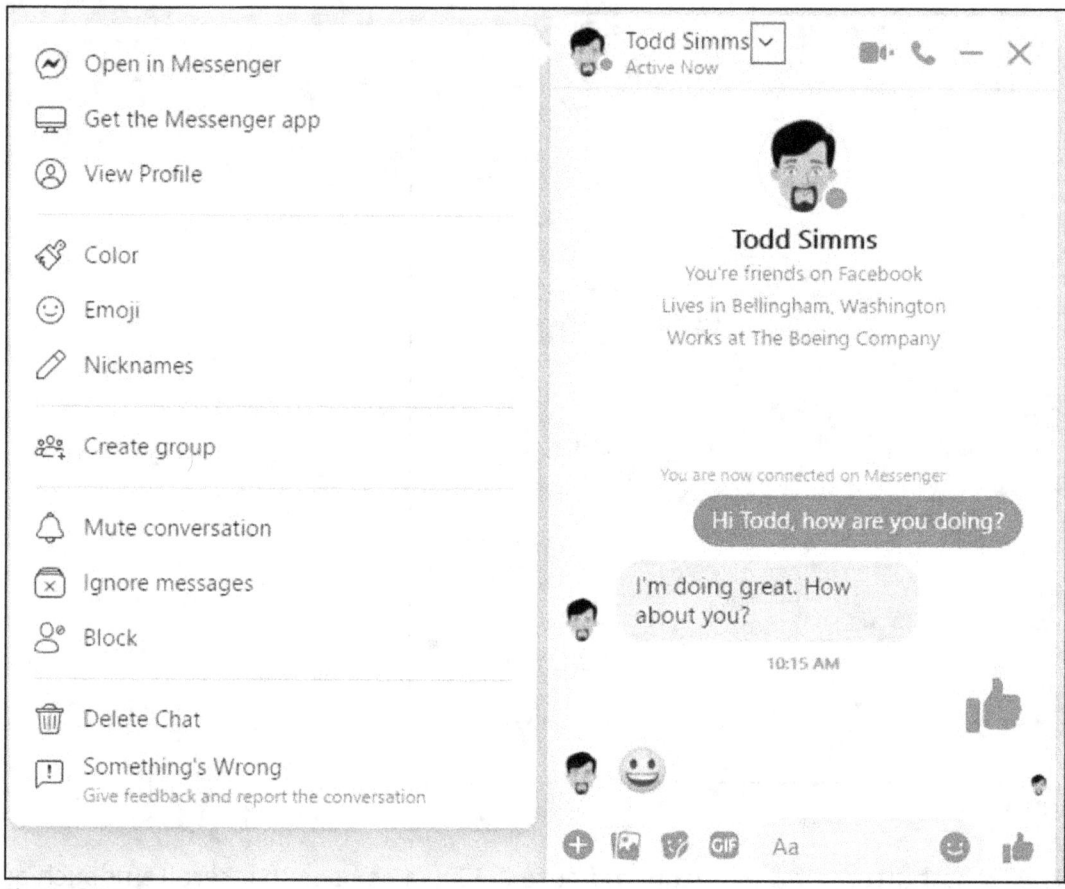

Figure 2.24

Creating Posts
One of the main things that people do with Facebook is share things that they feel their friends might be interested in seeing. For example, if you are on vacation at a nice resort, you might share pictures of the hotel or the beach. Or if your

Chapter 2 – Facebook

grandchild got a soccer trophy you might post that so your friends can see their accomplishment. Others will create posts to support a cause such as donating to a local animal shelter.

The process of creating a post is simple and only takes a few steps to do so. At the top of your Facebook Feed you will see a section with a box that says *What's on your mind* where you can type in something you wish to share. You will also see that you can do things such as start a live video feed, add a photo or video from your computer or smartphone and share how you are feeling at the moment.

Figure 2.25

Once you click in the box to start typing you will then have additional choices for things you can add to your post. At the top of the post, you can choose if you want to share your post with just your friends, specific friends, everyone (public) and so on.

Figure 2.26

35

Chapter 2 – Facebook

At the bottom, you can add photos, videos, tag friends, check into a location and so on. I will add a photo from the dog park and tag its location and figure 2.27 shows what my post will look like before I actually click on the Post button to make it live.

Figure 2.27

Chapter 2 – Facebook

After my post is live, it will show up in my feed as well as on my friend's feeds so they can see what I have been up to. When Todd logged into his account, my post was shown in his feed as seen in figure 2.28.

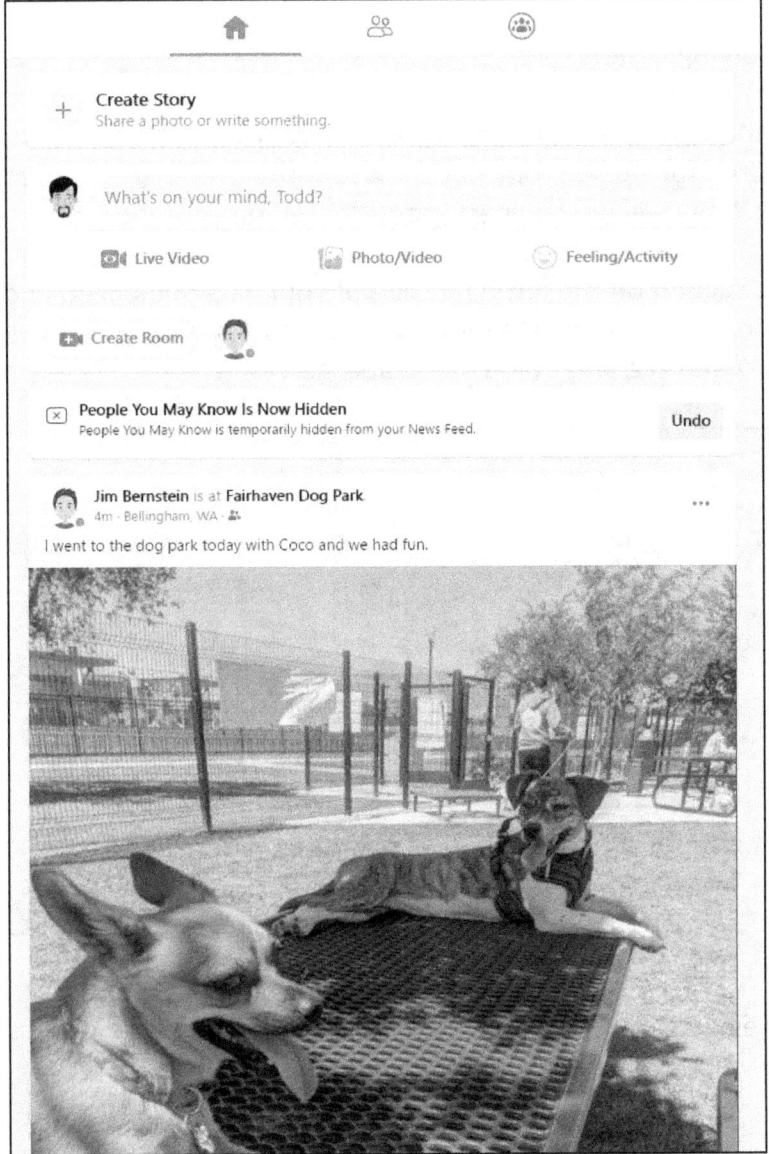

Figure 2.28

If your friends have a lot of friends, then your post might not be shown or may get buried with all the other things they have going on in their feed so you can't assume that every post you make will be seen by all your friends. But if your friends click on your name to view your profile, your posts will be shown to them in chronological order.

Chapter 2 – Facebook

You will also notice that you see posts that are not from your friends or groups in your feed. When this happens, you can either ignore them or click on the ellipsis at the top right of the post and choose to hide the post or hide all posts from that particular person or group.

Joining Groups and Following Others

Groups are a great way to connect with other people with similar interests or to find information on a topic you are interested in. Facebook has thousands of groups, and you can search for these groups or browse through the groups that they recommend to you. They will also suggest groups based on your location.

You can find the Groups section on the left hand side of your Facebook page and when you click on it, you will see suggested groups and also a search box. I will search for animal shelters and see what type of results I get.

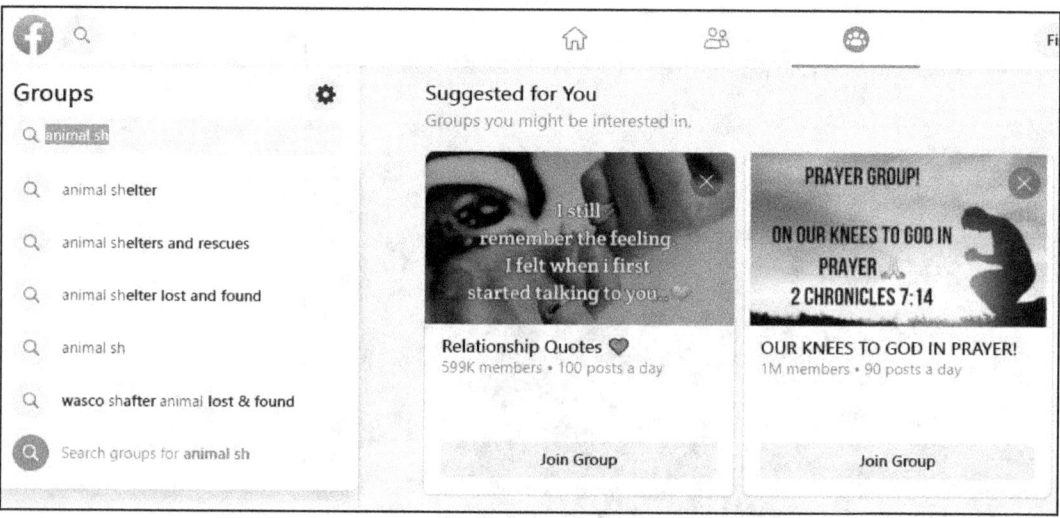

Figure 2.29

I can thing filter by all results, groups and group posts. I will choose the groups option and narrow it down by typing in the city I want to find groups for.

Chapter 2 – Facebook

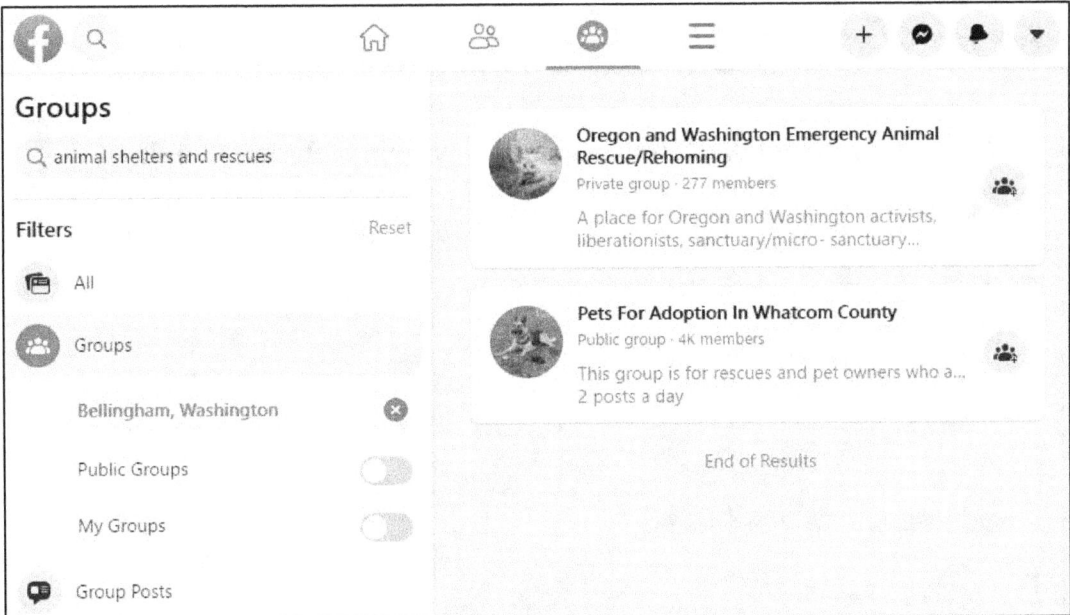

Figure 2.30

To join a group, I can click on the join button to the right of the group name. Many times, it will show a status of pending because you will need to get approval from the group administrator. You might even get a popup screen with some questions that you will need to answer before being allowed to join.

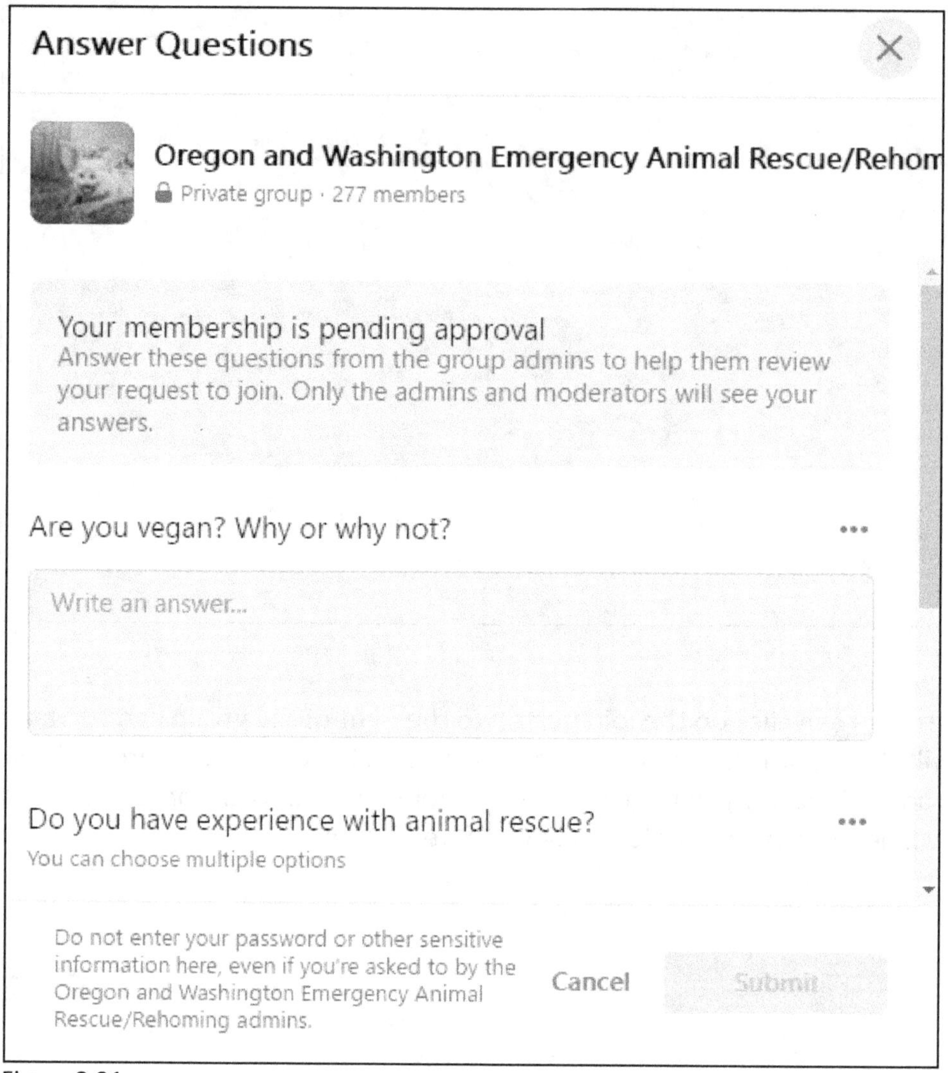

Chapter 2 – Facebook

Figure 2.31

You will be informed whether or not you were accepted to the group and then you will be able to participate in that group once you are an official member. It will also show up in your groups section.

Another thing you might want to do is follow or like a person or group to get updates from them that will then show up in your feed. For example, if I wanted to keep up with the band The Rolling Stones to get information on things like new albums or tour dates, I could do a search for them and find the result I am looking for.

When going through the search results, you might find many groups or pages that are on the topic you are looking for. You will have to determine which one is the

Chapter 2 – Facebook

one you want to follow and also whether or not it's the "official" page for that particular topic.

Figure 2.32 shows one of the results from my search. It shows there are over 18 million followers and that the tag name for this page is @therollingstones. It also shows the website below that. Judging by this information it appears that this is the official Rolling Stones page and if I want to follow this page, I can click on the + icon at the upper right corner of this result. Once I do that the + will turn into a checkmark indicating I am now following The Rolling Stones on Facebook. When you follow a person or group, you do not need to worry about getting approval from them first.

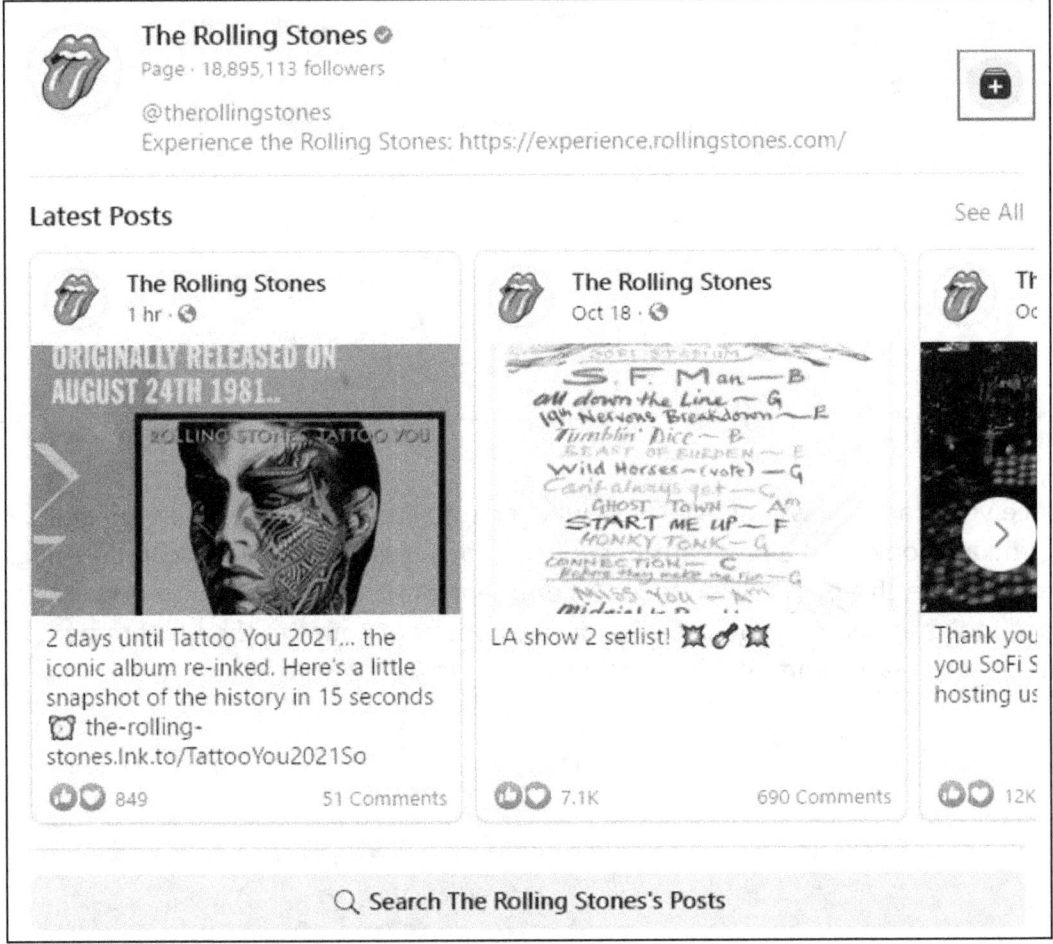

Figure 2.32

If I were to go to the *Pages* icon on the left side of the main Facebook screen and then click on *Liked Pages*, I would be shown all of the pages that I am following. I could then click on the ellipsis next to the word Following to change my settings, share the page with others, block the page and so on. If I were to click the *Following* button, I can make it so I am not following them anymore. I can also click it again to start following them once more.

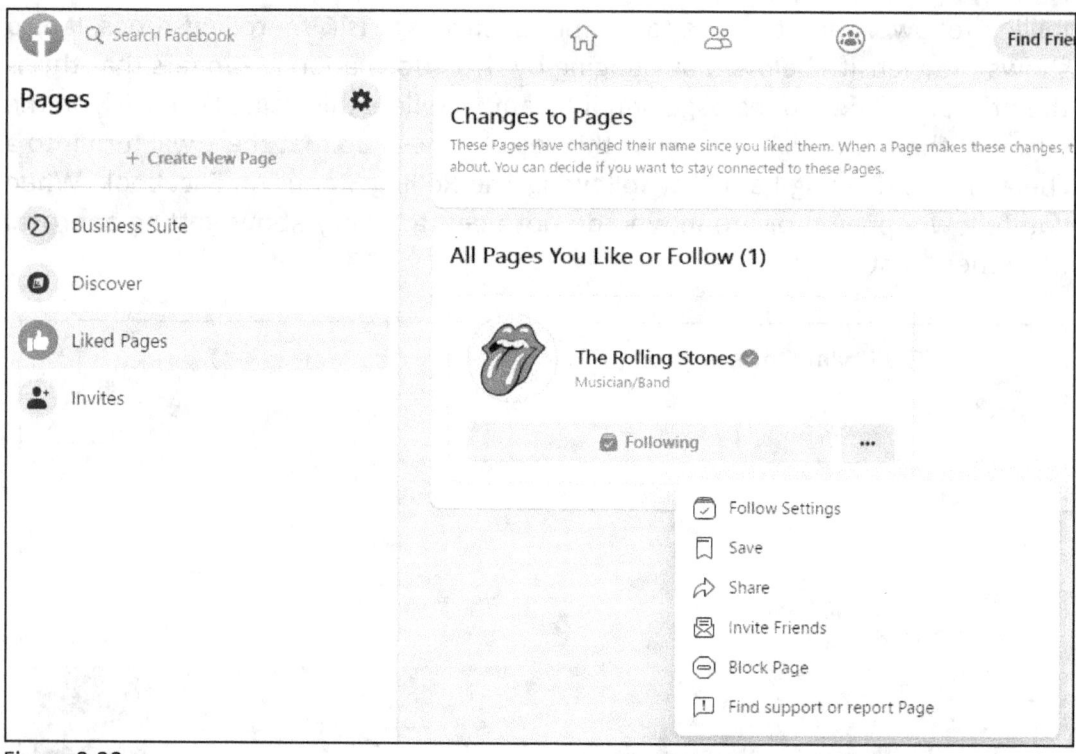

Figure 2.33

Once you start following pages, you will begin to see their posts show up in your main Facebook feed along with posts from your friends. Then you can do things such as give the post a like, make a comment on it or share it with your other Facebook friends. You can also click on the comment count at the bottom right of the post to read comments from other people (figure 2.34).

Chapter 2 – Facebook

Figure 2.34

Games

Facebook is not just about posting your life story and keeping up with your friends. It's also about doing fun things such as playing video games. In fact, for many people that is the only thing they do with Facebook!

To get to the Facebooks games you can click on the *Play Games* icon on the left side of the page. From there you will be shown some games that Facebook thinks you might like. You will also have game categories on the left side of the page if you want to narrow down your search to a specific type of game. There is also a search box if you happen to know the name of the game you want to play.

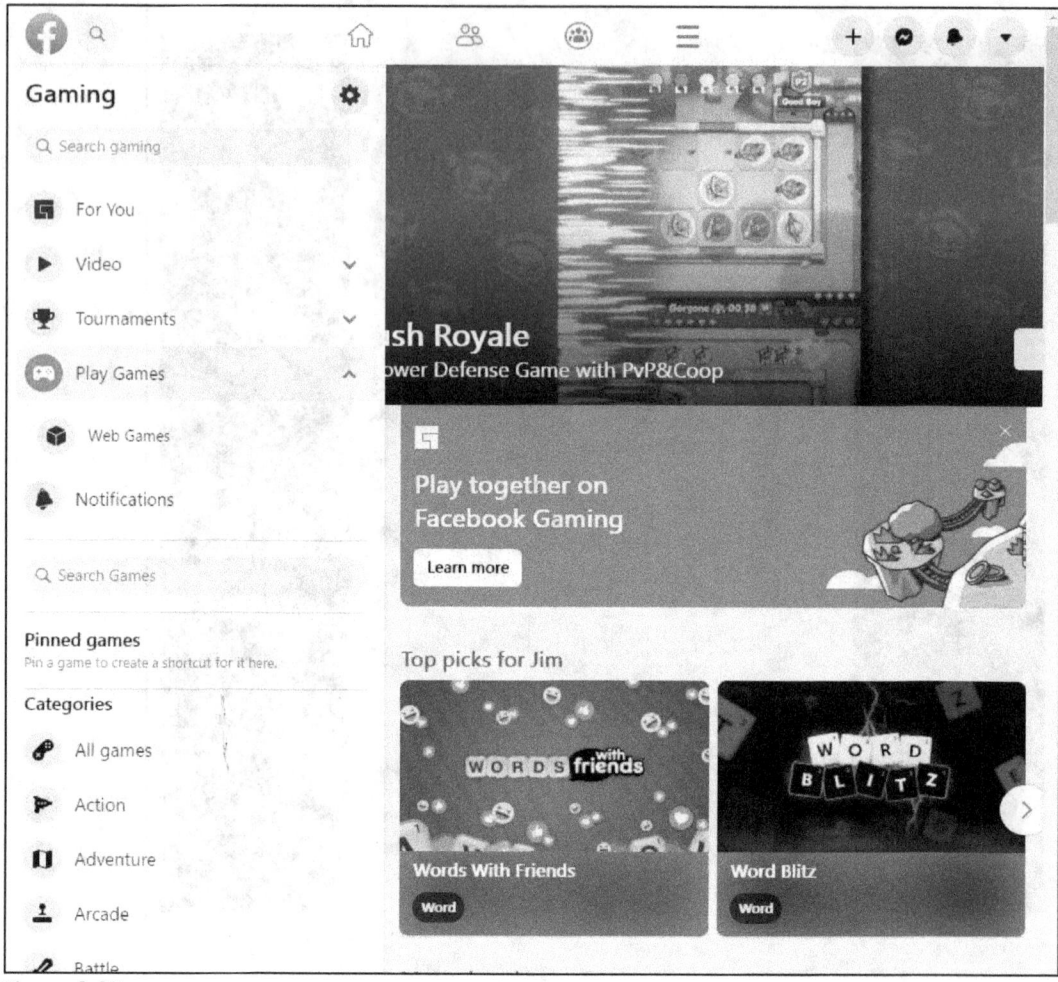
Figure 2.35

I will choose the *Arcade* category and then click on the game called Snake Mania. Once I am there, I can click on the *Play Now* button to start the game and even click on the *Pin* button to have Facebook create a shortcut to the game so I can find it again later if I want to play again. I can also share the game with my friends if I think they might want to play it as well.

Chapter 2 – Facebook

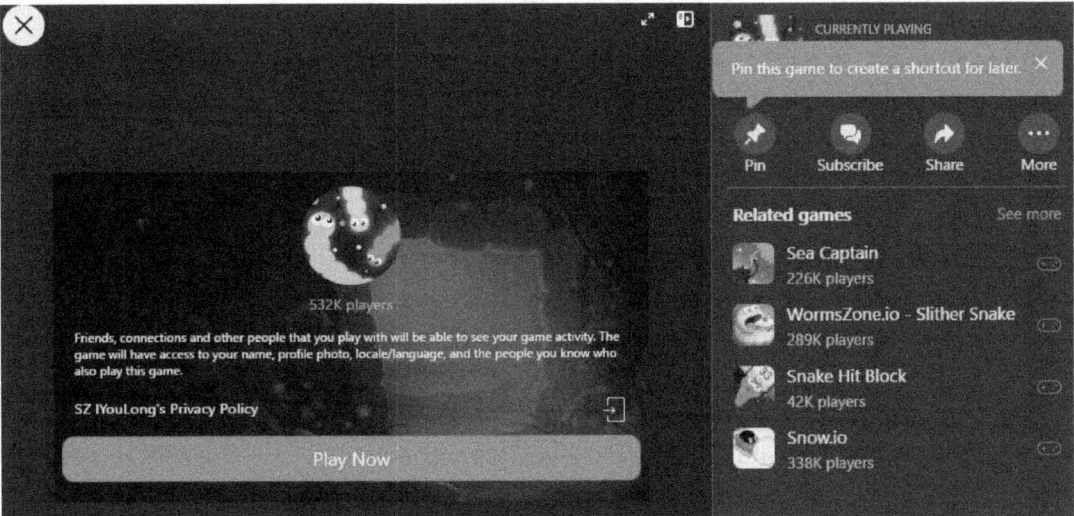

Figure 2.36

After I click on *Play Now*, the game will start and I can start having fun. This game even shows the top scores from others who have played the game today. To exit the game, I can click on the X at the top left of the screen.

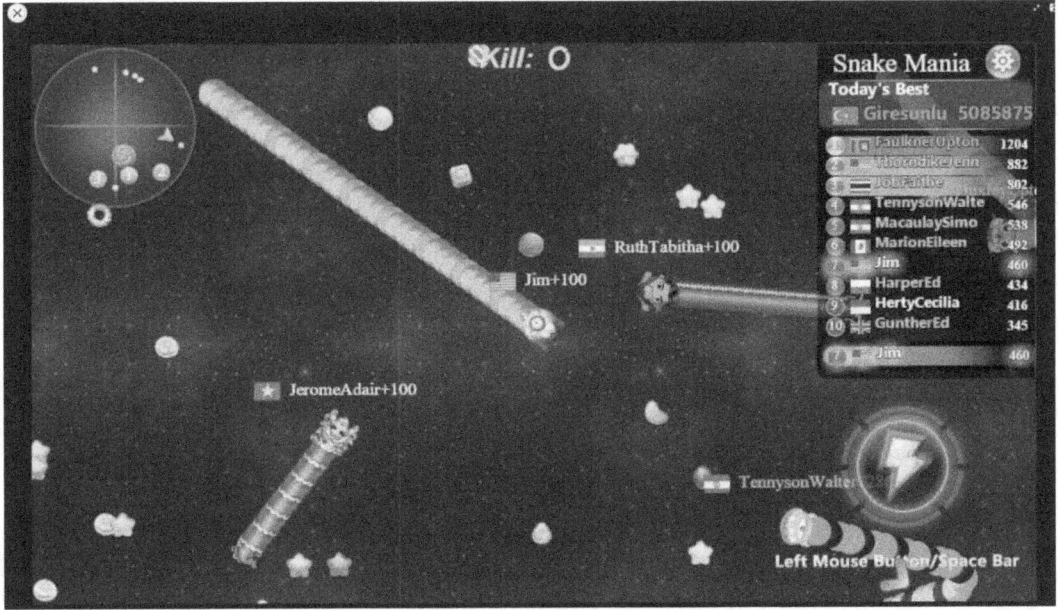

Figure 2.37

When playing games, just remember that the process for playing them will not always be the same and there will be a learning curve each time you try a new one. Also keep in mind that some games will be single player games while others you can play with your Facebook friends.

Chapter 2 – Facebook

Facebook Marketplace
Buying and selling items online is a very popular thing to do these days and I'm sure you have heard of websites such as Craigslist and eBay or maybe even used a phone app such as OfferUp to buy or sell something.

The Facebook Marketplace works in a similar fashion to those other sites and is a place where you can buy just about anything and also sell items you don't have a need for anymore. You can find the Marketplace icon on the left side of the page just like you have gone to find most other Facebook features.

Once you are there you will see items for sale in your local area as well as categories on the left hand side that you can use to narrow down the results. There is also a search feature at the top where you can search for specific items if needed.

Chapter 2 – Facebook

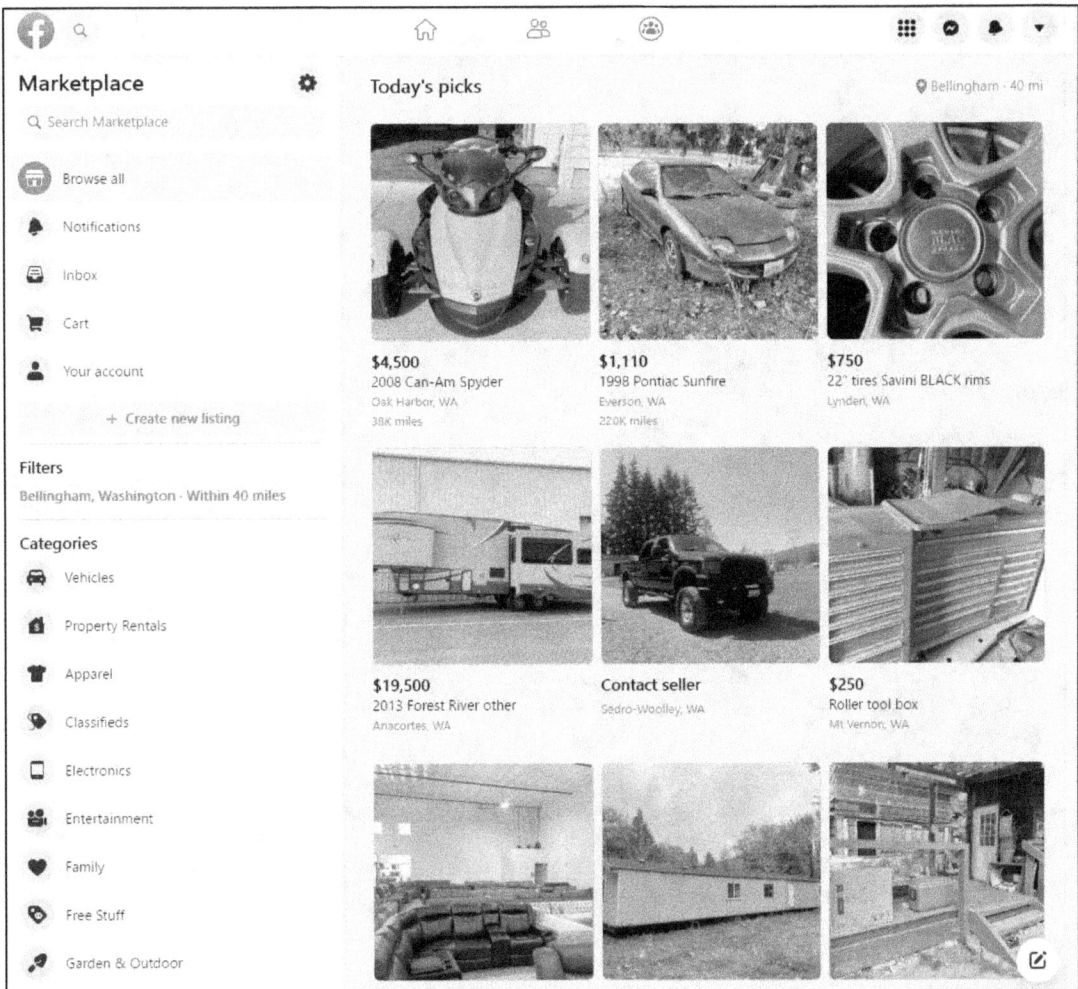

Figure 2.38

If you need to change the search area or narrow it down a bit, then you can click on the city name in the *Filters* area and change the location or search are in miles.

Chapter 2 – Facebook

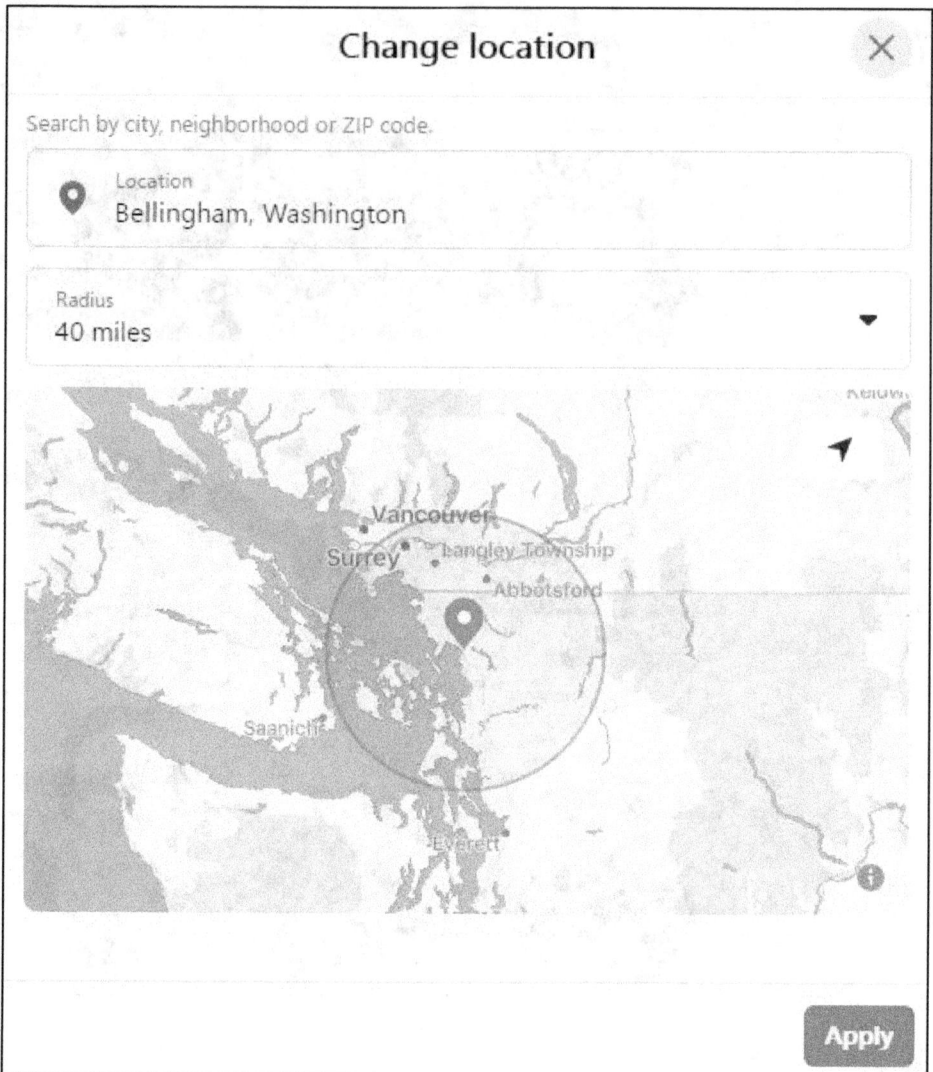

Figure 2.39

If I were to search for mountain bikes for example, I would be shown all the results in my search area, and I can then click on each listing I want to view. I can also sort the results by things such as condition, price, date listed and availability.

Chapter 2 – Facebook

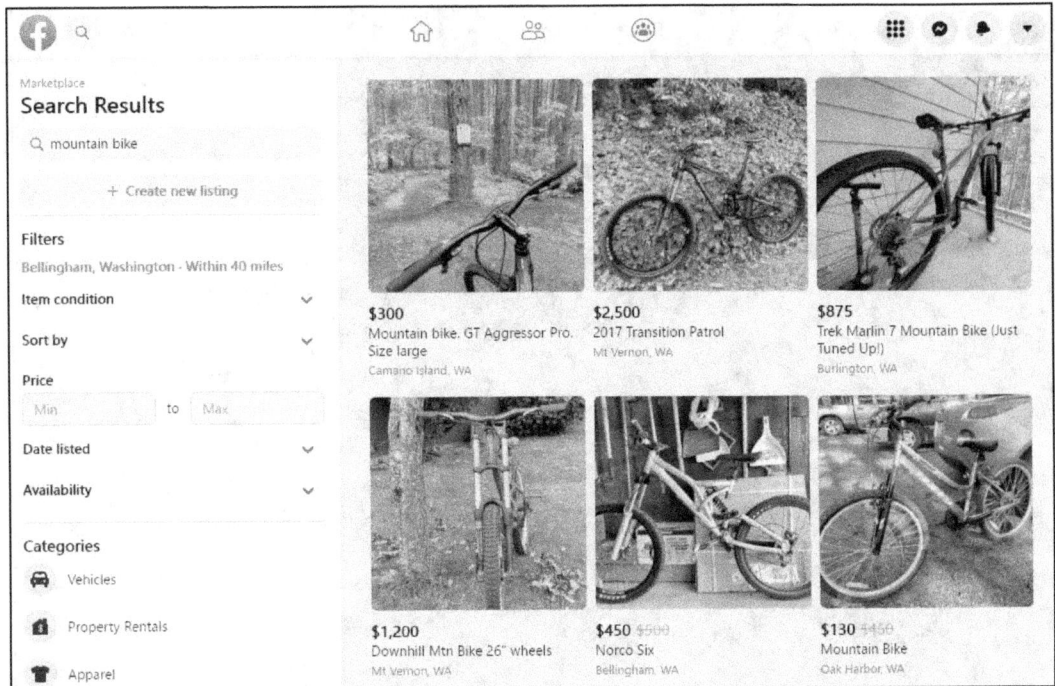

Figure 2.40

When I click on a particular listing, I will be able to see more information about the item as well as any additional photos. There is also a place to send the seller a message as well as save the post for viewing later and also a share icon in case you want to send the post to a friend.

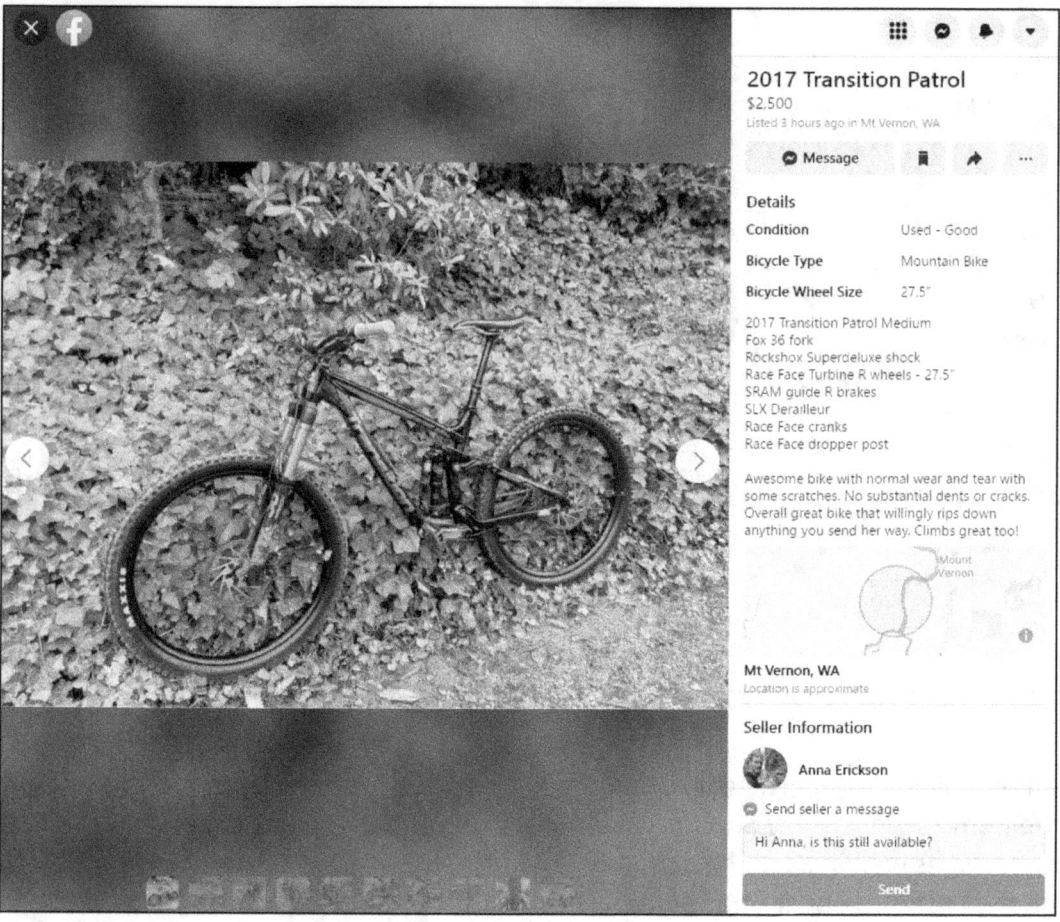

Figure 2.41

If you want to sell your own item, you can click on the *Create a new listing* button as seen at the top of figure 2.40. Then you can choose which category your listing should be placed in. So if I was going to sell a mountain bike, I would choose the *Item for Sale* category.

Chapter 2 – Facebook

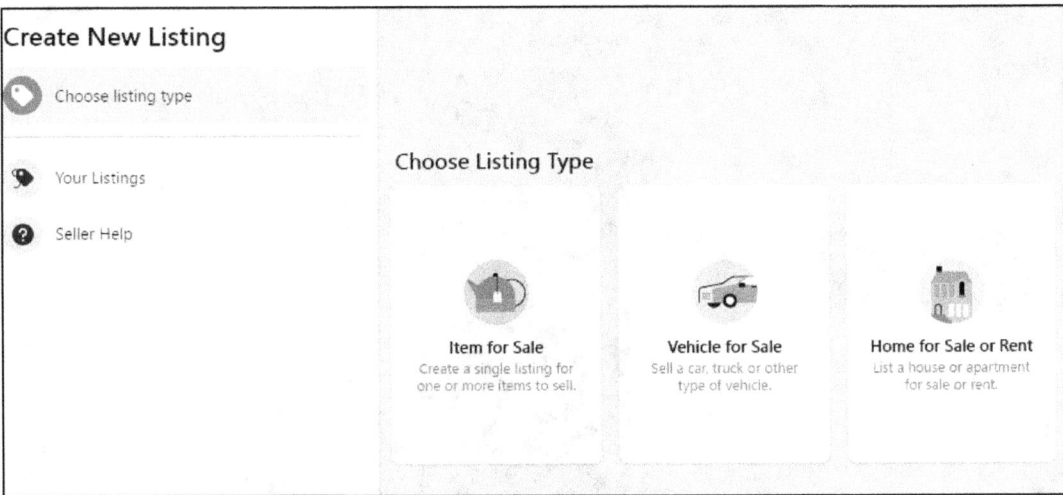

Figure 2.42

Then I would need to add a title, description, price and any photos etc. I might want to use.

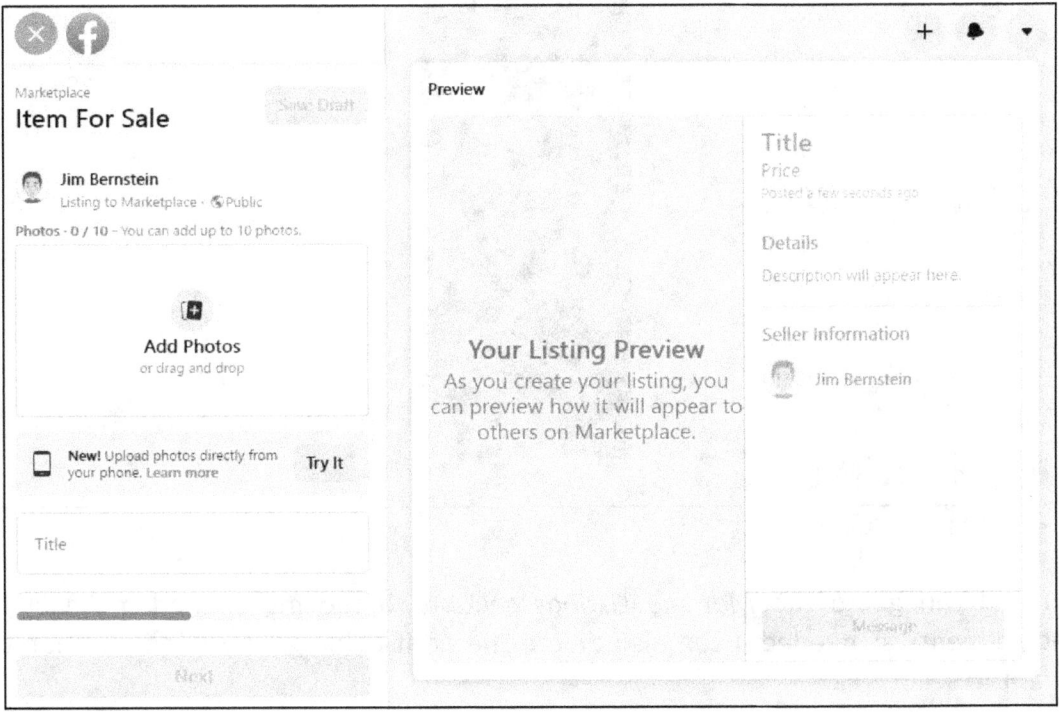

Figure 2.43

After I added all the required information, I would click the *Next* button and finally Publish on the next screen.

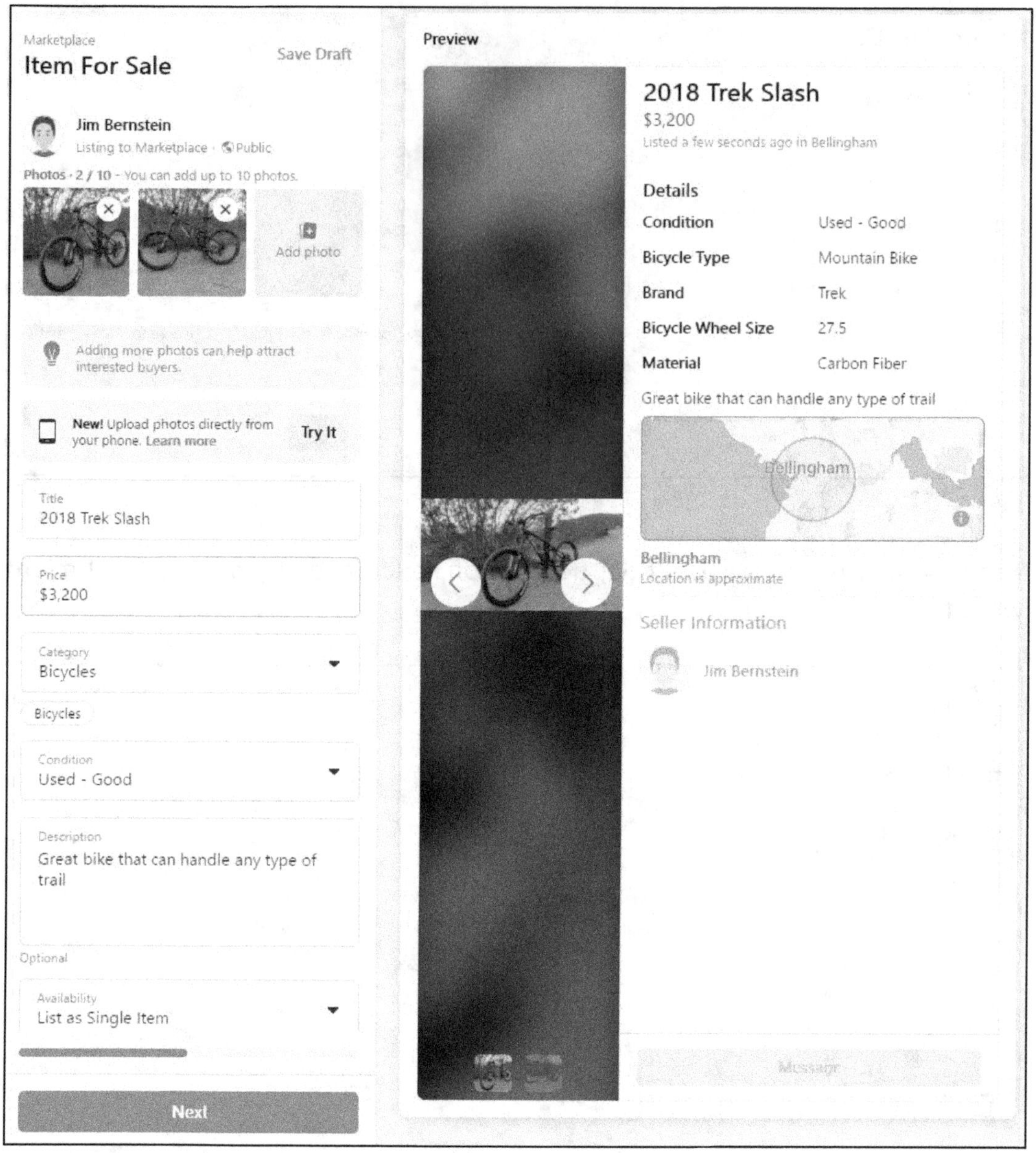

Chapter 2 – Facebook

Figure 2.44

Then I can go to the *Manage Listings* section to see my ad and make any adjustments as needed. I can also delete the ad if I change my mind and don't want to sell it.

Chapter 2 – Facebook

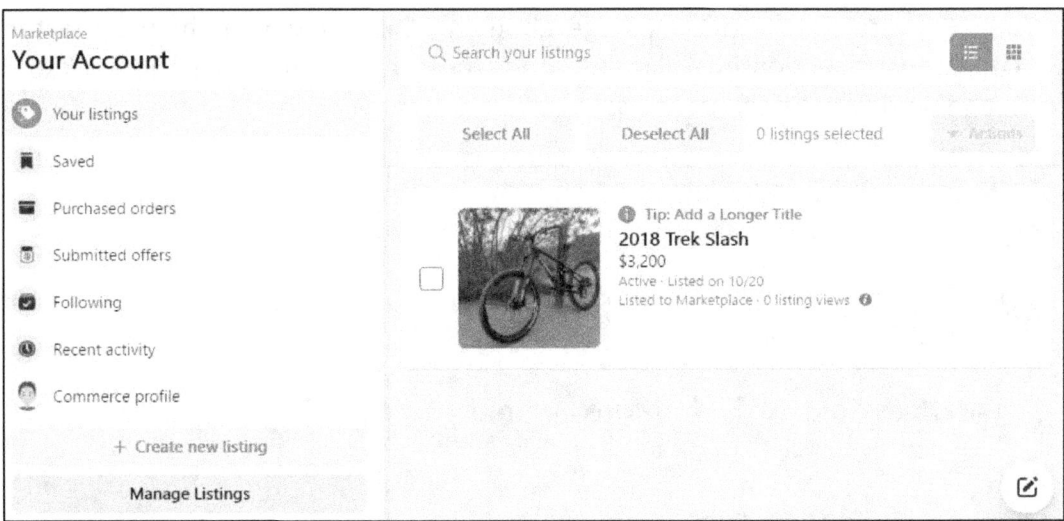

Figure 2.45

Now when someone searches for my bike in my area, it will come up in the search results.

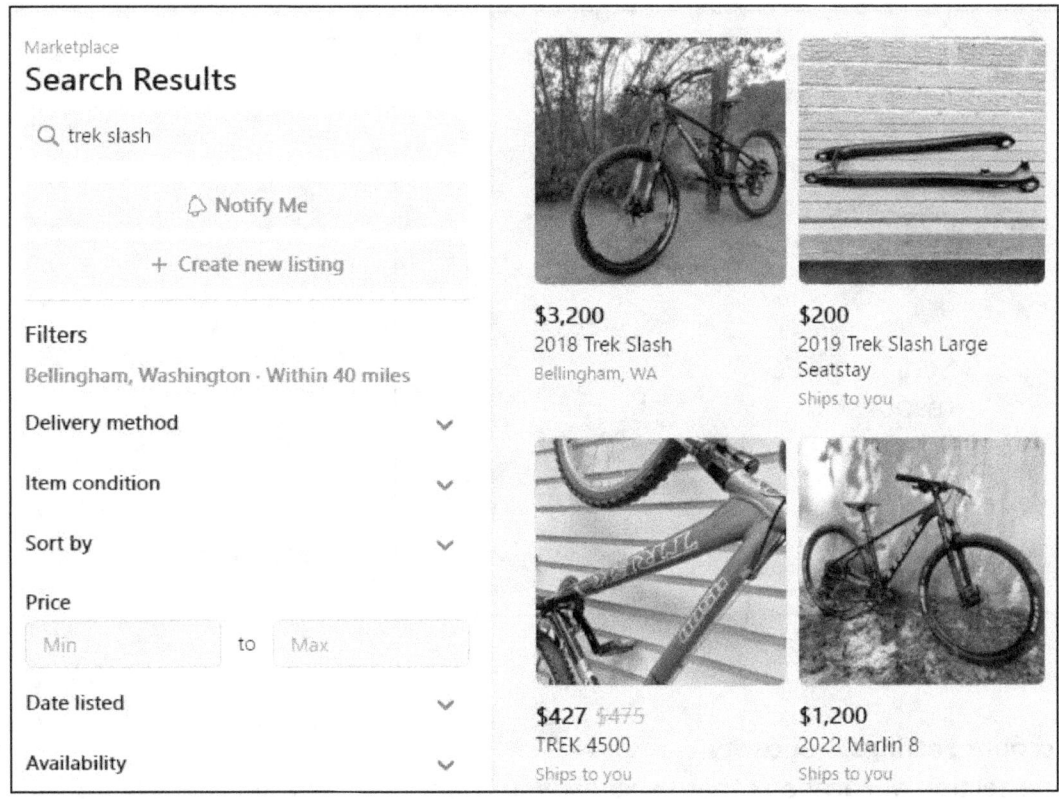

Figure 2.46

If Todd were to send me a message about my bike, it would show up in the chat\messenger section just like any other message. Then we can go back and forth and work out a deal for the sale.

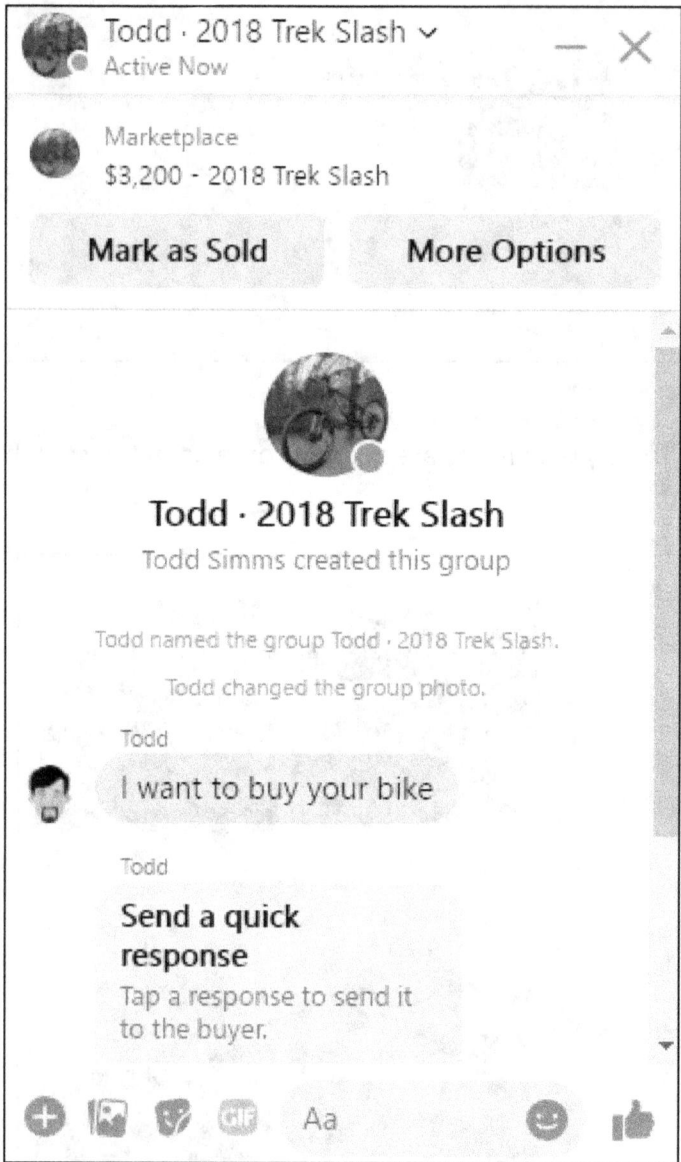

Figure 2.47

Account Settings & Security

One section of Facebook that I suggest you check out is the settings and privacy area because you might want to make some adjustments here as to what kind of information people can see about you.

Chapter 2 – Facebook

There is a lot to this area, but you shouldn't have to go through every single setting to make your account secure. To get to these settings you will need to click on the down arrow at the top right of the page and then click on *Settings & Privacy*.

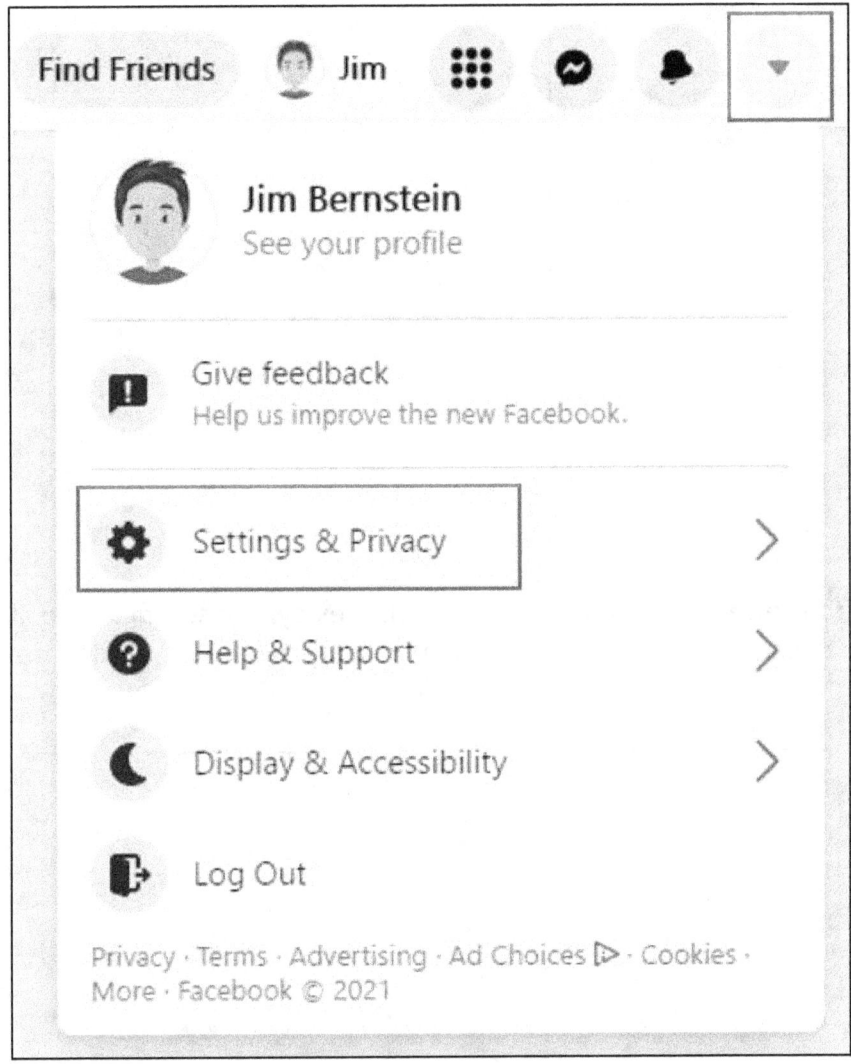

Figure 2.48

From the next menu that opens, you can click on *Settings*.

Chapter 2 – Facebook

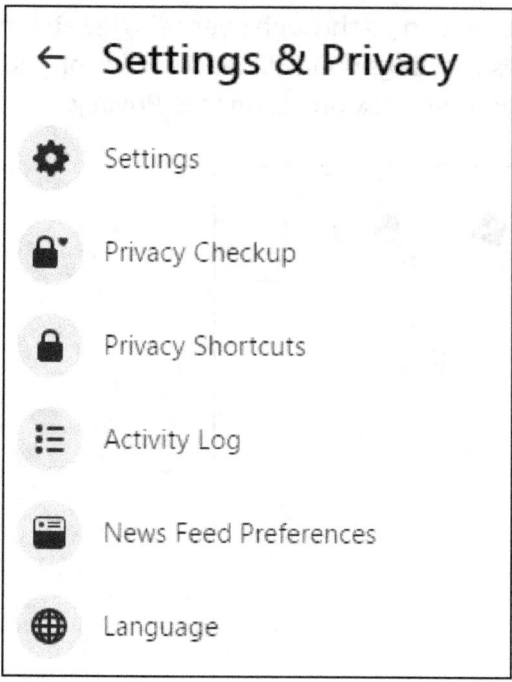

Figure 2.49

Next, I would go to the *Security and Login* section and review the settings here. If you ever need to change your password, you can do so from here by clicking the *Edit* button.

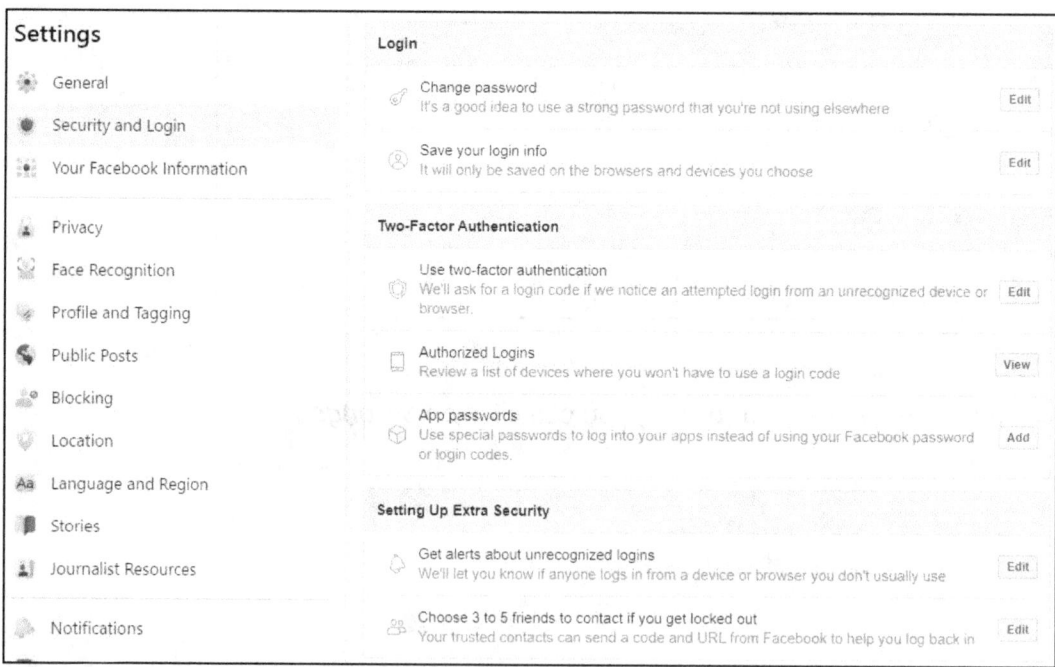

Figure 2.50

Chapter 2 – Facebook

If you want to add some extra security to your login then you can enable two-factor authentication to have a text message sent to your phone with a code every time you log in. This might be too much effort for many people but if you are really into security then this might be for you!

The section labeled *get alerts about unrecognized logins* can be used to notify you if someone has been trying to log into your account from a different device than you normally use. Just keep in mind that if you enable this and then sign into your account from a different computer such as a friends then you will get an alert warning you of a potential unauthorized login attempt.

The last section you might want to look at is at the bottom of figure 2.50 where it says *choose 3 to 5 friends to contact if you get locked out*. This can be used to help you out if you get locked out of your account and don't remember your password. Otherwise, it can be really hard to get your account back if you don't have the proper information to give Facebook to let you back in. Here you would choose some of your friends that you trust that can help verify your identity to Facebook to get you back into your account.

I also recommend reviewing the *Privacy* section since that determines things such as who can see your posts, who can send you friend requests, who can see your friends list, who can email you and so on.

Chapter 2 – Facebook

Settings	Privacy Settings and Tools			
General	Privacy Shortcuts	Check a few important settings Quickly review some important settings to make sure you're sharing with the people you want.		
Security and Login				
Your Facebook Information		Manage your profile Go to your profile to change your profile info privacy, like who can see your birthday or relationships.		
Privacy				
Face Recognition		Learn more with Privacy Basics Get answers to common questions with this interactive guide.		
Profile and Tagging				
Public Posts	Your Activity	Who can see your future posts?	Friends	Edit
Blocking		Review all your posts and things you're tagged in		Use Activity Log
Location				
Language and Region		Limit the audience for posts you've shared with friends of friends or Public?		Limit Past Posts
Stories				
Journalist Resources		Who can see the people, Pages and lists you follow?	Public	Edit
Notifications	How People Find and Contact You	Who can send you friend requests?	Everyone	Edit
Mobile				
		Who can see your friends list?	Public	Edit
Apps and Websites				
Games		Who can look you up using the email address you provided?	Everyone	Edit
Business Integrations		Who can look you up using the phone number you provided?	Everyone	Edit
Ads				

Figure 2.51

Another area you might want to check out is the *Profile and Tagging* section. Here you can tell Facebook who is allowed to do things such as post on your profile, see your posts, share your posts, tag you in posts and so on.

Chapter 2 – Facebook

Settings	Profile and Tagging			
General	Viewing and Sharing	Who can post on your profile?	Friends	Edit
Security and Login		Who can see what others post on your profile?	Friends	Edit
Your Facebook Information				
Privacy		Allow others to share your posts to their stories?	On	Edit
Face Recognition				
Profile and Tagging		Hide comments containing certain words from your profile	Off	Edit
Public Posts				
Blocking	Tagging	Who can see posts you're tagged in on your profile?	Friends of friends	Edit
Location		When you're tagged in a post, who do you want to add to the audience of the post if they can't already see it?	Friends	Edit
Language and Region				
Stories	Reviewing	Review posts you're tagged in before the post appears on your profile?	Off	Edit
Journalist Resources				
Notifications		Review what other people see on your profile		View As
Mobile				
		Review tags people add to your posts before the tags appear on Facebook?	Off	Edit
Apps and Websites				

Figure 2.52

If you want to take the easy route when it comes to privacy settings, then you can go through the *Privacy Checkup* from the main menu as seen in figure 2.49. This area is broken down into categories that you can click on to review the settings related to each of the categories.

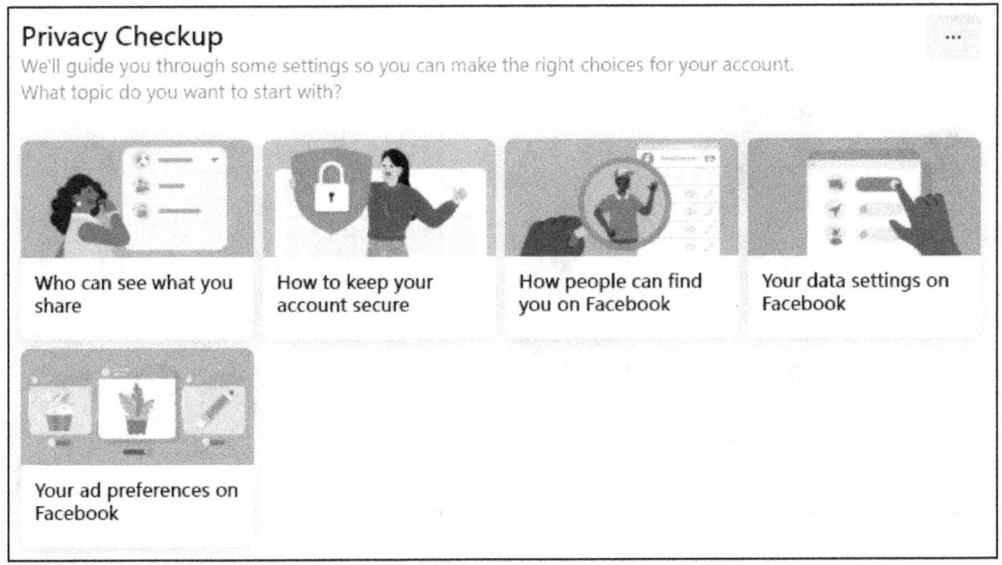

Figure 2.53

Chapter 2 – Facebook

Facebook Mobile App
Since smartphones have become more popular than computers these days, it makes sense that you might want to access your Facebook account from your mobile device so you can stay in touch no matter where you might happen to be.

Facebook has an app that you can install on your smartphone or tablet and access the same features that you are used to using on your desktop computer. All you need to do is go to the Play Store (Android devices) or App Store (iPhones & iPads) and do a search for Facebook.

When you find it, just make sure that it is the official Facebook app and not something with Facebook in the title trying to fool you into thinking you are installing the Facebook app itself. It should have Facebook as the company name under the name of the app as seen in figure 2.54.

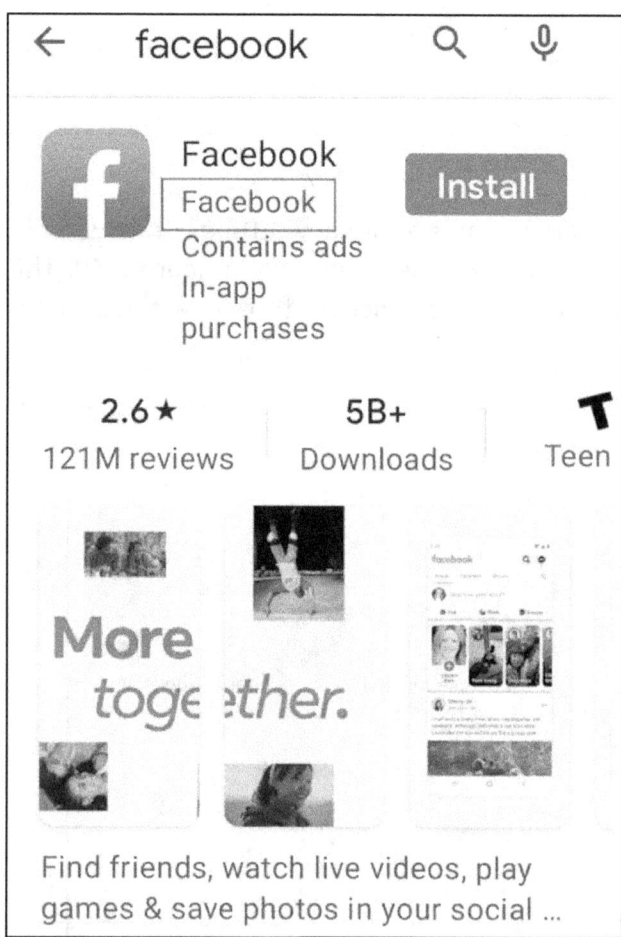

Figure 2.54

Chapter 2 – Facebook

Then all you need to do is install the app, open it and log in with your name and password. You will then see an interface that looks similar to what you would see on your computer.

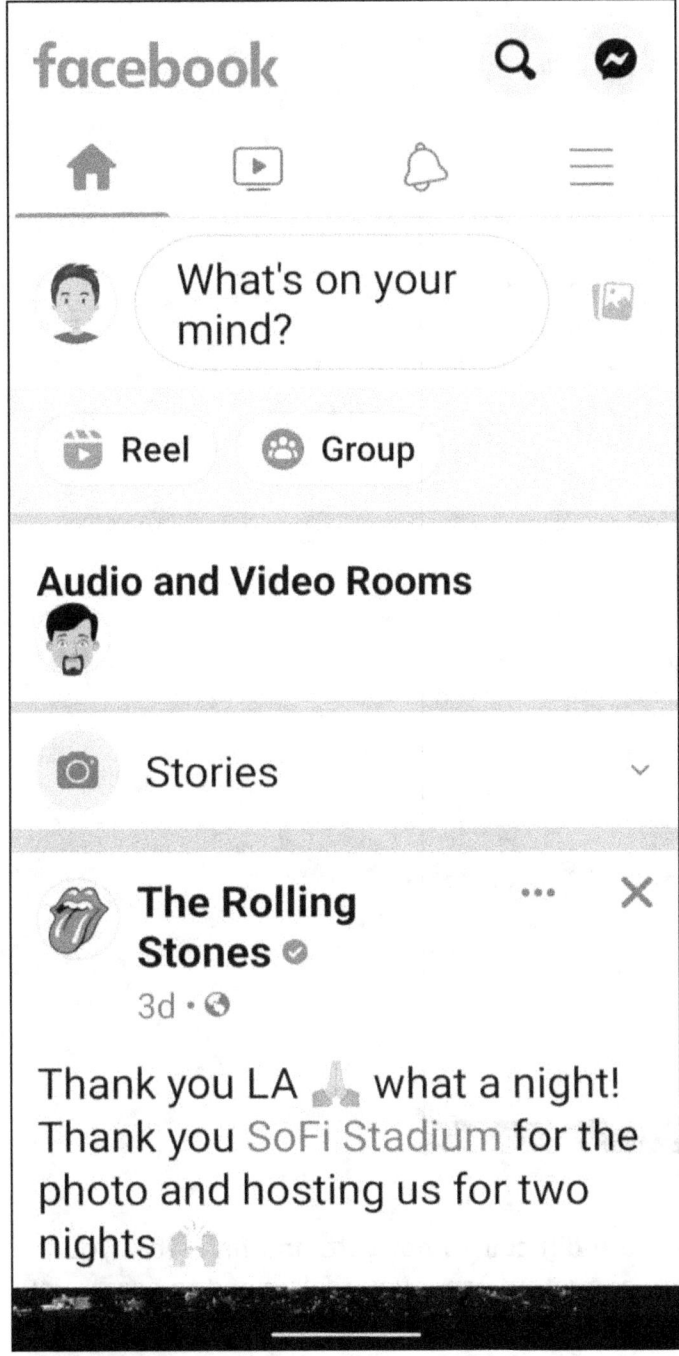

Figure 2.55

Chapter 2 – Facebook

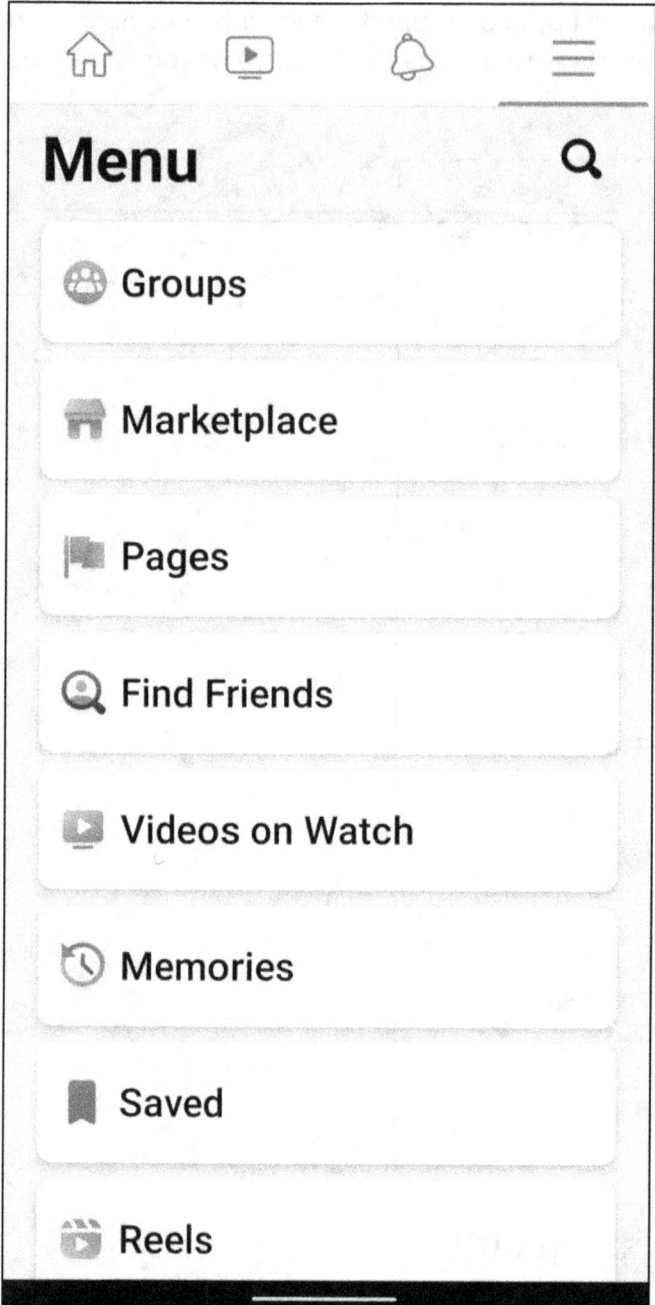

Figure 2.56

The mobile app will be a little more difficult to navigate and find what you are looking for, but it should be easy enough to use if you really need to access your account when you are away from your computer.

Chapter 2 – Facebook

 If you plan on using the Facebook mobile app to send messages to your friends, then it will most likely require you to also install the Facebook Messenger app in order to do so. It is also a free app that is easy to download and install.

Deleting Your Account
If you find that Facebook is not for you, or you end up spending so much time on it that you start to ignore your friends and family that you actually see in person then you might want to think about deleting your account.

If you think you only need a break from Facebook, you can deactivate your account which shuts it down but also gives you an option to activate it again in case you change your mind and want to come back.

To get to these two choices you will need to go back to the settings area I discussed in the last section and look for a setting called *Your Facebook Information*. Once you are there you will see the option called *Deactivation and deletion* and you would click on *View* to access these options.

Figure 2.57

63

Next, you will see that you can choose to either deactivate or delete your account. If you deactivate your account, your account will be disabled, and your name will be removed from things like posts and other shared features.

If you choose the delete option, then everything you shared and uploaded will be removed and you won't be able to get them back. Plus, any instant message history will be erased.

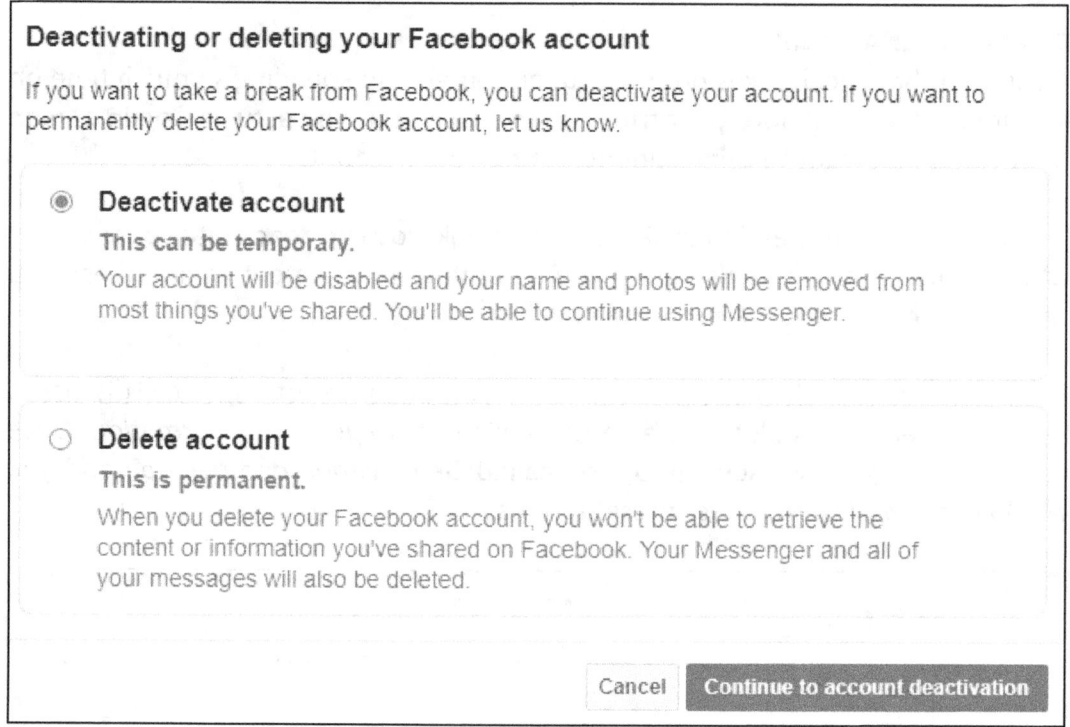

Figure 2.58

So be absolutely sure you want to delete your account before doing so, otherwise it will be a lot of work to start from scratch because you will need to add all of your friends back and upload any photos etc. that you shared all over again.

Chapter 3 – Instagram

If sharing things like what you had for dinner and how your grandson got an A on his science project is a little too much for you and you would rather just share pictures of all the exciting things you do, then Instagram might be for you.

Instagram Overview
Instagram is used for sharing photos with people who "follow" you. When you create an account and upload pictures, nobody will see them except for yourself unless they follow you or unless your photo happens to randomly appear in someone's feed.

As you start to follow more people and more people start to follow you, the more images you will see in the app and of course the more notifications you will receive as well. Most people use their smartphones with Instagram that is where most of their photos are kept. You can however, post photos you might have on your computer.

You also have the ability to share videos from your smartphone with your Instagram followers, so you are not just restricted to photos. Plus there are additional sharing features such as Feeds and Stories which I will be getting into later in this chapter.

Signing Up for an Account
Just like with any other type of social media account, Instagram requires that you create an account so you have an actual login that you will use each time you use the app.

There are a couple of ways you can create an account and whichever way you want to use will work just fine. Since Facebook owns Instagram, you can use your Facebook credentials to sign up and log into your Instagram account. But if you don't want your Instagram account tied to your Facebook account or don't have a Facebook account then you can sign up using an email address and phone number.

If you do decide to connect your Facebook account and log in that way, then you can go to the Instagram website (Instagram.com) on your computer and click on the Signup link to start the process. On the signup screen you would then click on *Log in with Facebook* button to begin the process.

Chapter 3 – Instagram

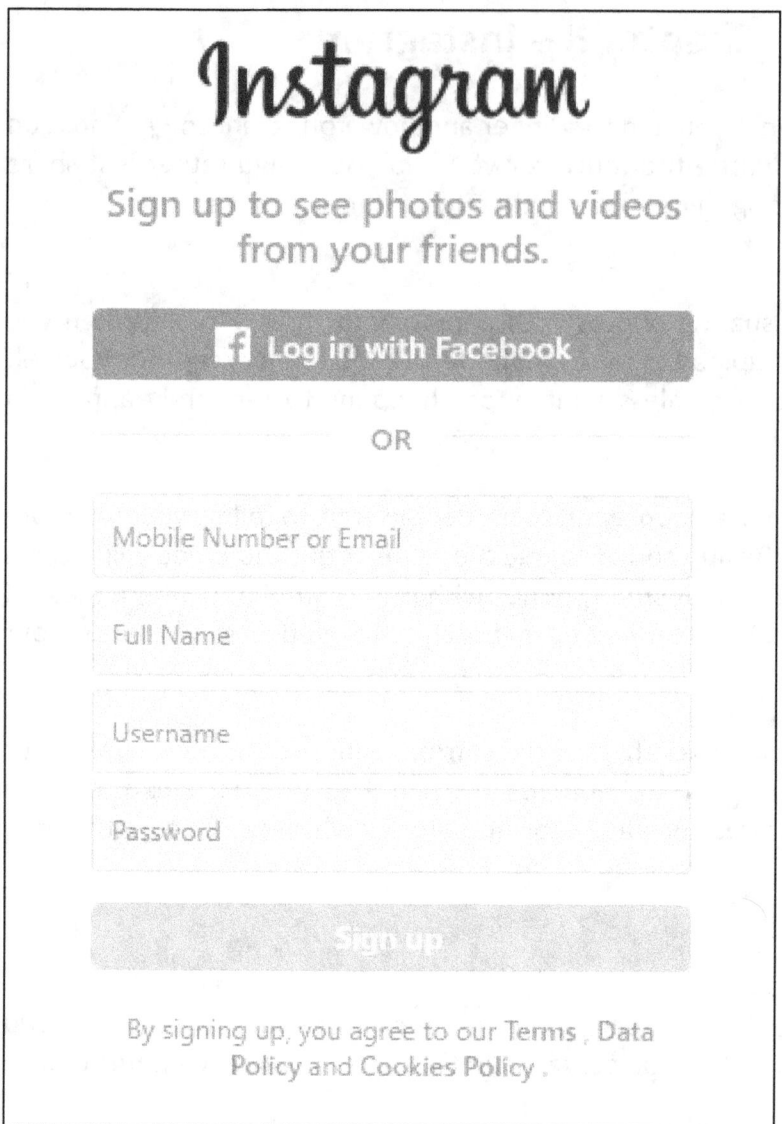

Figure 3.1

Then you would be asked to log into your Facebook account but if you were already logged in then you would see a screen similar to figures 3.2 and 3.3 and continue from there.

Chapter 3 – Instagram

Figure 3.2

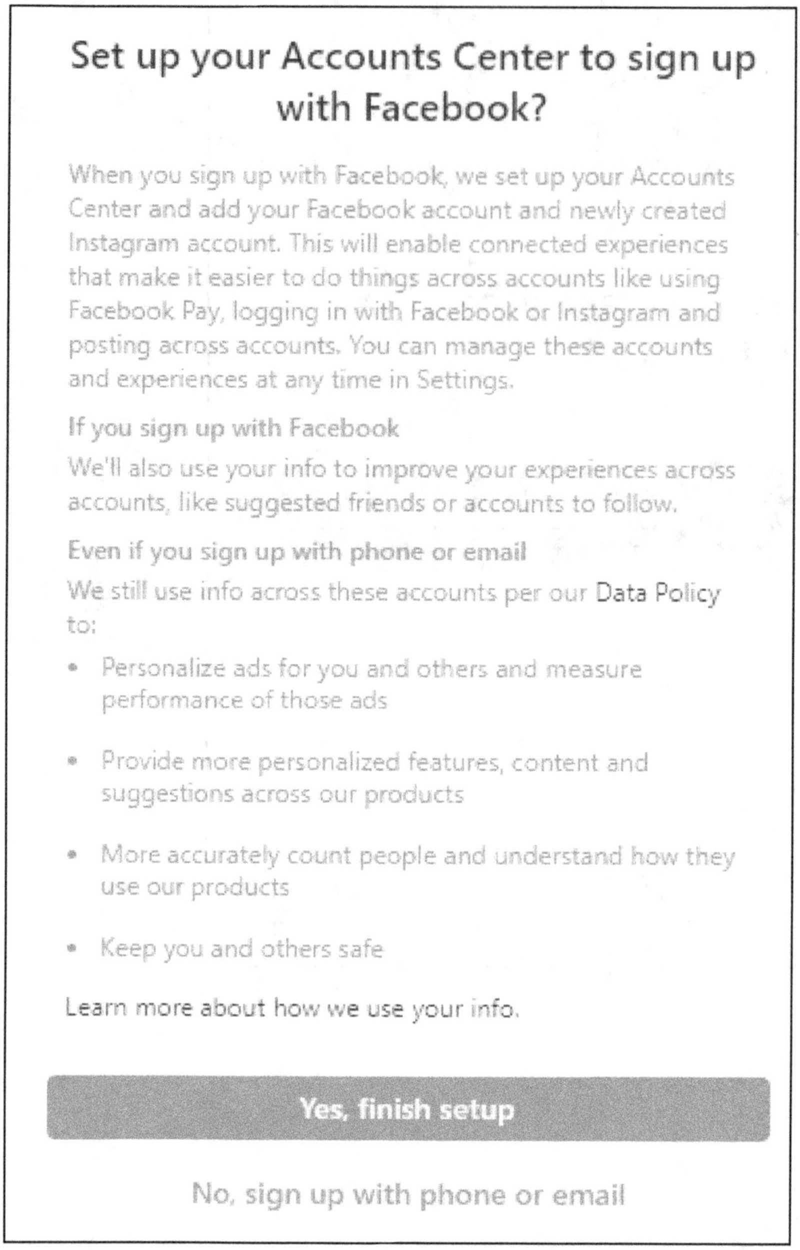

Chapter 3 – Instagram

> **Set up your Accounts Center to sign up with Facebook?**
>
> When you sign up with Facebook, we set up your Accounts Center and add your Facebook account and newly created Instagram account. This will enable connected experiences that make it easier to do things across accounts like using Facebook Pay, logging in with Facebook or Instagram and posting across accounts. You can manage these accounts and experiences at any time in Settings.
>
> If you sign up with Facebook
>
> We'll also use your info to improve your experiences across accounts, like suggested friends or accounts to follow.
>
> Even if you sign up with phone or email
>
> We still use info across these accounts per our Data Policy to:
>
> - Personalize ads for you and others and measure performance of those ads
>
> - Provide more personalized features, content and suggestions across our products
>
> - More accurately count people and understand how they use our products
>
> - Keep you and others safe
>
> Learn more about how we use your info.
>
> **Yes, finish setup**
>
> No, sign up with phone or email

Figure 3.3

For my example, I am going to create a new account as if I do not have a Facebook account or don't want to use my Facebook account for login purposes. So I will add my phone number or email address and name and also create a unique username and provide a secure password. If the username you choose is already taken, you won't see the checkmark next to what you typed in and you will need to come up with something else.

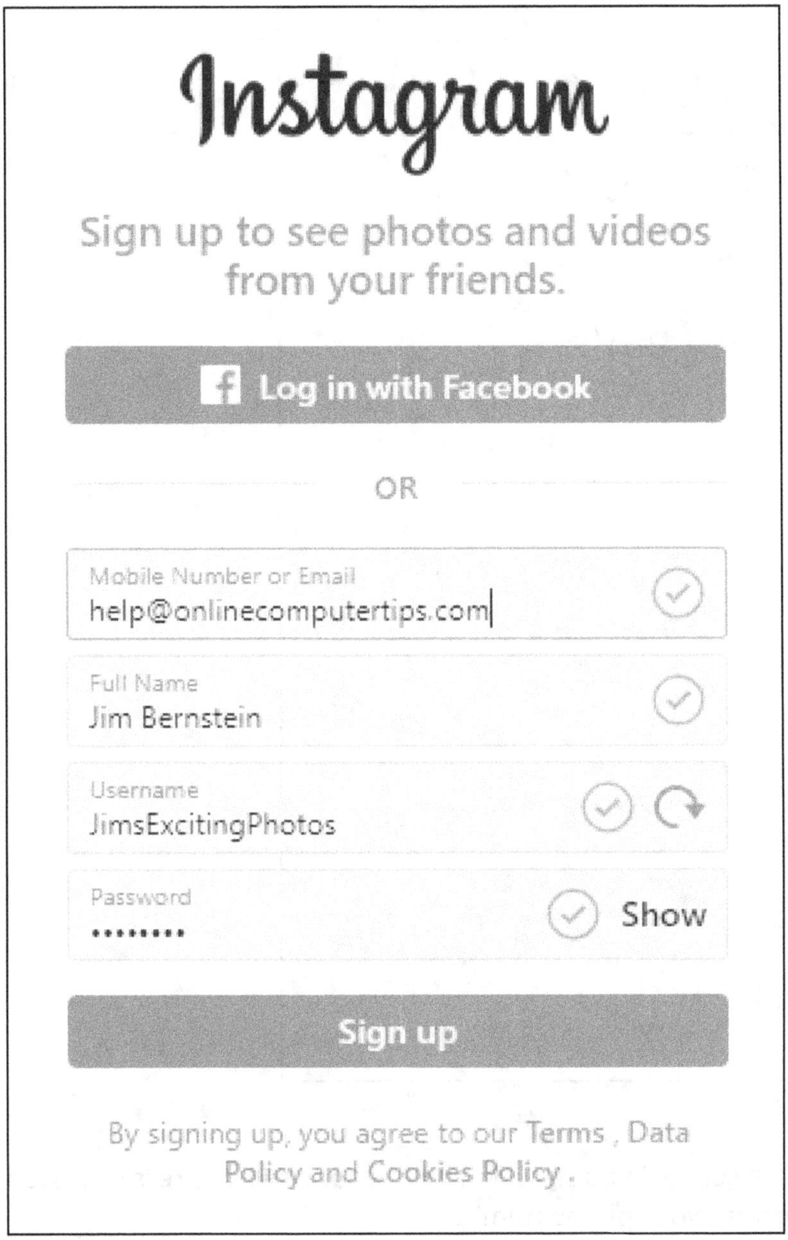

Chapter 3 – Instagram

Instagram

Sign up to see photos and videos from your friends.

Log in with Facebook

OR

Mobile Number or Email
help@onlinecomputertips.com

Full Name
Jim Bernstein

Username
JimsExcitingPhotos

Password
•••••••• Show

Sign up

By signing up, you agree to our Terms, Data Policy and Cookies Policy.

Figure 3.4

Then you will need to provide your birthday or at least a fake one that you will remember. Just be sure to make far enough in the past so you are at least 18 years old!

Chapter 3 – Instagram

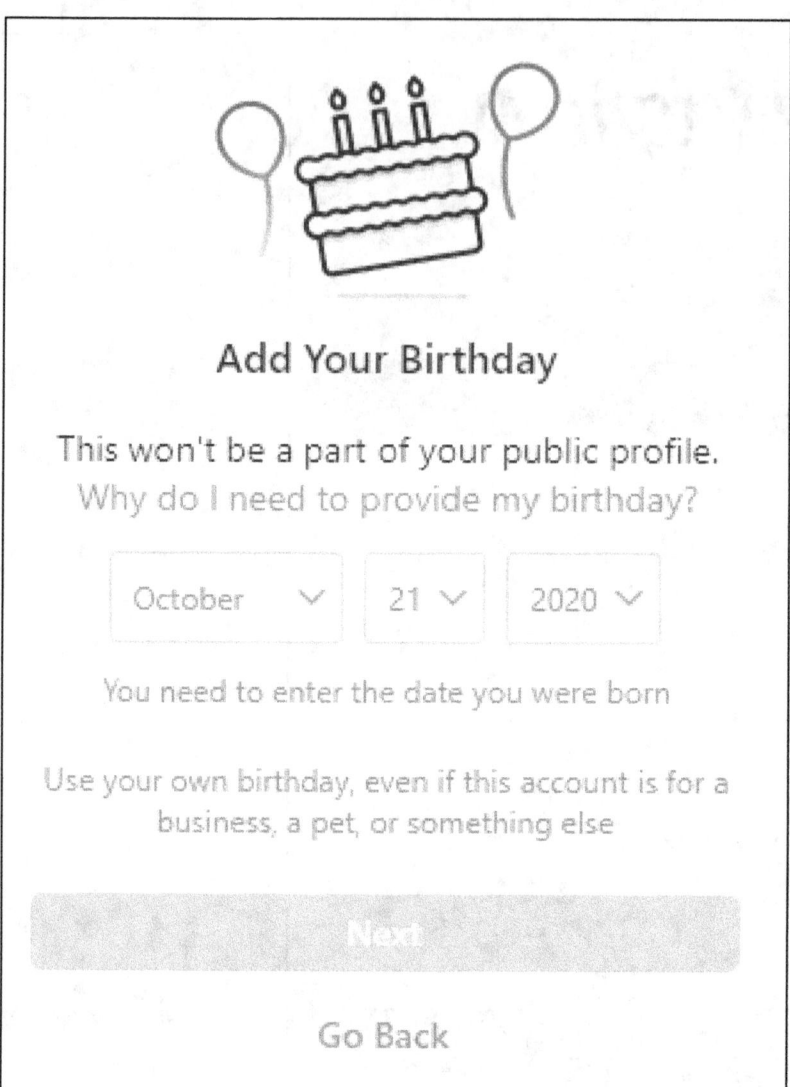

Figure 3.5

You will then be emailed a code if you signed up with your email address or texted a code if you signed up with your phone number.

Chapter 3 – Instagram

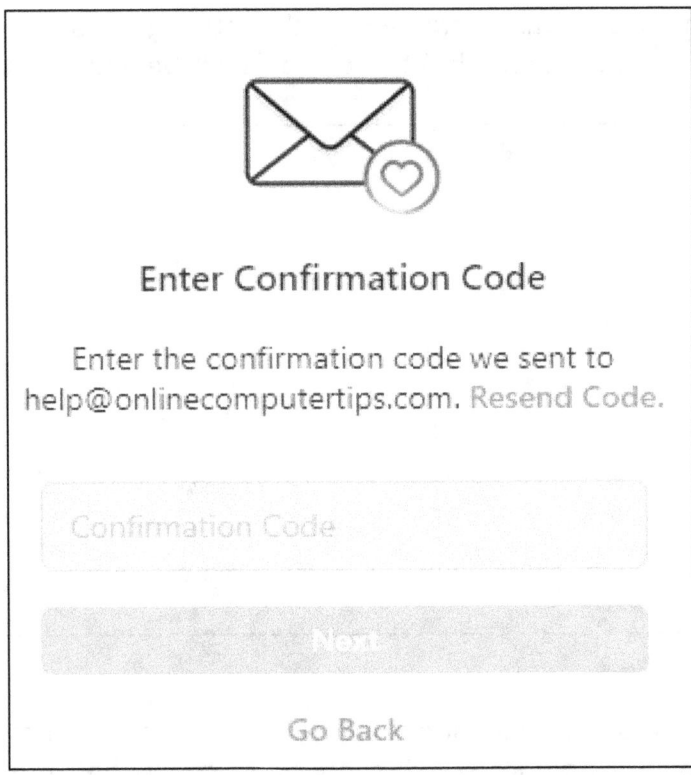

Figure 3.6

Then you will be asked if you want to turn on notifications so you will be alerted whenever someone you follow uploads a new picture or likes or comments on one of yours.

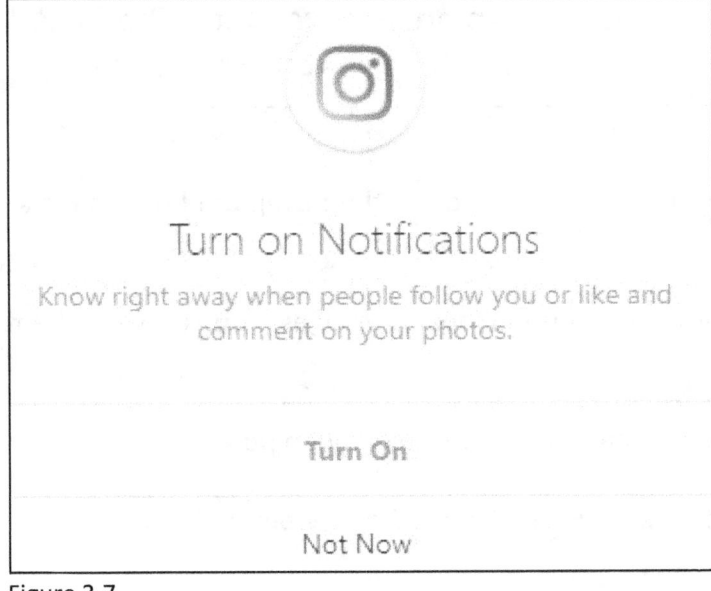

Figure 3.7

Chapter 3 – Instagram

You will then be shown some people that Instagram thinks you might want to follow but the odds that you really want to follow these people will be slim.

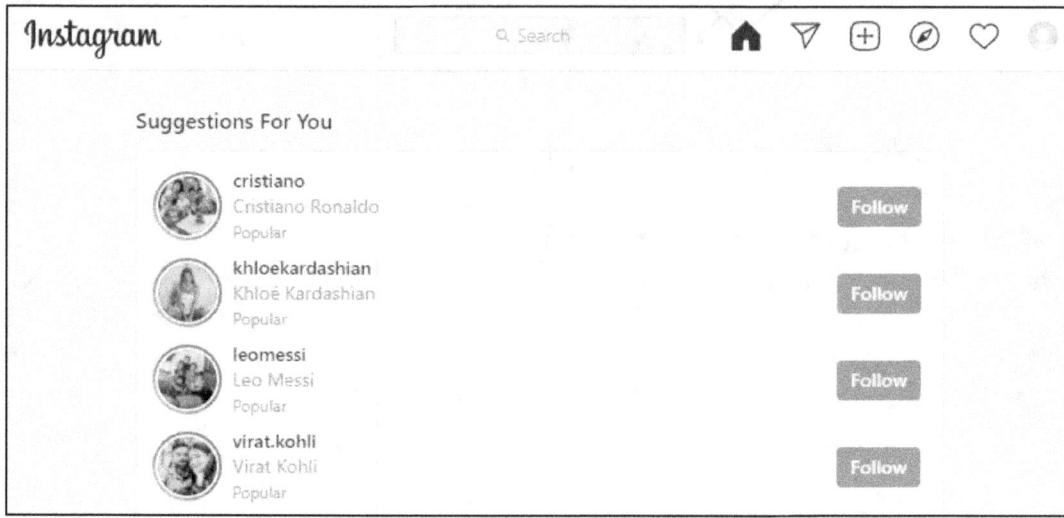

Figure 3.8

At the top right of the page, you will find various items that will take you to different areas of your Instagram account. I will show you how to find this information on your smartphone later in the chapter.

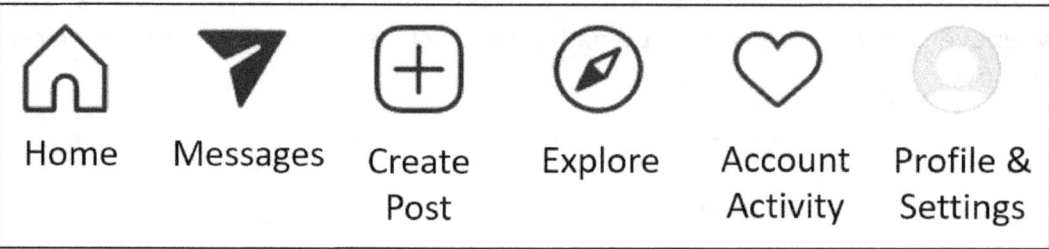

Figure 3.9

- **Home** – You can click this button to take you to the Instagram home page at any time.

- **Messages** – If people have sent you personal messages, you can view them here.

- **Create Post** – Come here to create a new photo or video post.

- **Explore** – Check out photos and videos from other people that you might be interested in.

72

Chapter 3 – Instagram

- **Account Activity** – Here you will find which of your photos or videos were liked or commented on by others.

- **Profile & Settings** – Here is where you can do things like edit your profile, change your password, phone number or email address, manage contacts, adjust security settings and so on.

Installing and using the Instagram App
You can install the Instagram app on your smartphone or tablet the same way you did for the Facebook app. Just make sure you are installing the real app and not some third party application with a similar name.

You can find the app in the Play Store (Android devices) or the App Store (iPhones and iPads). Then you will simply install it, open it up and then sign in with your username and password.

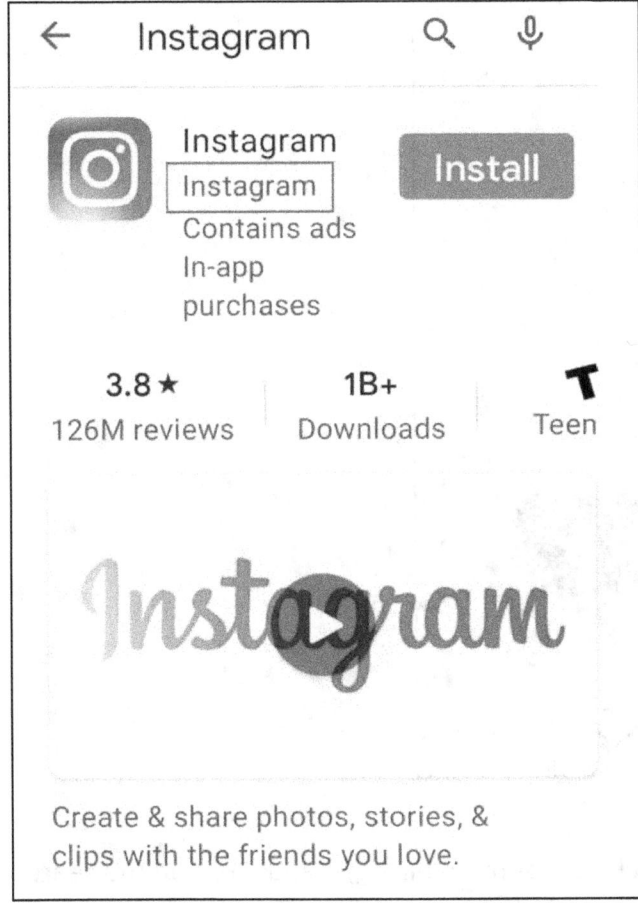

Figure 3.10

Chapter 3 – Instagram

Once you are logged in, you will see a similar looking interface with the same icons as seen in figure 3.9. The mobile app will also offer you suggestions of people to follow that you are most likely not interested in.

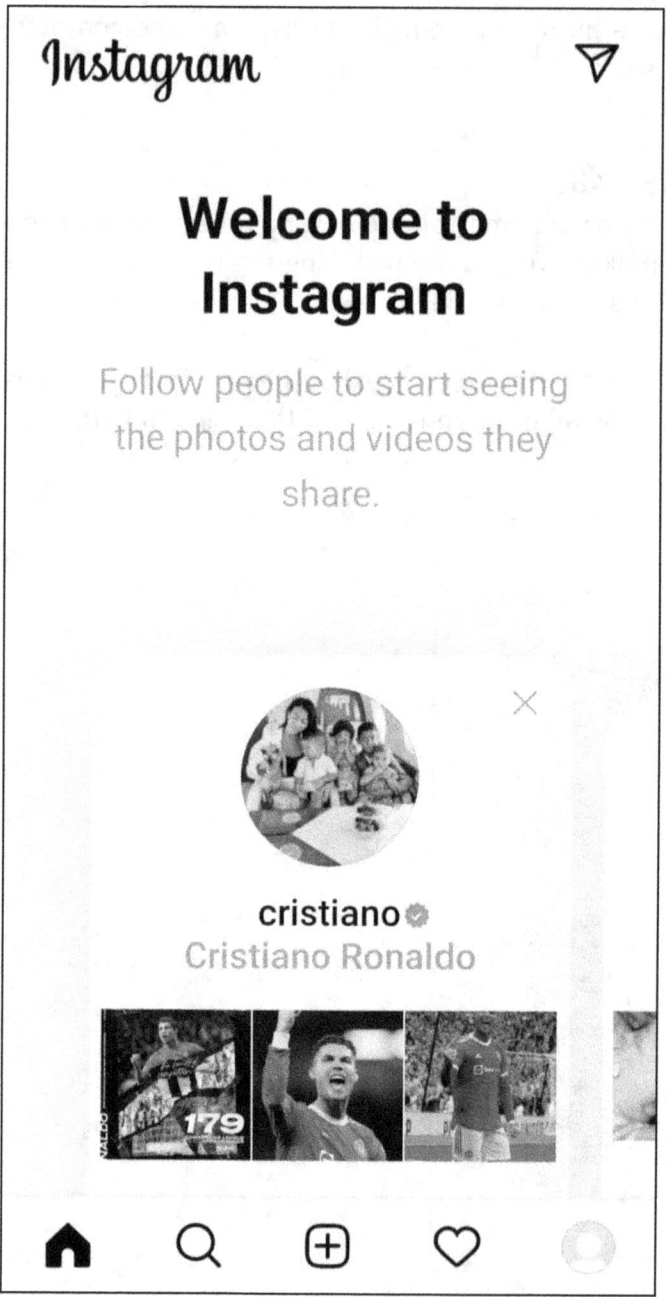

Figure 3.11

If I wanted to search for a topic such as mountain biking, I would tap on the search magnifying glass icon and type in my search.

Chapter 3 – Instagram

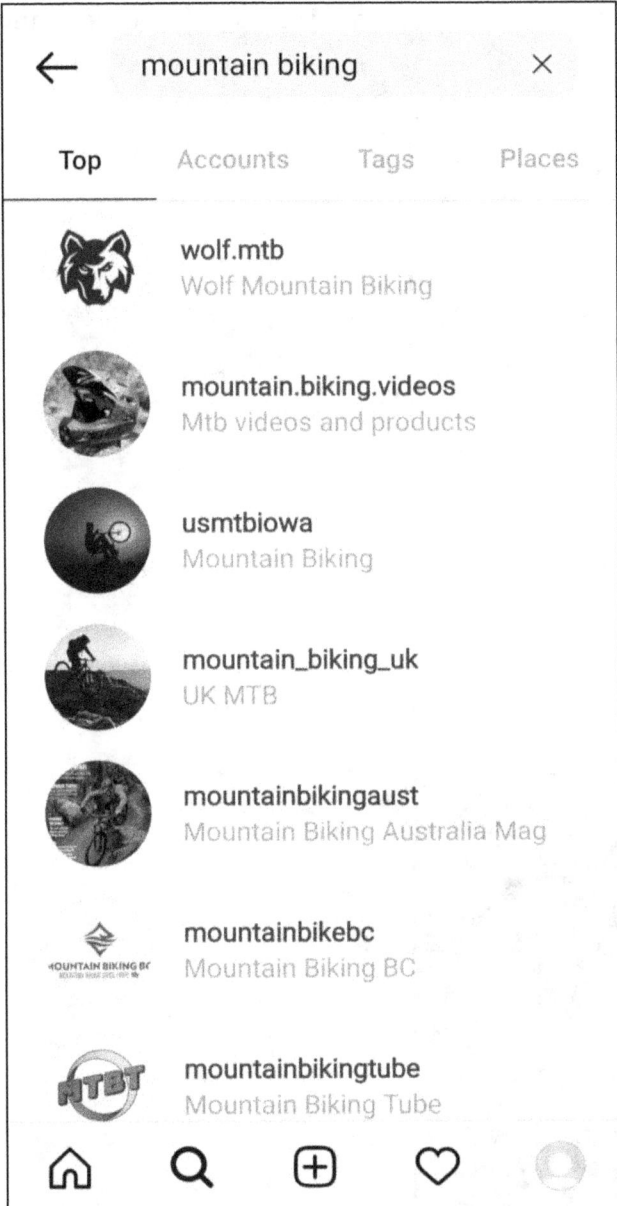

Figure 3.12

Let's say that the user named **mountain.biking.videos** seems interesting to me. To view their photos and videos I would then tap on their name, and I would then be shown all of their posts in chronological order.

I can also see information about their account such as how many posts they have, how many followers they have and how many people they are following themselves. And if I decide I like their content, I can tap on the *Follow* button to have notifications sent to my phone whenever they make a new post. Tapping on

Chapter 3 – Instagram

the *Message* button will let you send them a personal message. Whether they reply or not is up to them.

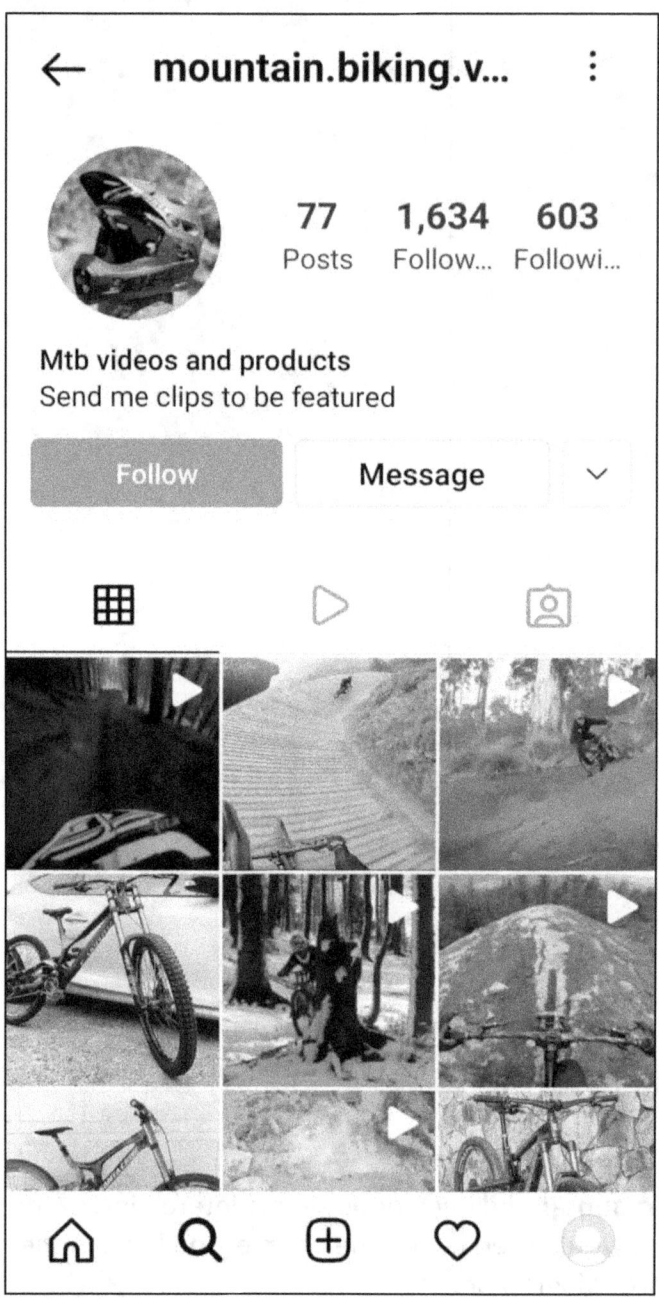

Figure 3.13

If you look at the icons above the pictures in figure 3.13 you will see that there is one with 9 boxes. This is where all their latest posts of different types will show up. The next icon that looks like a play button is where you will find video posts.

Chapter 3 – Instagram

And the last icon indicates posts where this user was mentioned. You may see other types of icons here depending on what account you are looking at and what types of posts they are making.

If you were to click on the three vertical dots at the top right of the app, you would get some additional options as shown in figure 3.14.

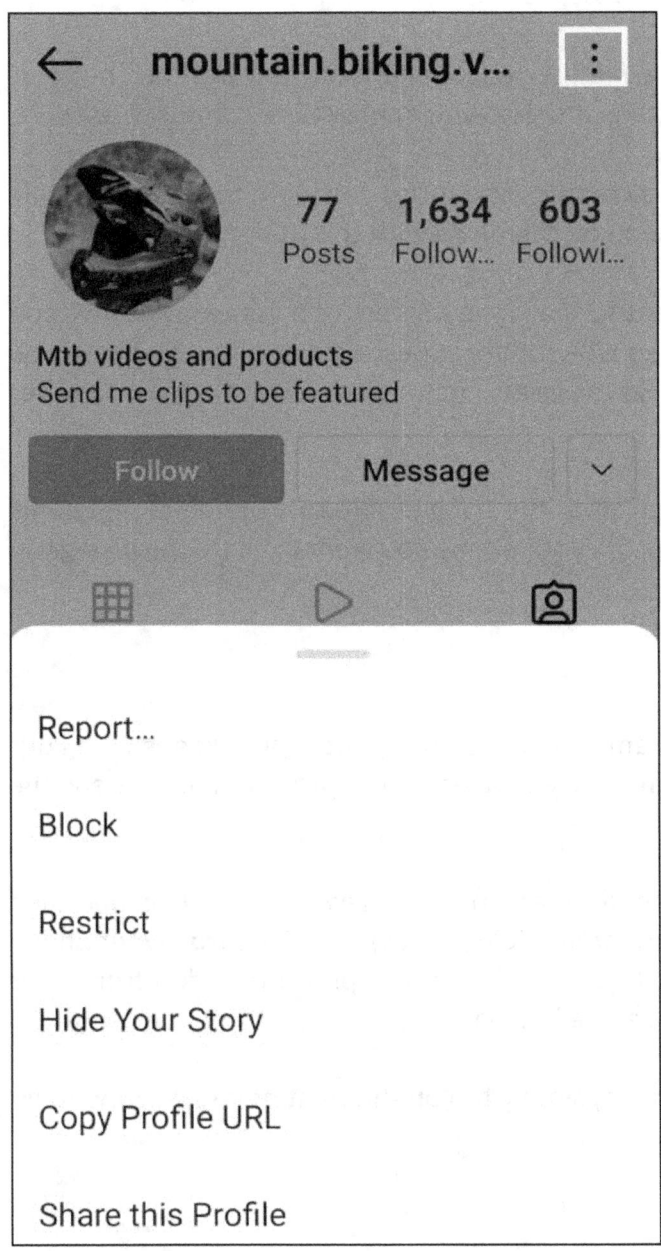

Figure 3.14

Chapter 3 – Instagram

Here is what each of these options will do.

- **Report** – If you see that someone is making inappropriate posts, you can report them to Instagram so they can take action on the user account.

- **Block** – Use this option to prevent a user from viewing or commenting on your posts as well as sending you messages.

- **Restrict** – This option will allow a user to comment on your post etc. but only you and them will be able to see it unless you approve the comment itself.

- **Hide Your Story** – If you have created any stories and want to prevent certain users from viewing them, then you can do so with this option.

- **Copy Profile URL** – If you want to share the address of a user with others, you can have Instagram copy their URL (Uniform Resource Locator) and then you can paste it into an email, text message, chat and so on and send it to other people.

- **Share this Profile** – This is similar to the Copy Profile URL option except it will allow you to choose which app on your phone you want to share the Instagram profile with.

Sharing Photos and Videos
The whole point of using Instagram is to share your photos and videos with your followers and hopefully gain some new followers in the process. Fortunately, the process is fairly easy to do.

From the main screen you will need to tap on the *+ Create Post* button and then you will be able to choose a photo (or multiple photos) or a video from your phone or take a new one on the spot to share. To share a photo or video from your computer you would click on the same button.

Once you select your photo or video, simply tap on the right pointing arrow to go to the next screen.

Chapter 3 – Instagram

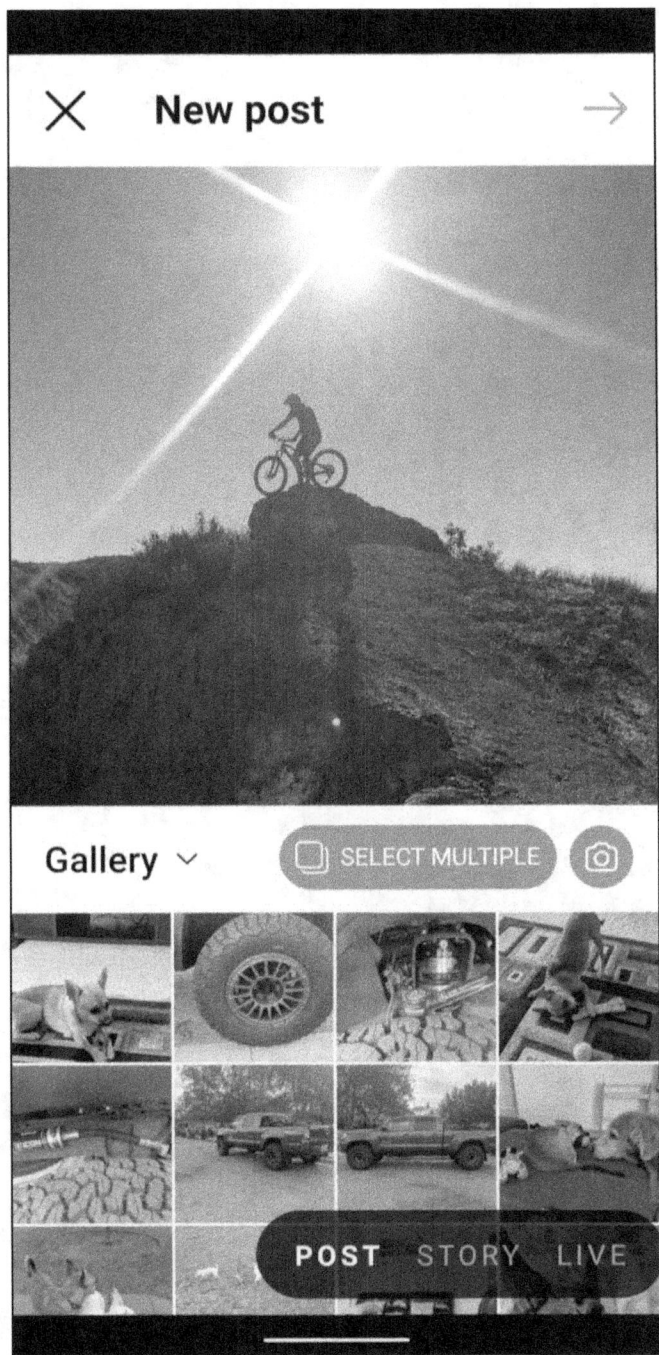

Figure 3.15

Next, you will have the opportunity to add a filter to your image or make adjustments such as changing the brightness, contrast, color and so on (figure 3.16). If you want to keep things the way they are, simply tap on the right pointing arrow once again.

Chapter 3 – Instagram

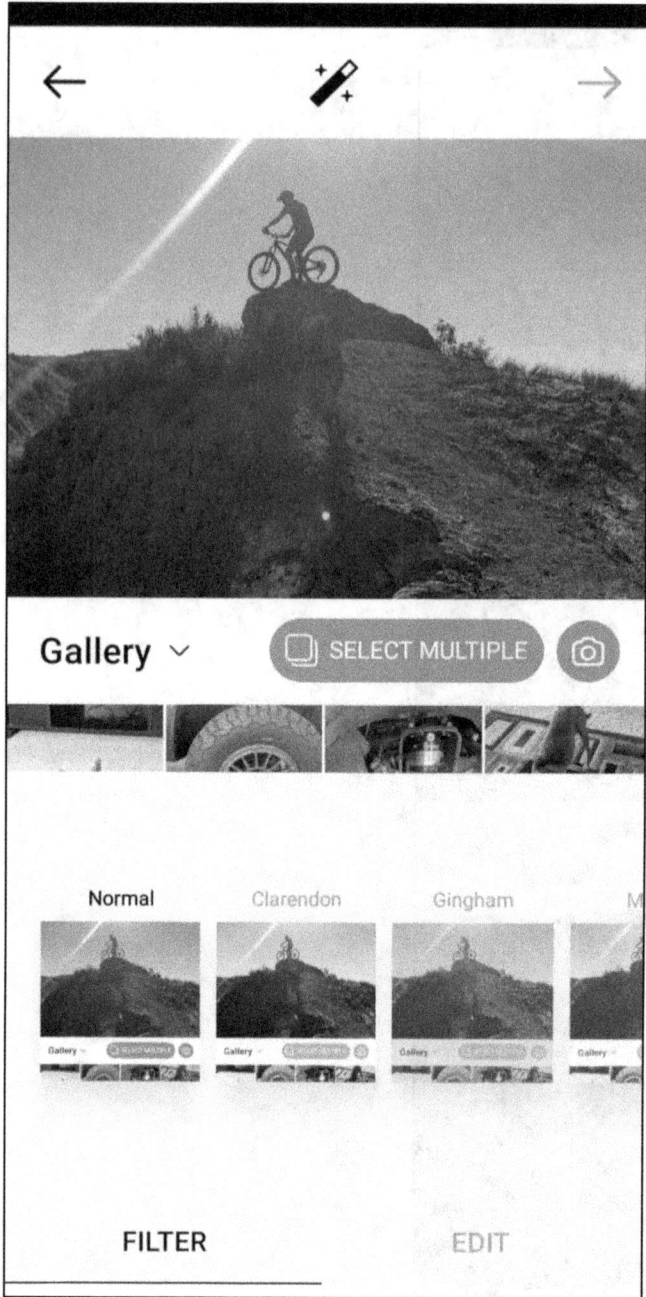

Figure 3.16

Next, you will add a caption to your post as well as add any additional information you want to be shown on your post. If you have location services enabled on your phone, then Instagram can read where the picture was taken or where your phone is currently located to add it to the post. Or you can manually type in the location if you wish to share that as well.

Chapter 3 – Instagram

If you have other accounts such as Facebook, Twitter or Tumblr enabled on your phone then you can share your post to those platforms at the same time. If everything looks good, tap on the checkmark to make your post live on your account.

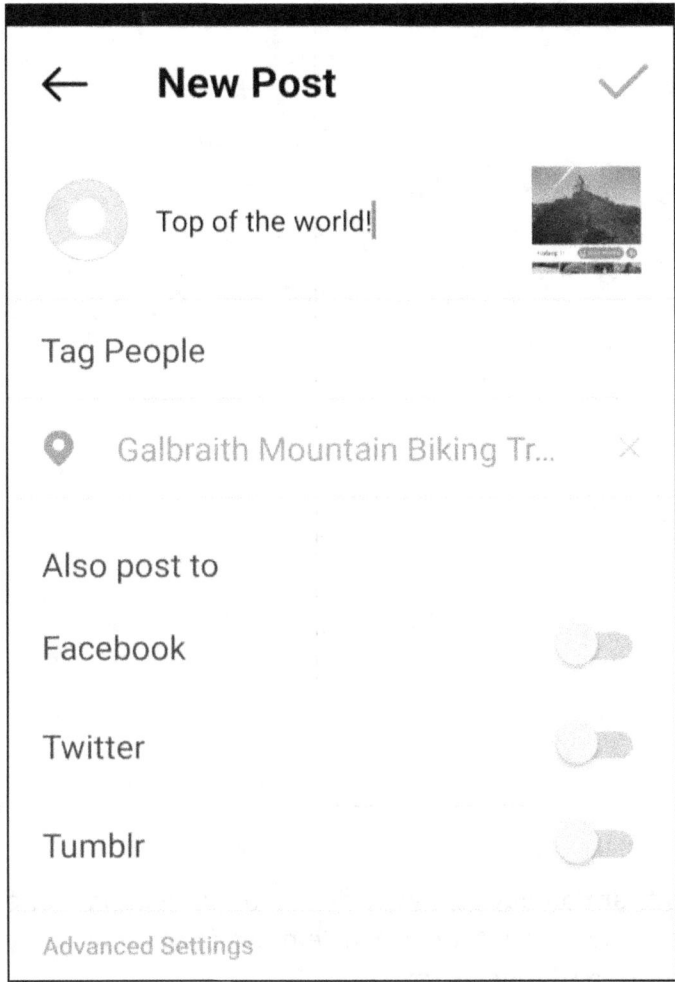

Figure 3.17

Adding a Profile Picture
Before I get into people following you and you following others, I would like to quickly go over how to add a profile picture to your account. If your goal is to get as many followers as you can then you will want to make your account stand out. Or if you just want your friends and family to be able to recognize your account from a picture then that is another reason to add one to your profile.

Chapter 3 – Instagram

To add a photo, tap on the profile icon at the lower right hand side of the app and then tap on the *Edit Profile* button. Then you would tap on *Change Profile Photo*. This procedure works the same way if you are doing it on your computer in a web browser.

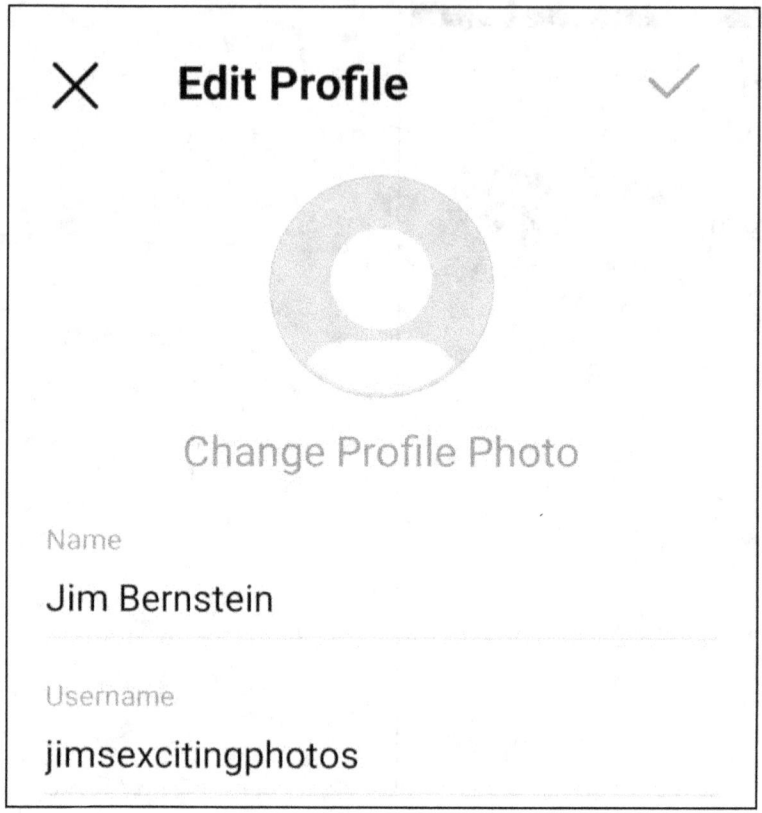

Figure 3.18

Then you can add a new photo that you have on your device or even import one from Facebook. Now you can see my account looks a little more exciting with my profile picture rather than the boring silhouette icon.

Chapter 3 – Instagram

Figure 3.19

Following Others and Follow Requests
If you post a bunch of pictures and videos on Instagram and nobody sees them then what's the point of having an account, right? In order to have others see what you are sharing they will need to follow you unless the rare chance that one of your posts shows up in their feed or search results.

To follow someone, you will need to find their username and then tap on the *Follow* button. I will search for my friend Todd Simms and thanks to his profile pictures, I instantly recognize his account.

Chapter 3 – Instagram

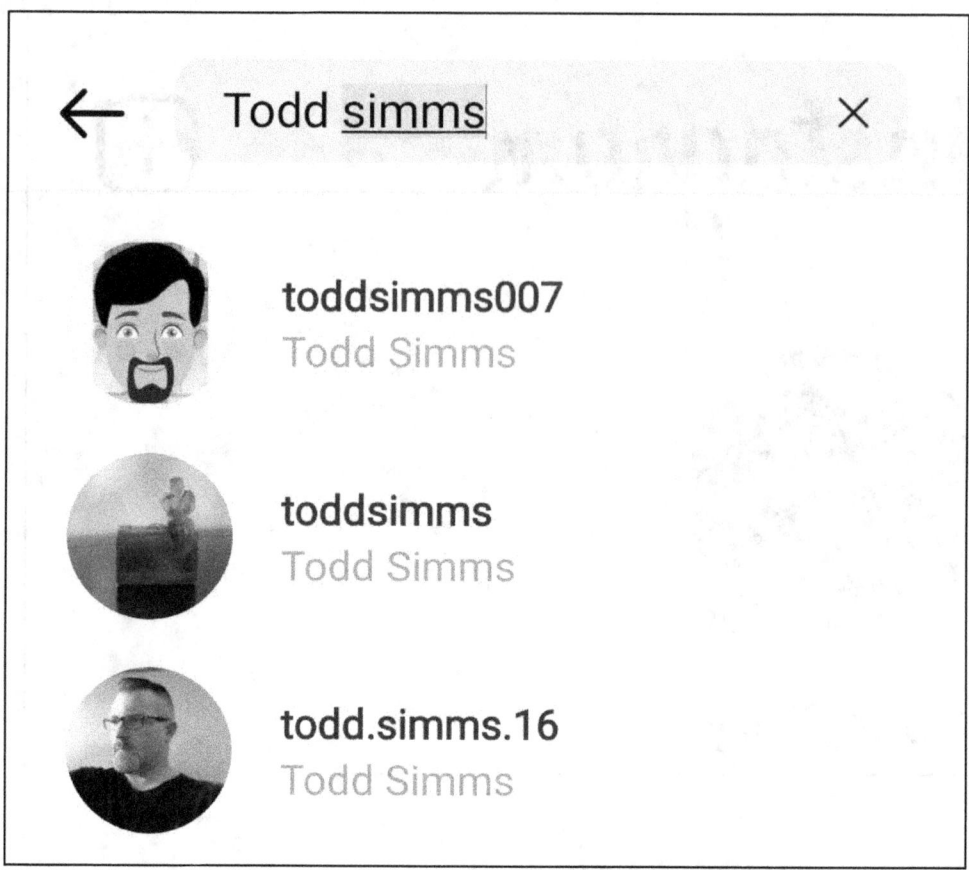

Figure 3.20

When I go to Todd's account, I can see his posts because they are public and if I tap on the *Follow* button, I will then be following Todd.

Chapter 3 – Instagram

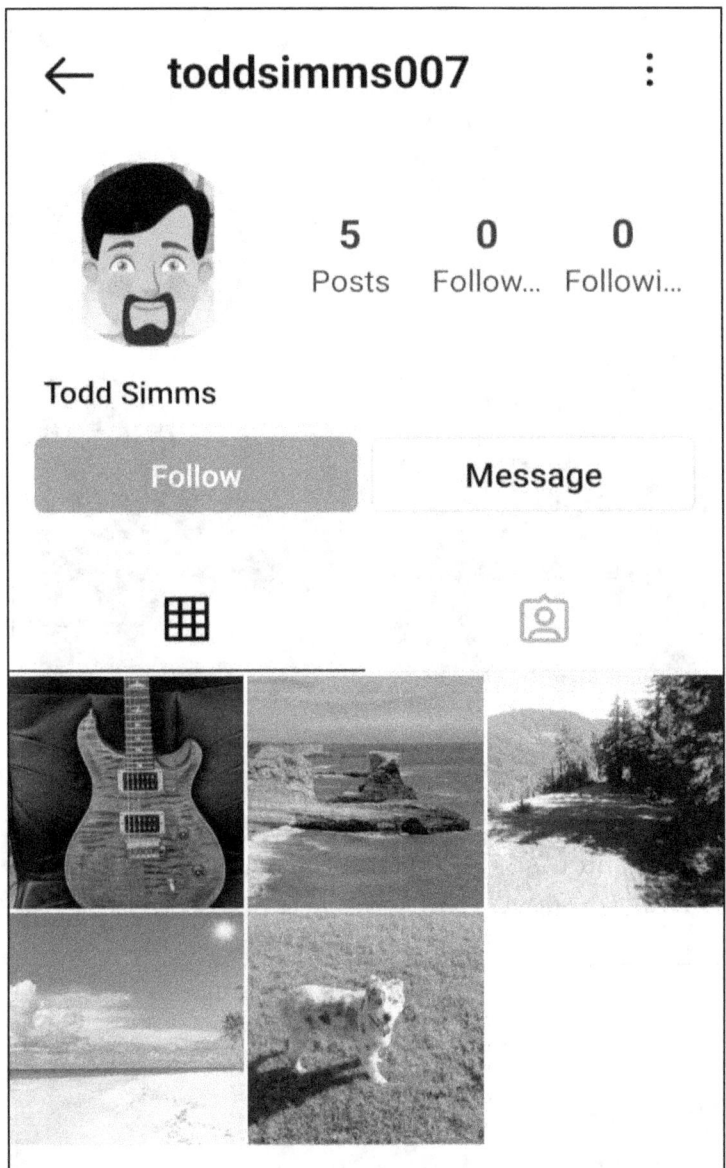

Figure 3.21

Now when Todd looks at his account, he will see that he has a new follower and also has a new notification letting him know that I am now following him. In this example, I am using Instagram on my computer. Todd can then click on the word follower to see who is following him.

Chapter 3 – Instagram

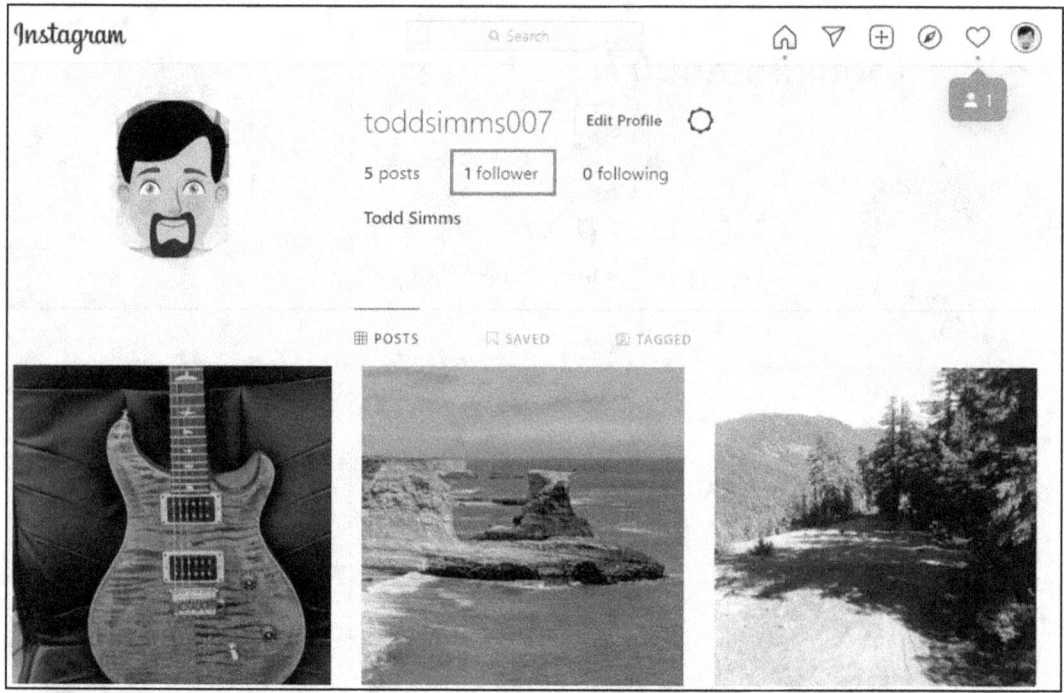

Figure 3.22

For my next example, I am going to make my account private to show you what happens when you try to follow a private account. Once again from my computer I am going to my profile settings and then the *Privacy and Security* settings and will check the box that says *Private Account*.

Figure 3.23

Chapter 3 – Instagram

To get to these same settings in the Instagram app on your phone you would tap on the 3 vertical bars and then choose *Settings* and then *Privacy* and turn the privacy setting on.

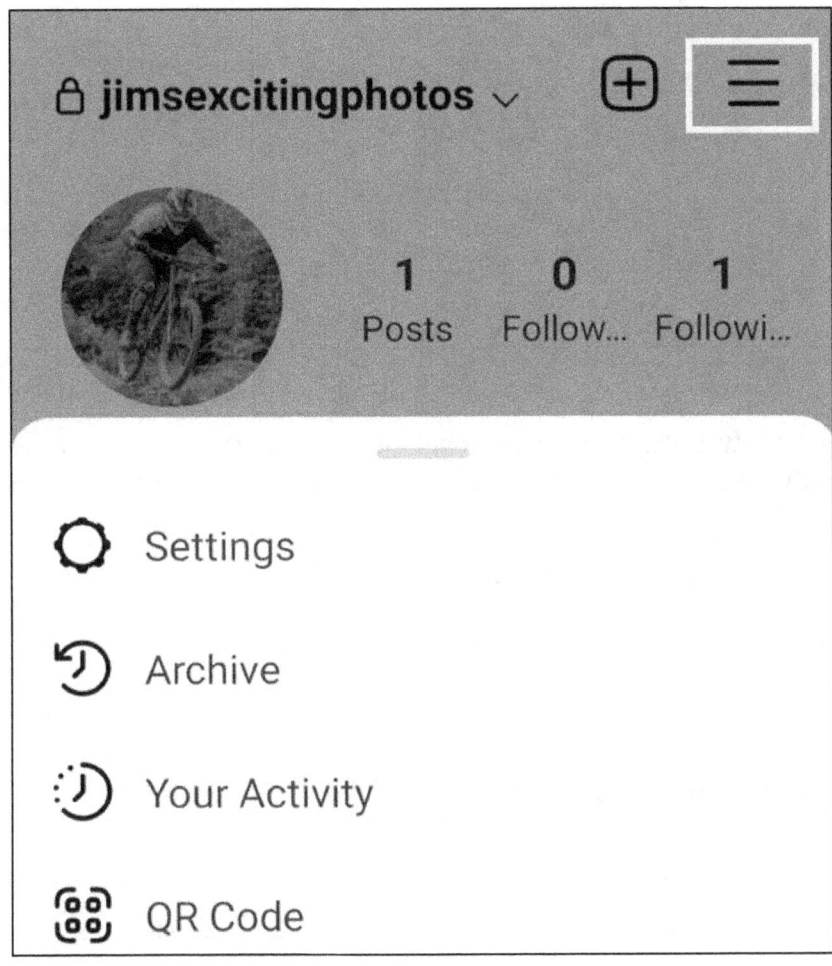

Figure 3.24

If Todd wants to follow my account, he can search for me and when he finds me, he will see that my account is private but can still click on the *Follow* button to send a request to follow me. In this example, the button says *Follow Back* because I am following him as well.

Chapter 3 – Instagram

Figure 3.25

Now the Follow (or Follow Back) button will change to Requested and I will be shown a notification when I log into my Instagram account that Todd wants to follow me (figure 3.27).

Figure 3.26

I can then choose to either confirm or delete this request.

Chapter 3 – Instagram

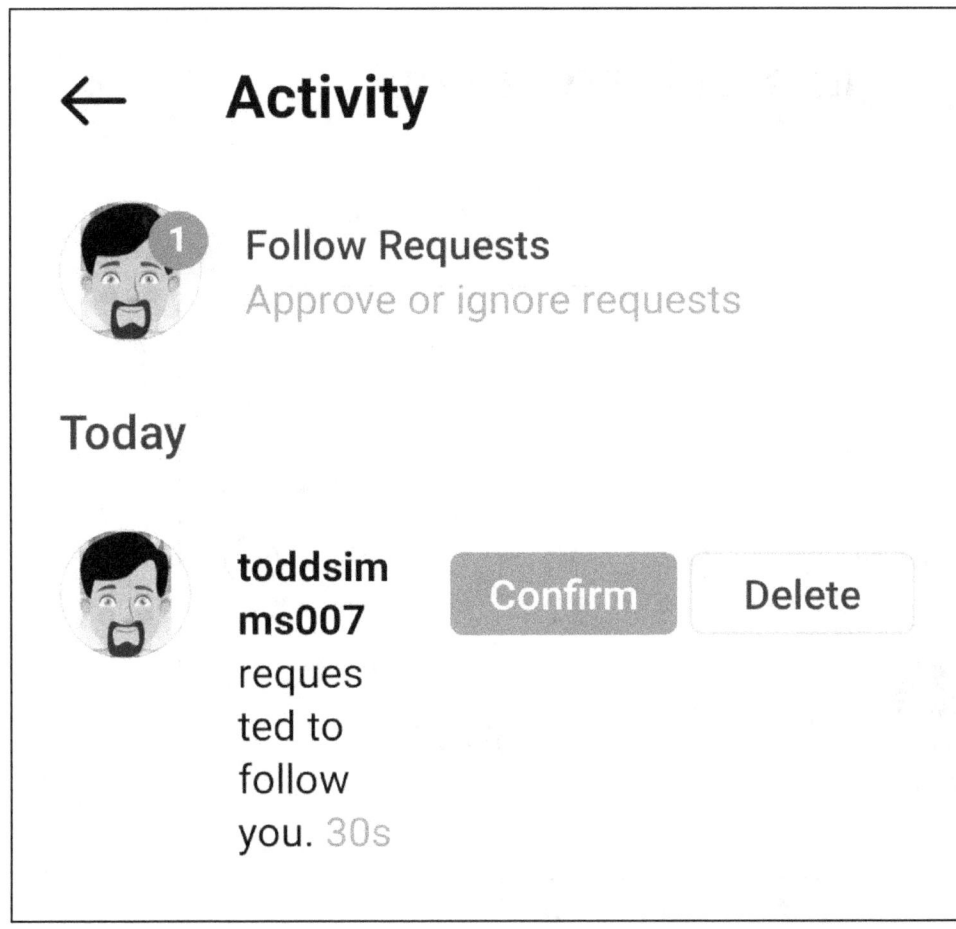

Figure 3.27

I will allow Todd to follow me by tapping on the *Confirm* button and now Todd will be following me and will receive notifications when I create new posts.

If you are following someone and decide you don't want to follow them anymore, you can click or tap on the profile icon, then on the word Following and find the person in your list that you want to unfollow. From there all you need to do is click or tap on the Following button to unfollow that user.

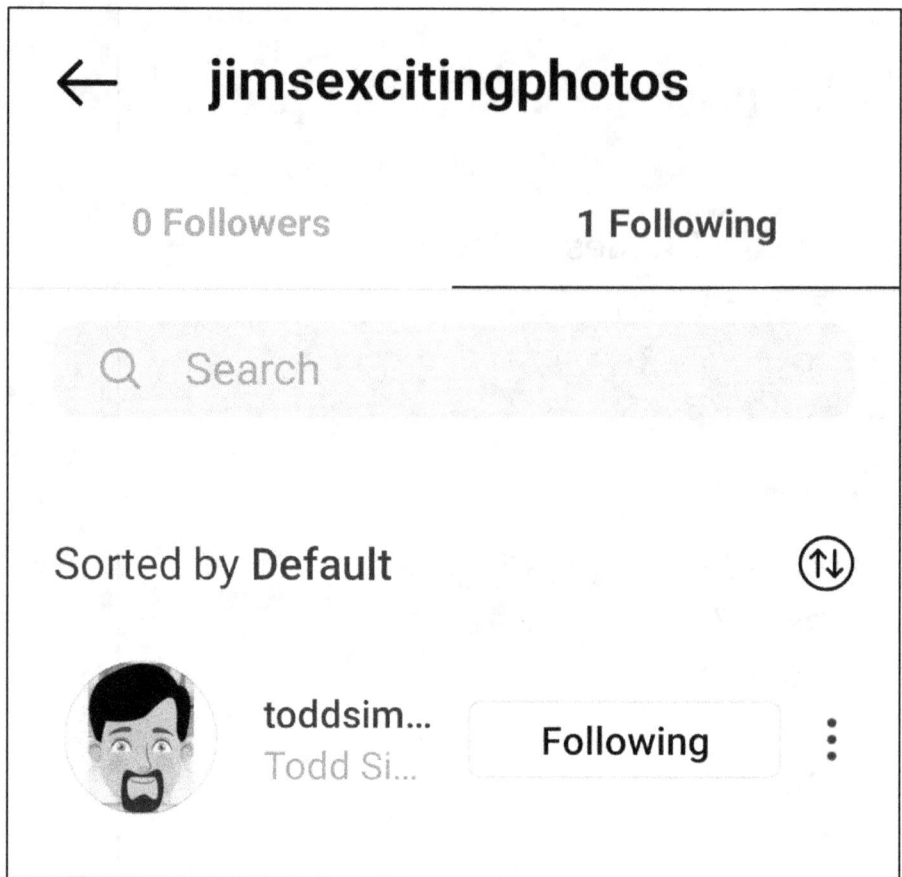

Figure 3.28

You can also stop someone from following you by going to the *Followers* section and then clicking or tapping on *Remove*.

Liking and Commenting on Posts
Once you start following people and performing searches for photos and videos you are interested in viewing, you will find yourself wanting to show the user who posted the videos that you think they did a good job and that you like their work. This is where likes and comments come into play.

Let's say I was checking out Todd's account and looking at the pictures he posted and really like the one of his new guitar. When I view the post there will be three icons underneath the picture as seen in figure 3.29.

Chapter 3 – Instagram

The heart icon will give that post a like, the speech bubble icon will let me comment on the picture and the paper airplane icon will let me send Todd a personal message.

Figure 3.29

Chapter 3 – Instagram

I will now give the photo a like and also make a comment on it. When Todd goes to his Instagram account (as shown from a web browser on his computer), he will see my like and comment in his notification area.

Figure 3.30

When Todd opens that particular post with the picture I liked and commented on (figure 3.31), he will also see my like and comment. Notice to the right of my comment that there is another heart where Todd can like my comment. Then Todd can make his own comment as well. Yes, I know there is a lot of liking and commenting going on here!

Chapter 3 – Instagram

Figure 3.31

 You might have noticed the **#prsguitars** in the description of the post. This is called a **hashtag** and is used to make your post come up in searches when someone searches for the keyword after the # symbol.

Chapter 3 – Instagram

Instagram Feed and Search

As you start to follow more people on Instagram, you will begin to notice that your main screen, or your feed will show more and more videos and pictures. This is because Instagram will show content from those you follow and put the photos it thinks you would be the most interested in at the top of your feed.

Your feed can be accessed by tapping or clicking on the home icon. Since the account I made for myself is new and I am only following Todd Simms, I will only see the photos that he has shared. As I begin to follow other users, their photos will eventually end up in my feed as they post new content.

If you would like to see photos and videos from other users that you are not following or are looking for other people to follow with similar interests to yours, you can use the search feature. Figure 3.32 shows how the search feature works from the Instagram website on a computer. If I type in Australian Shepherd, it will bring up a listing of posts regarding that topic that I can scroll down and view.

Figure 3.32

If you notice the first result in the search says **#austrailianshepherd** and has over 8 million posts that is because it's showing results from users who have used the #austrailianshepherd hashtag in their post so it would come up when people like myself search for Australian Shepherd. If I click on that result, I will be shown posts

Chapter 3 – Instagram

from multiple Instagram users and not just one like I would see if I were to click on something from the other search results.

If I perform the same search on the phone app, I will get similar results but if I tap on *See All Results*, I will be shown some additional categories as seen in figure 3.4.

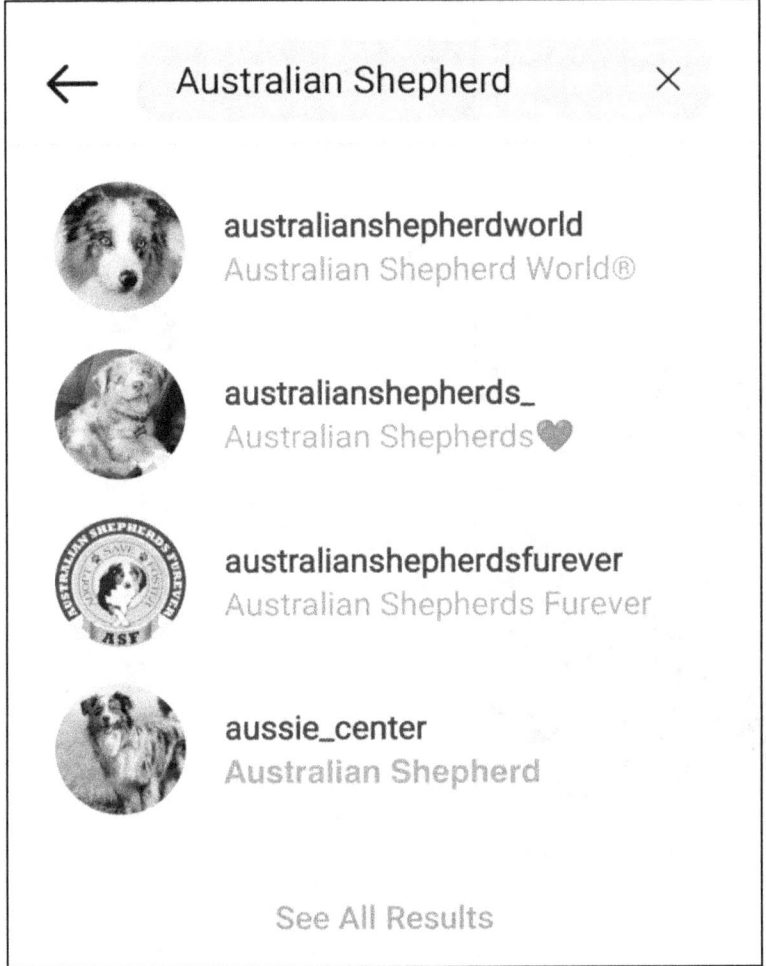

Figure 3.33

As you can see, there are the top results, user accounts that are about Australian Shepherds, posts that have Australian Shepherds tagged, and also places where you can find Australian Shepherds. At the top I can even shop for Australian Shepherd related products.

Chapter 3 – Instagram

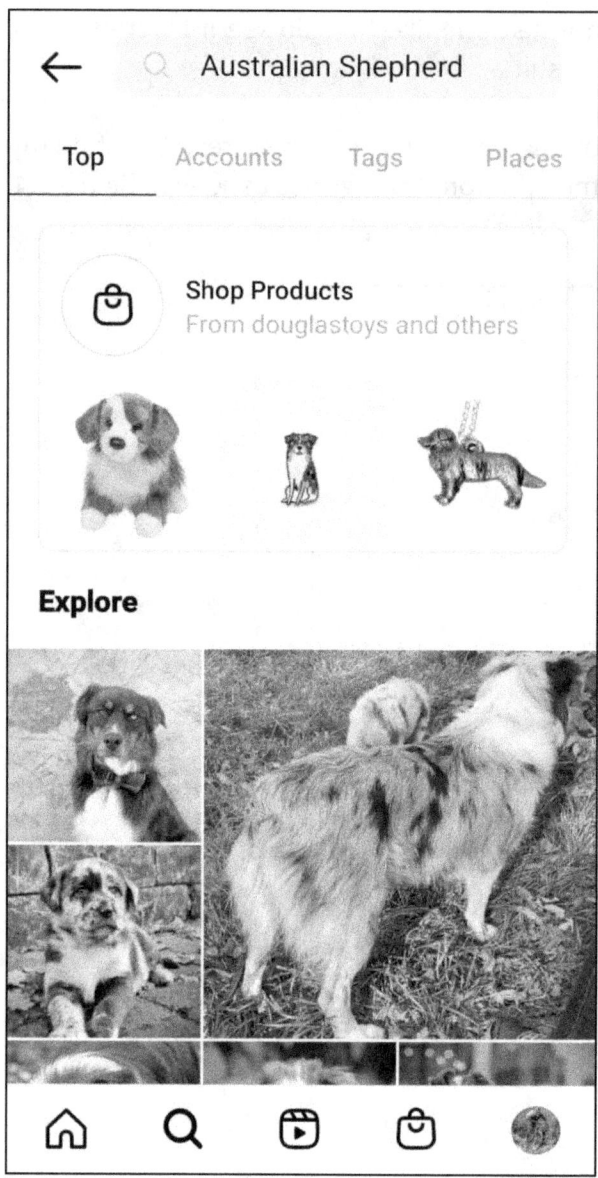

Figure 3.34

The larger post in figure 3.34 is actually a video and if I were to tap on that I would be able to scroll through various Australian Shepherd video clips.

Reels
Speaking of video clips, Instagram also includes what they call Reels, which are short video clips that you can create and add visual effects to at the same time. When you are in the main search area of the app, you will see a Reels section that you can tap on to scroll through other users' Reels.

Chapter 3 – Instagram

Figure 3.35

Once you view a particular video and start to scroll through the others, you will begin to notice that the videos are closely related to each other. Instagram will pay attention to what type of videos you watch the longest and then start to show you more videos that are related to that content. So if you tend to spend a lot of time watching cat videos, you will start to notice more and more of them in this area. You can also get to the Reels section from the video play button icon at the bottom center of the app.

Chapter 3 – Instagram

If you want to create your own Reel, you can start a new post and you will see the Reels option at the bottom right of the app. Then you can get your camera ready to film the subject of your Reel and preview music or visual effects from the icons at the left side of the screen as seen in figure 3.36. Then when you have everything looking the way you like, you would press the record button at the bottom of the screen to record your Reel. Then if you like the way it looks, you can share it to your feed so your followers can watch the video.

Figure 3.36

Chapter 3 – Instagram

Notification Settings

Just like with most apps, Instagram will want to send you popup notifications for just about any occasion, such as when someone likes one of your pictures or creates a new post etc. Fortunately, it is easy to adjust these settings so you will only see the notifications you want to see.

From the Instagram website on your computer, you would click on your profile icon, go to *Settings* and then *Push Notifications*. Then you can scroll through the various categories and change the settings for the ones you want to adjust.

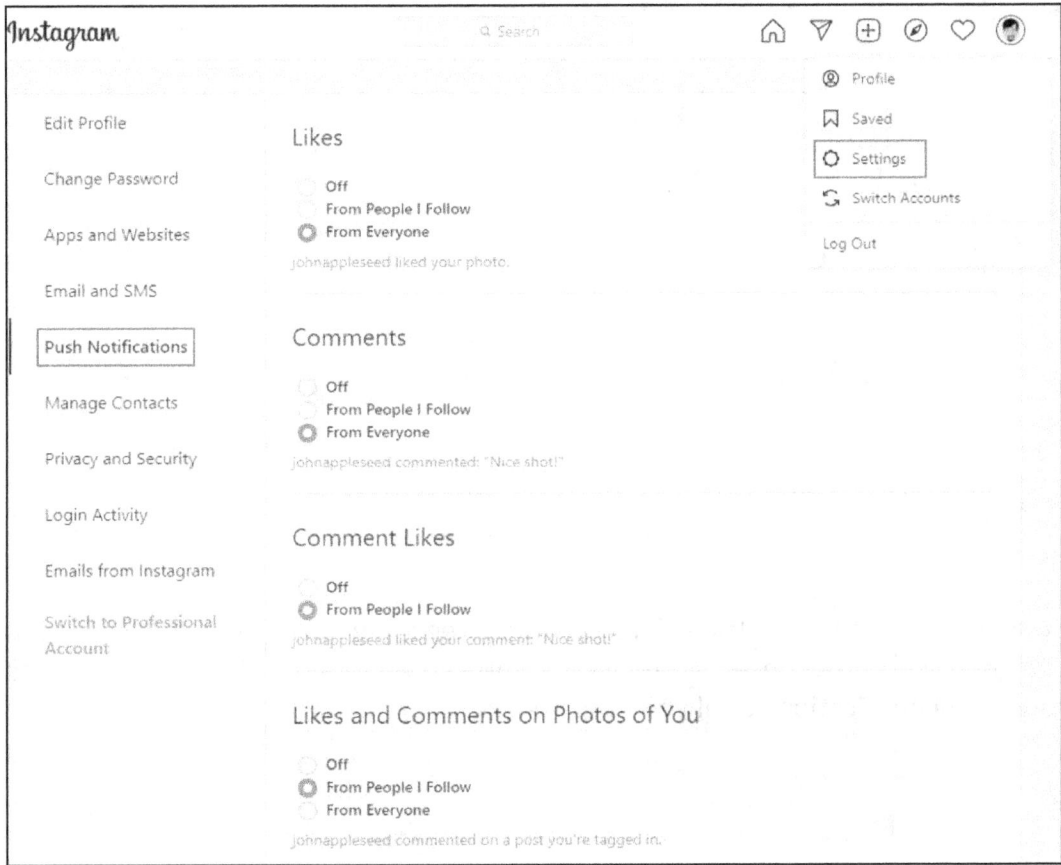

Figure 3.37

For the app, you will need to tap on the 3 vertical bars at the upper right and then choose *Settings* and then *Notifications*.

Chapter 3 – Instagram

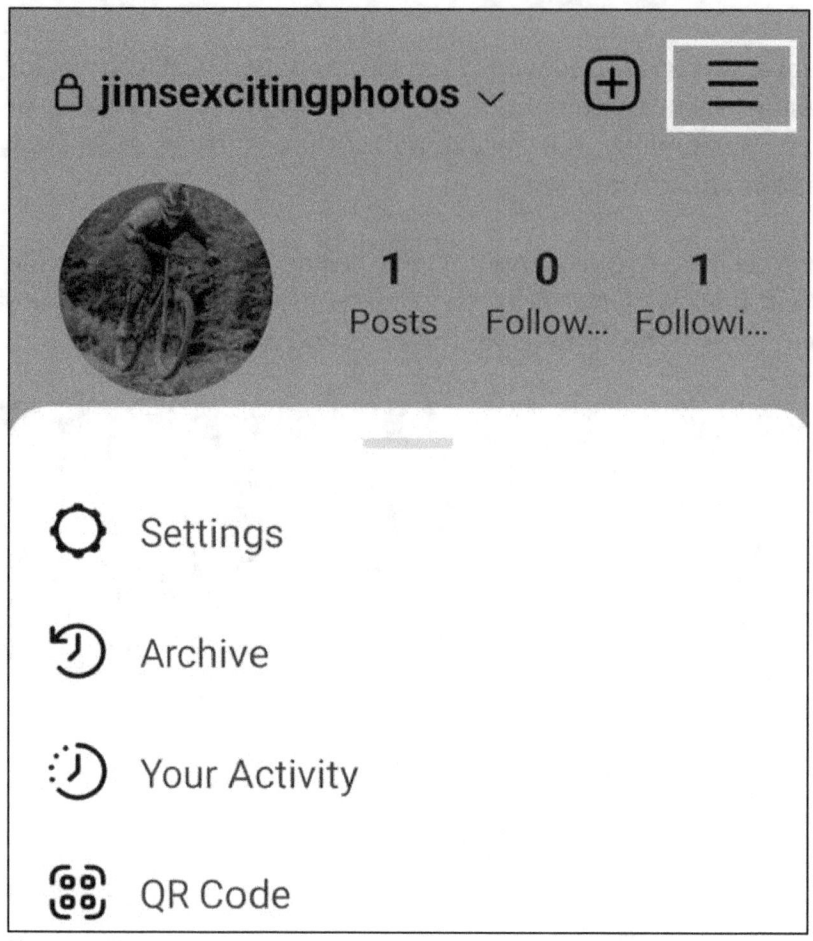

Figure 3.38

To change notification settings for a specific category, you will need to go into that category and make the adjustments. Or you can enable the *Pause all* option to turn off all notifications until you un-pause it.

Chapter 3 – Instagram

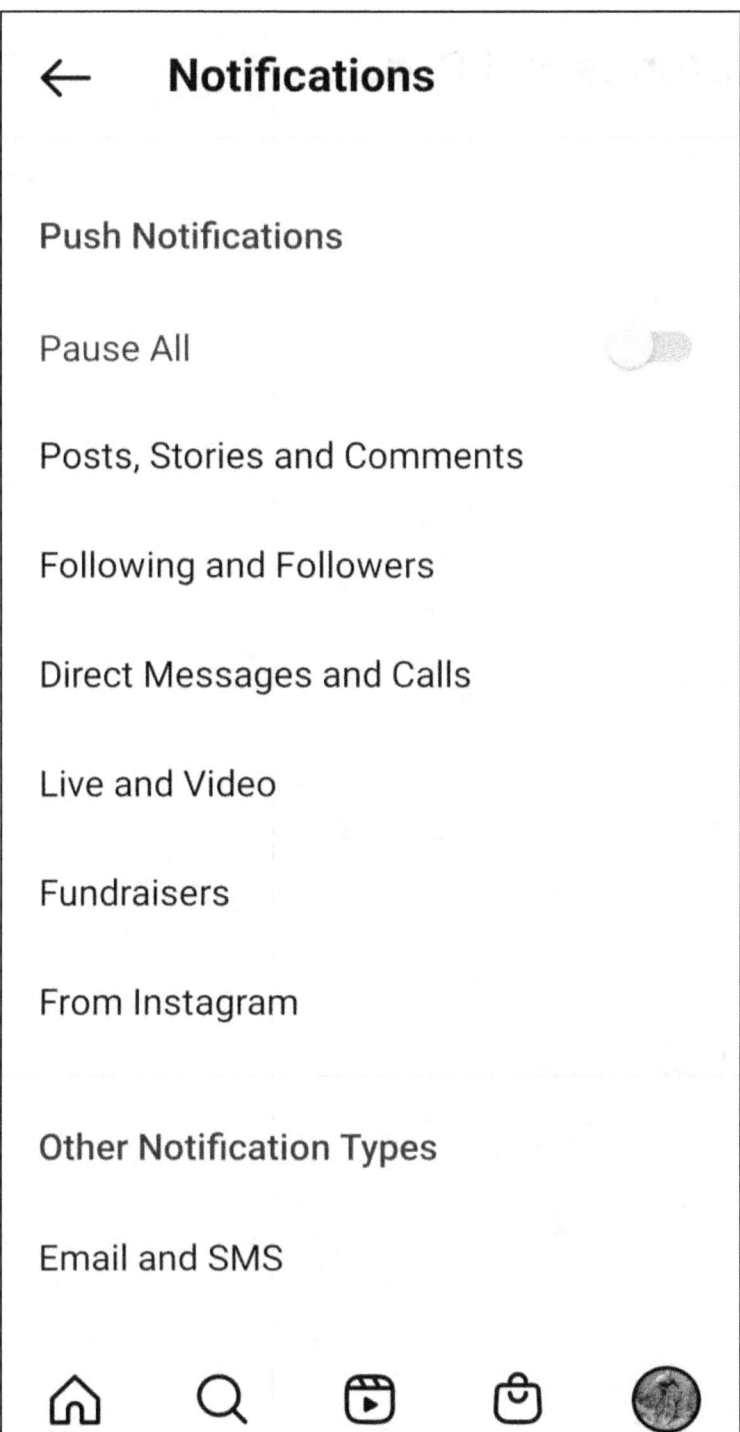

Figure 3.39

Chapter 3 – Instagram

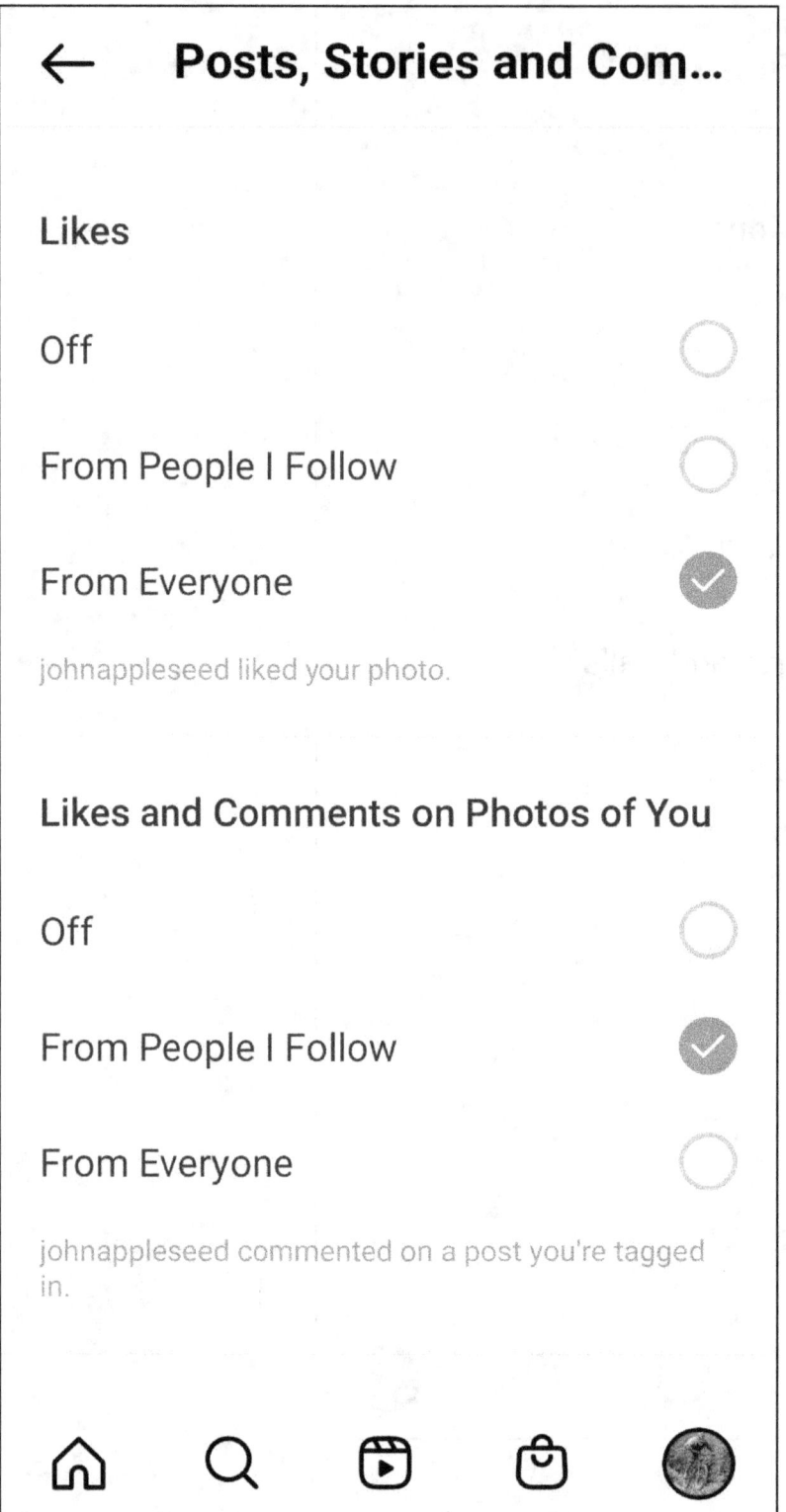

Figure 3.40

Chapter 4 – Twitter

For our next social media topic, I will be discussing Twitter and explaining how it works and how you can use it to see what people you are interested in have to say as well as share your views on any topic you wish to speak your mind about.

You can think of Twitter as an online news and social networking site where people share their views in short messages called Tweets. Twitter works the same way as Instagram does where your messages will be shared with those who are following you and you will also see messages from those you follow.

The Twitter Interface
You can use Twitter from a web browser on your computer or you can use the Twitter mobile app to read and create posts (Tweet). Once you create an account and login, you will see the same information on either platform even though they won't look exactly the same. Figure 4.1 shows the Twitter interface as seen from a web browser on a computer and figure 4.2 shows the interface as seen on a smartphone.

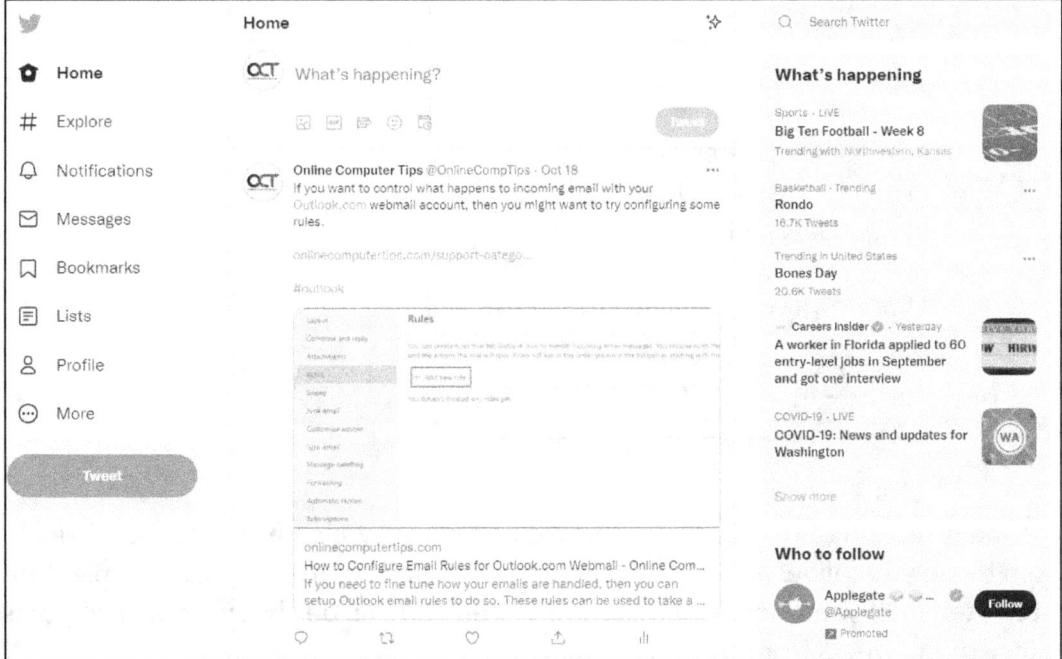

Figure 4.1

Chapter 4 – Twitter

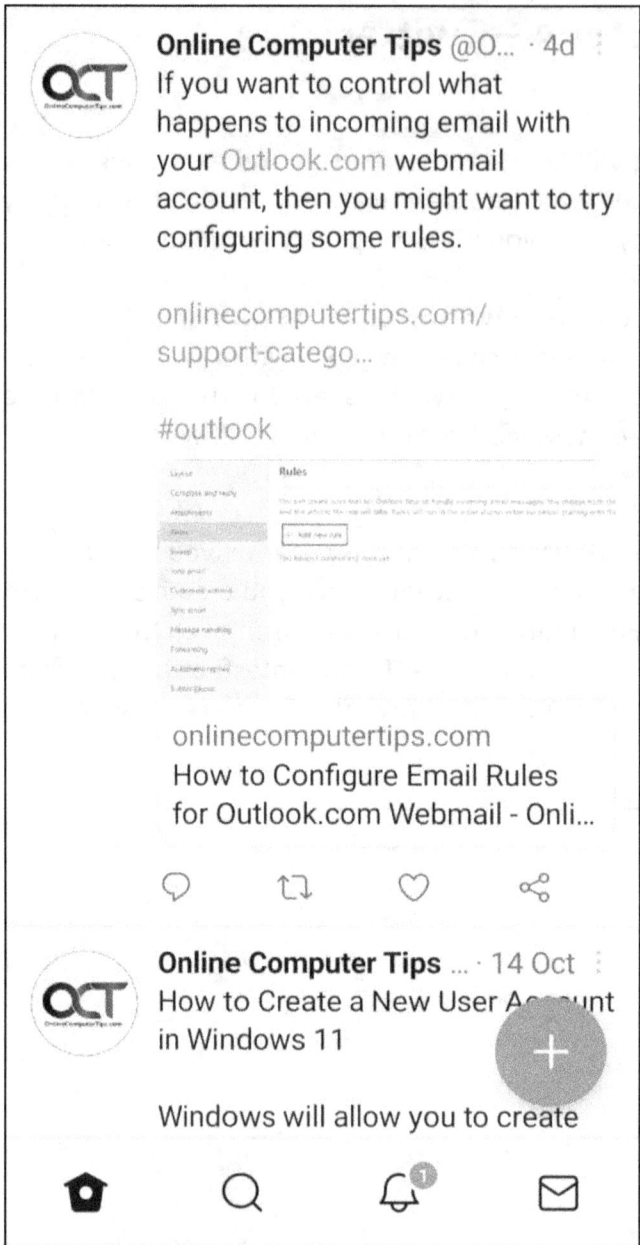

Figure 4.2

The main section of the Twitter interface is the feed which will show you Tweets from those you follow as well as Tweets from people Twitter thinks you might be interested in. If you select your username then you will be shown your own posts rather than Tweets from those you follow.

Chapter 4 – Twitter

On the left side of the web interface, you will have your various categories and settings such as notifications and messages. To see these same categories on the mobile app, you will need to click on your profile icon to bring up the menu.

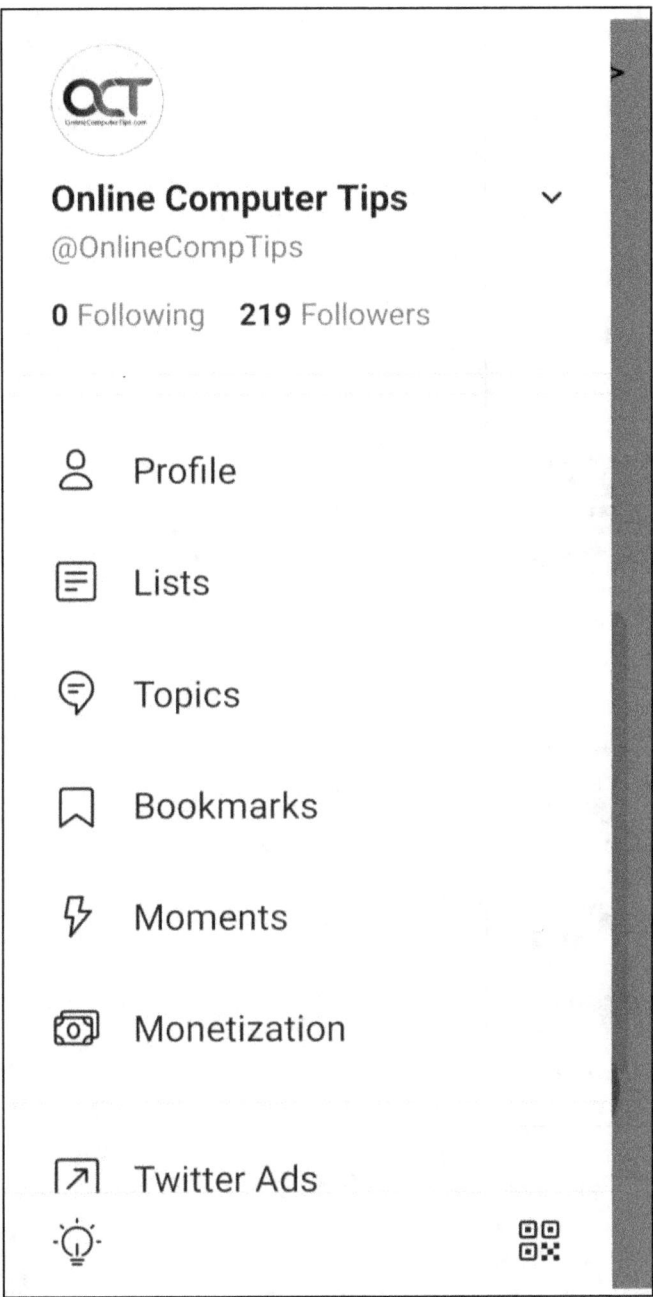

Figure 4.3

Chapter 4 – Twitter

On the right side of the web interface, you will see the latest stories and what is "trending" on Twitter. For the mobile app, you can click on the search magnifying glass and choose one of the categories such as trending or news etc.

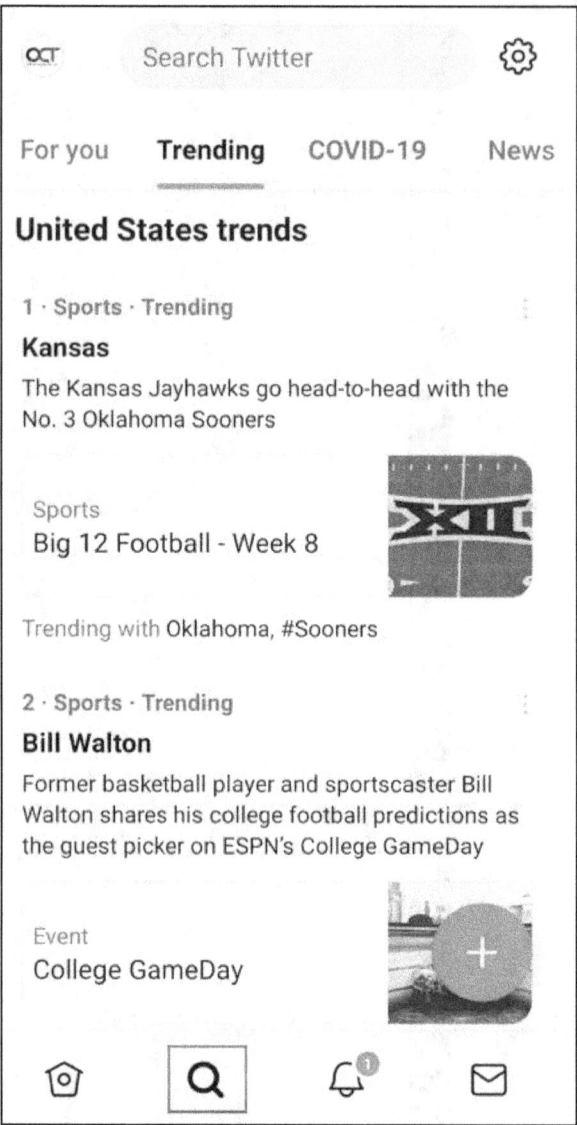

Figure 4.4

Signing Up for an Account
Once again, you will need to sign up for an account to use Twitter. You can still access Twitter and browse the latest events and search for topics without an account, but if you want to participate and create your own Tweets, you will need to sign up first.

Chapter 4 – Twitter

You can sign up for an account via the Twitter website on your computer or from the Twitter app on your smartphone or tablet. If you have an existing Google\Gmail account, you can use that to sign in as well as use your Apple account. If you would rather just create an account on its own, then you can sign up with your phone number or email address.

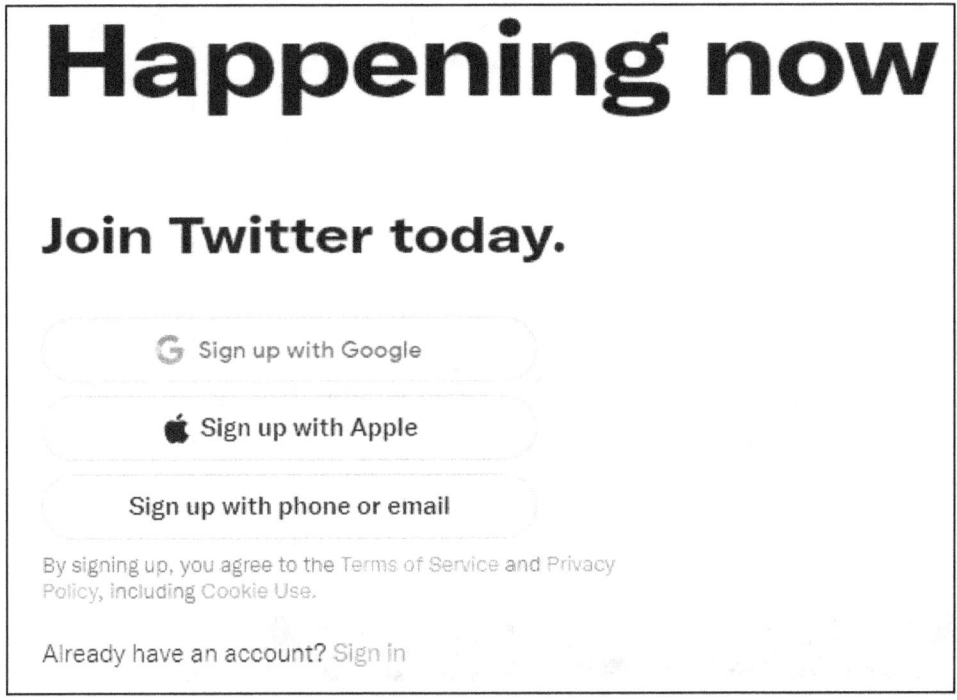

Figure 4.5

For this example, our friend Todd will be creating a new account for himself and will sign up using his email address. This process will be done via a web browser on a computer, but you can sign up through the app as well.

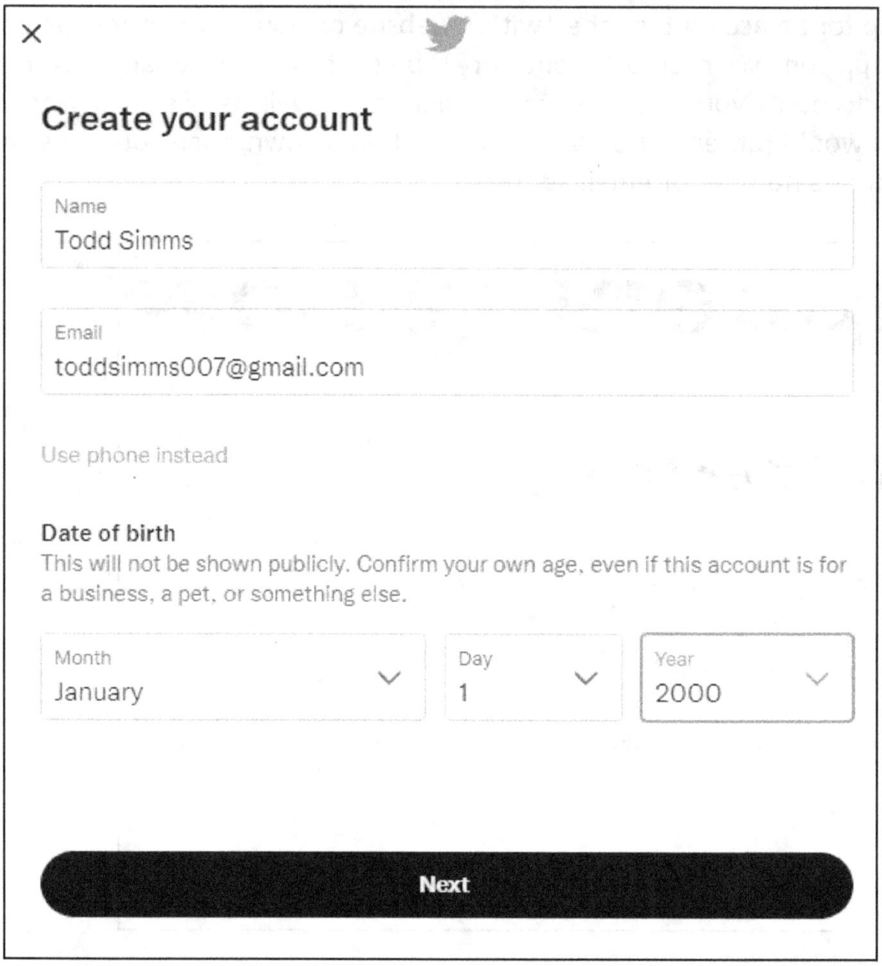

Chapter 4 – Twitter

Create your account

Name
Todd Simms

Email
toddsimms007@gmail.com

Use phone instead

Date of birth
This will not be shown publicly. Confirm your own age, even if this account is for a business, a pet, or something else.

Month: January   Day: 1   Year: 2000

Next

Figure 4.6

Twitter will send a verification code via email that will have to be entered into the next box to continue. Then you will be prompted to add your phone number to your account and then you will either receive a text or recorded phone message with your confirmation code. Finally, you will be asked to create a password and decide if you want to enable notifications or not. If you say yes and change your mind, you can always disable them later.

Twitter might then prompt you to select some categories that you are interested in and then will use this information to show you related Tweets in your feed.

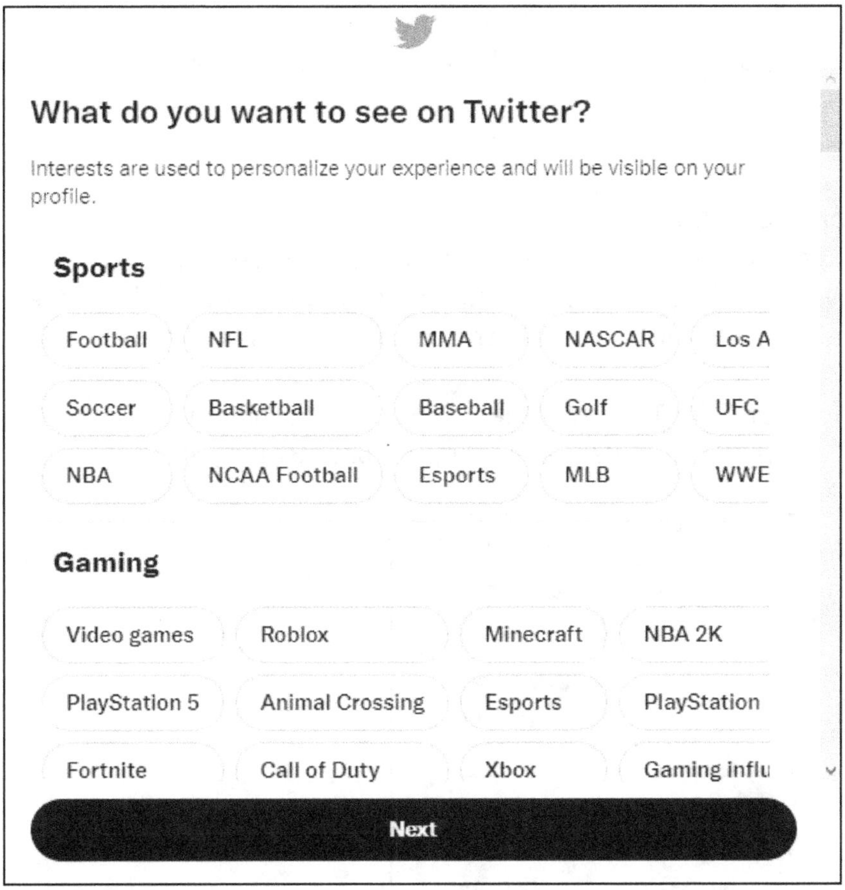

Chapter 4 – Twitter

Figure 4.7

Finally, you will be shown a suggested username based on your email address. If you don't like it, you can change it assuming it's not a name that is already in use.

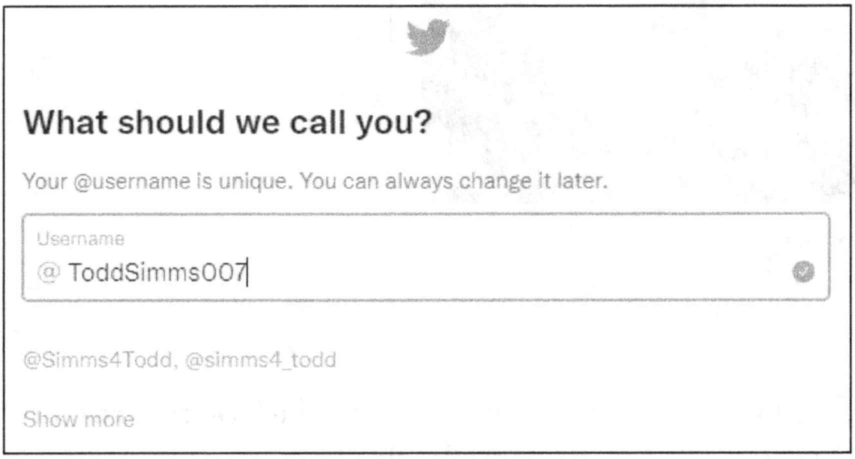

Figure 4.8

Chapter 4 – Twitter

After the account is set up, you will be taken to the main Twitter page where you really won't see too much except for a blank feed with some suggested people to follow.

Installing the Smartphone App
Since Twitter can be used on your computer or mobile device, I want to take a moment and go over installing the app on your smartphone or tablet. The process is exactly the same as it was for the apps in the other chapters I have discussed.

All you need to do is search for Twitter in the Play Store (Android) or the App Store (iPhone and iPad) and make sure it's the real app before installing it.

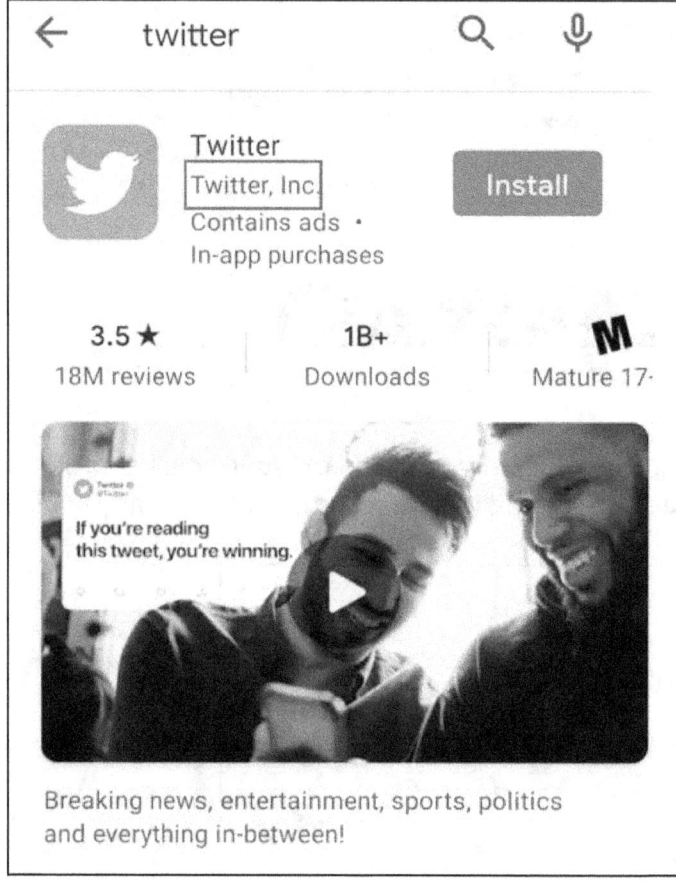

Figure 4.9

Next, you can log in with your username and password if you have created one or go through the signup process once you open the app itself.

Chapter 4 – Twitter

Profile Settings

Before we start using Twitter, I wanted to go over how to access your profile settings and add a profile photo. From the web interface, click on *Profile* over on the left and for the app, click or tap on your profile icon and choose Profile. Next, you will click or tap on the *Set up profile* button.

Figure 4.10

Then you will see an option to add a profile photo as well as a header photo just like we had for Facebook.

Chapter 4 – Twitter

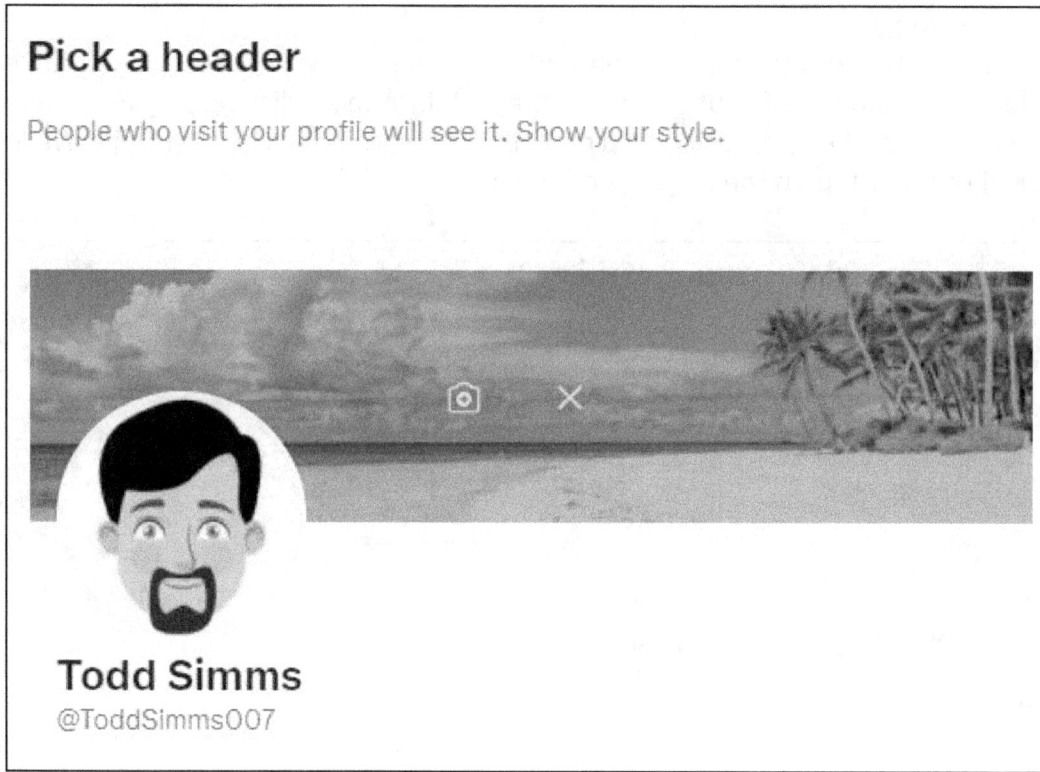

Figure 4.11

Next, you will be prompted to add some information for a bio for yourself which is optional. Figure 4.12 shows Todd's completed profile.

Figure 4.12

112

Chapter 4 – Twitter

Composing Tweets
Now that Todd has his profile complete, it's time to start speaking his mind and Tweeting to the rest of the world. For this example, I will be using the smartphone app.

When Todd opens the app, he will see that there is not much there but there is a + inside of a circle button which is used to create a new Tweet.

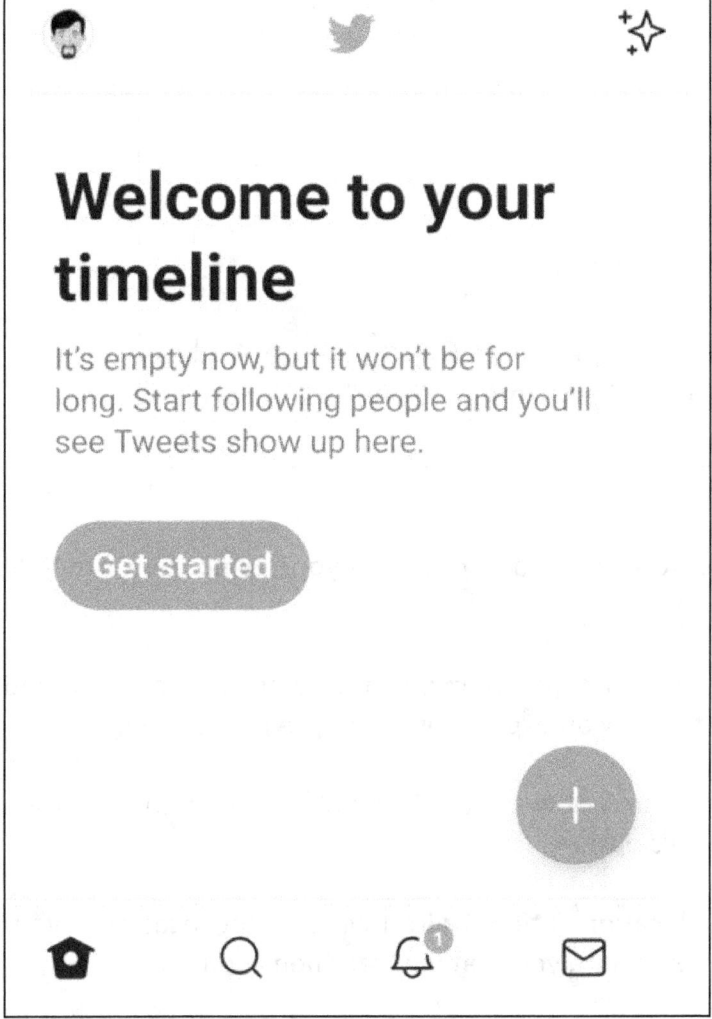

Figure 4.13

Under the text area where you type you will see various icons\buttons that will let you add various content to your Tweets.

Chapter 4 – Twitter

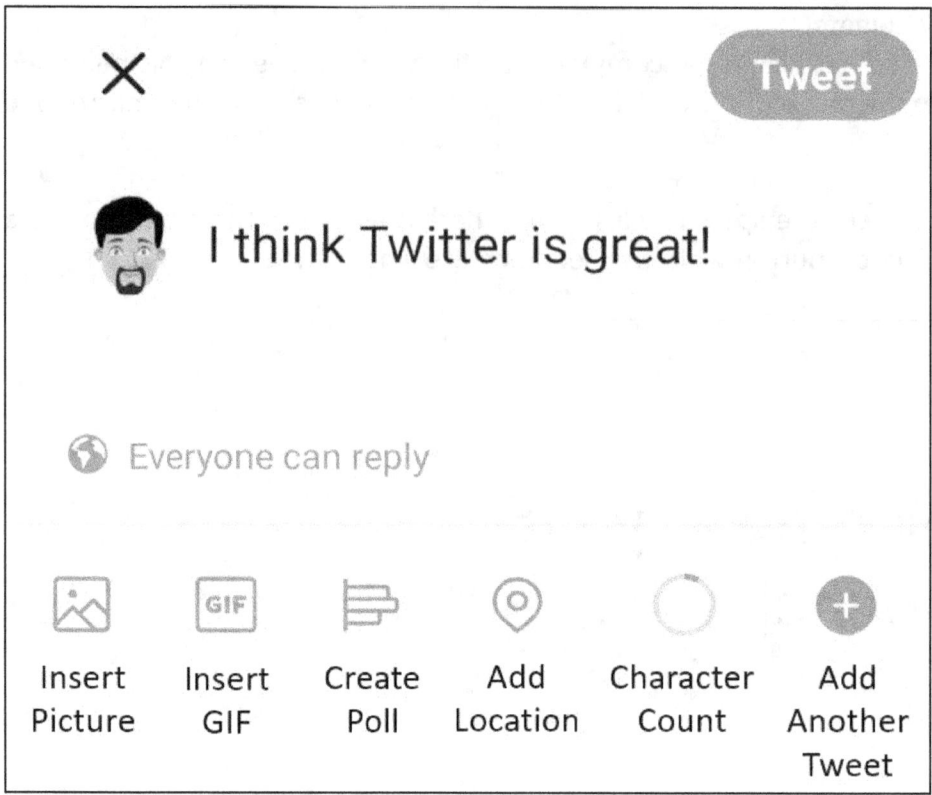

Figure 4.14

- **Insert Picture** – Here you can insert a photo from your computer or mobile device into your post\Tweet.

- **Insert GIF** – Twitter has many animated images that you can search for and then add to your Tweet to show an expression or maybe go for a laugh.

- **Create Poll** – If you want your followers to take a poll on a certain topic then you can create one with this option.

- **Add Location** – Using the location option, Twitter will take the location of your device and also find places around you that you can then add to your Tweet.

- **Character Count** – Twitter will only allow you to use up to 280 characters in a Tweet so this icon will show you how close you are getting to the maximum.

- **Add Another Tweet** – If you need to add an additional related or follow-up Tweet along with the main Tweet, then you can use this option.

Chapter 4 – Twitter

When you Tweet from your computer, you will notice that you have different options below the Tweet. For example, you will have an Add Emoji choice to add smiley's etc. and also an Add Schedule option that will allow you to compose a Tweet and the schedule when you would like it to go live (figure 4.16). You can also view and edit scheduled Tweets from here.

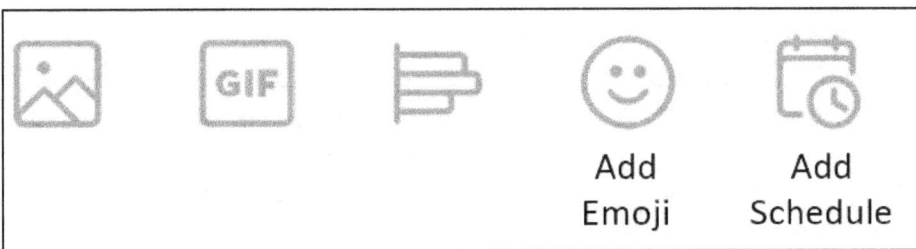

Figure 4.15

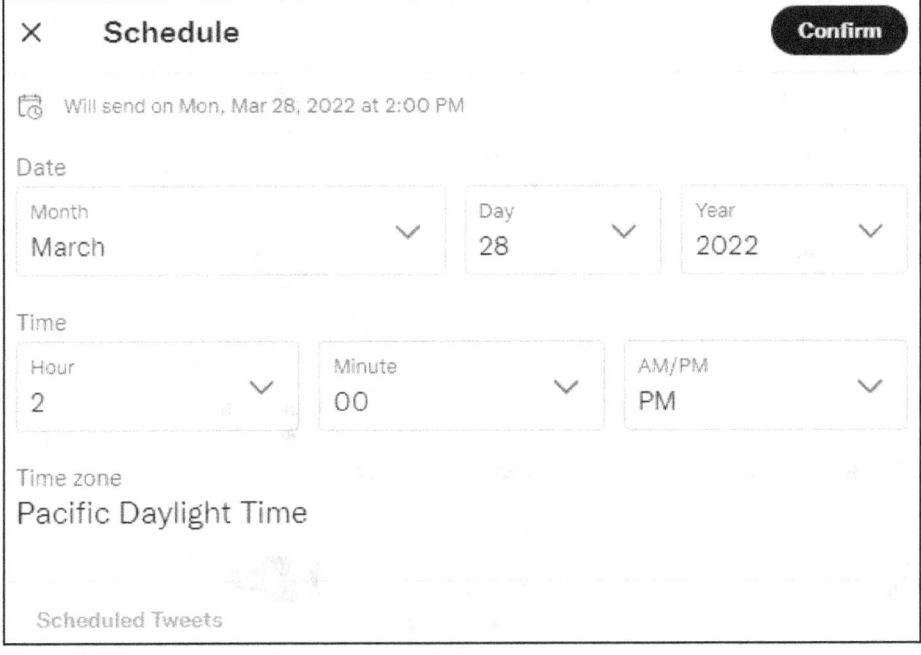

Figure 4.16

After you have all your options configured, simply click or tap the Tweet button to have your post go live. Then anyone who is following you will be able to see your Tweet. I will be going over how to follow someone later in this chapter.

Chapter 4 – Twitter

Hashtags

I have mentioned hashtags previously in this book but wanted to go over them again and show you how they apply to Twitter. Even though you can share photos on Twitter, it's mainly used to post comments and opinions on specific topics. It also uses the hashtag (#) feature to link your posts to a certain topic such as the Olympics I would search for *#olympics* and I would get the results shown in figure 4.17.

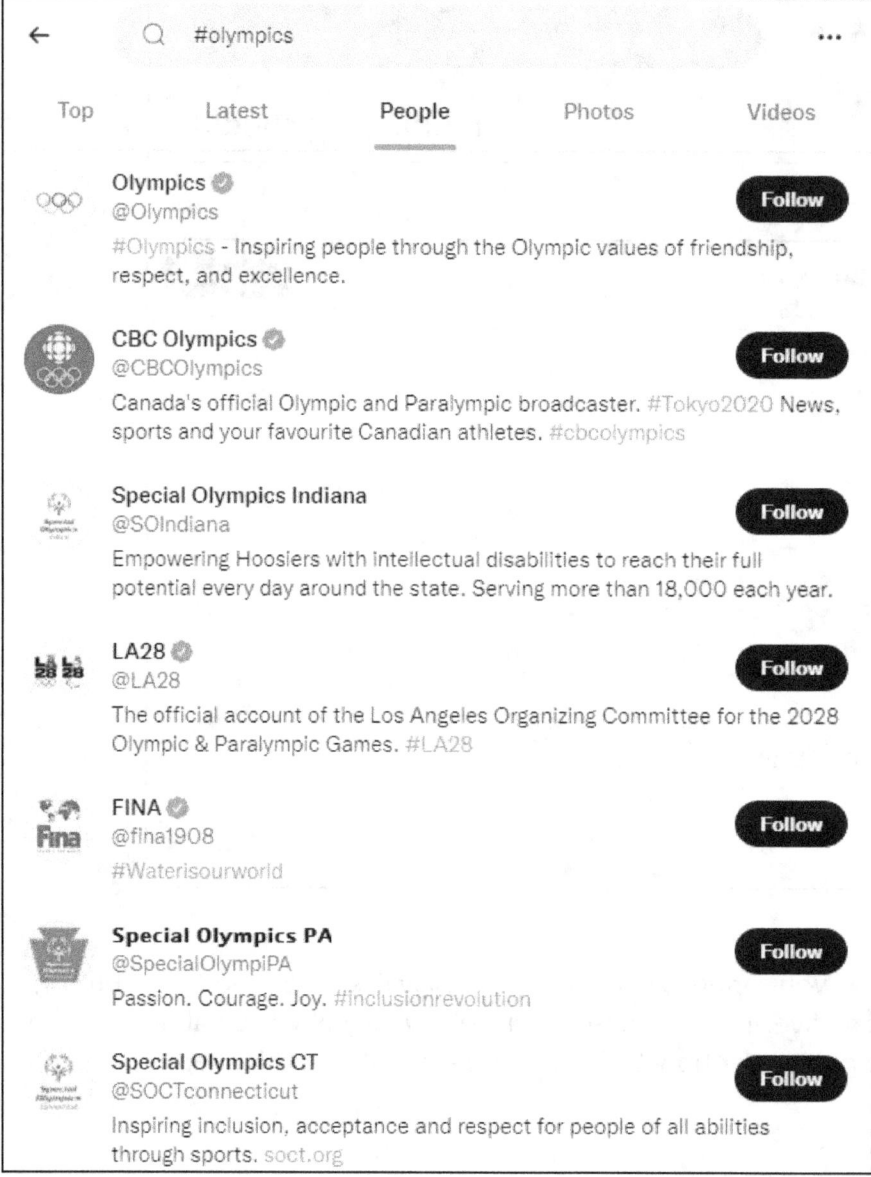

Figure 4.17

The reason I got these results are because these users added the hashtag *Olympics* in their Tweets which made them show up in my search results. If I search for Olympics without the # in front of it, I would get similar results but they won't be quite the same. I can also click on any hashtag within a Tweet to find more results that are using that hashtag.

So if you want your Tweets to be found by others searching for a term that you feel it is related to, you can add one or more hashtags to the end of your Tweet.

Following Others
Many people create Twitter accounts so they can follow what people and causes are saying to keep themselves informed. Other people don't follow anyone and only Tweet to share their information with anyone who is interested. Either way is perfectly fine so it's up to you whether or not you want to be a follower, be followed or both.

The following process is quite easy and all you need to do is find the account of the person or group you wish to follow. I am going to use another account to find the Twitter account of Todd Simms by searching for his name.

If I just search for Todd Simms, I will get a lot of results that I will need to go through to find the right one.

Chapter 4 – Twitter

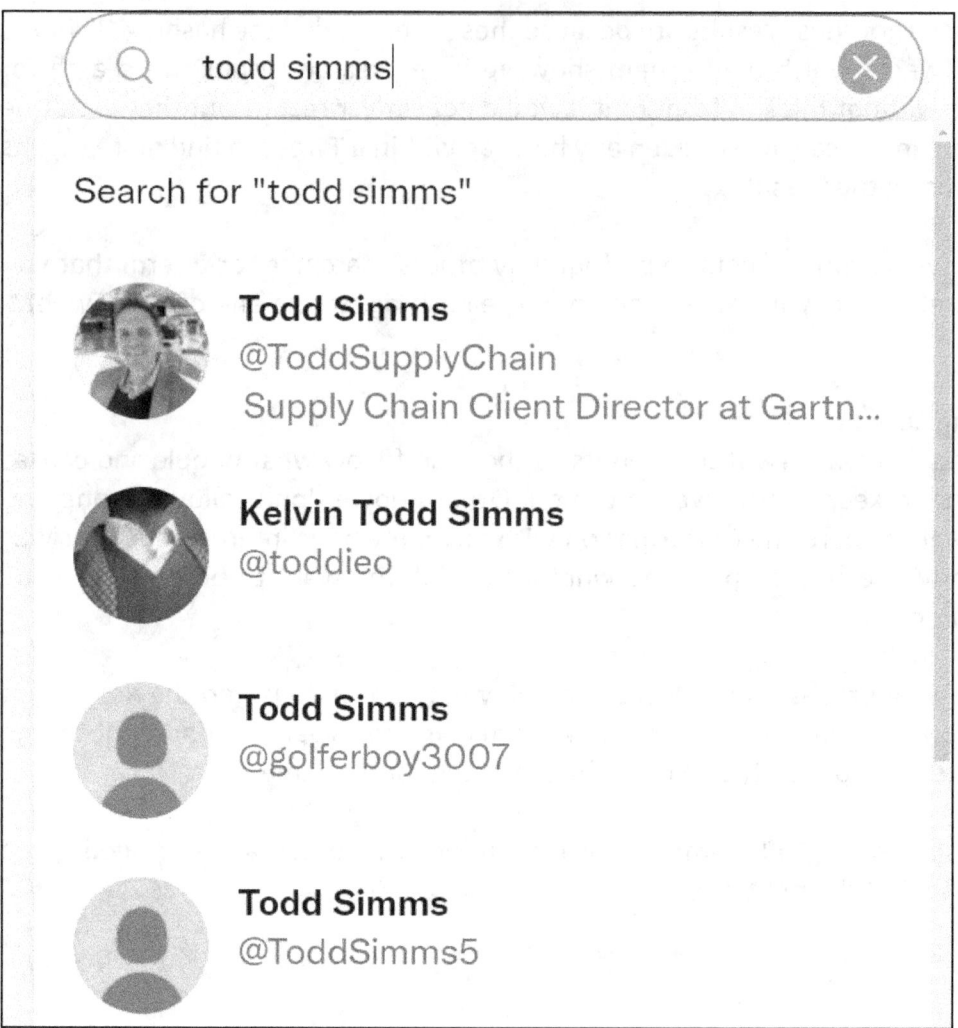

Figure 4.18

But if I know his username, I can search for that, and I will find him right away. Then I can click on his name to view his account and then click on the *Follow* button. The button will then change to say *Following*.

Chapter 4 – Twitter

Figure 4.19

Now when I go to my Twitter feed, Todd's new post will show up with its hashtag and animated GIF image.

Chapter 4 – Twitter

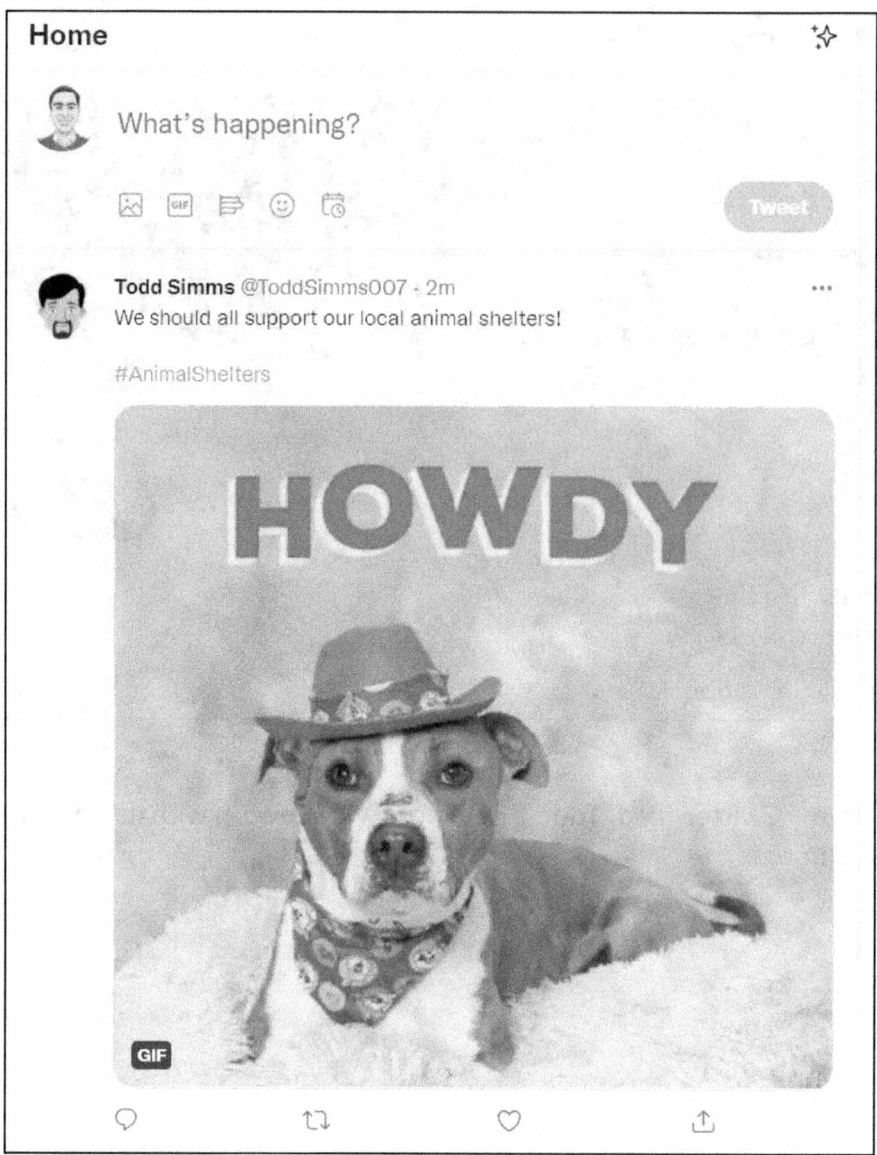

Figure 4.20

If I were to click or tap on the ellipsis (…) at the top of Todd's Tweet, I would have several options including unfollowing Todd, muting him so I don't get any notifications. Blocking his Tweets altogether and reporting any inappropriate posts he makes.

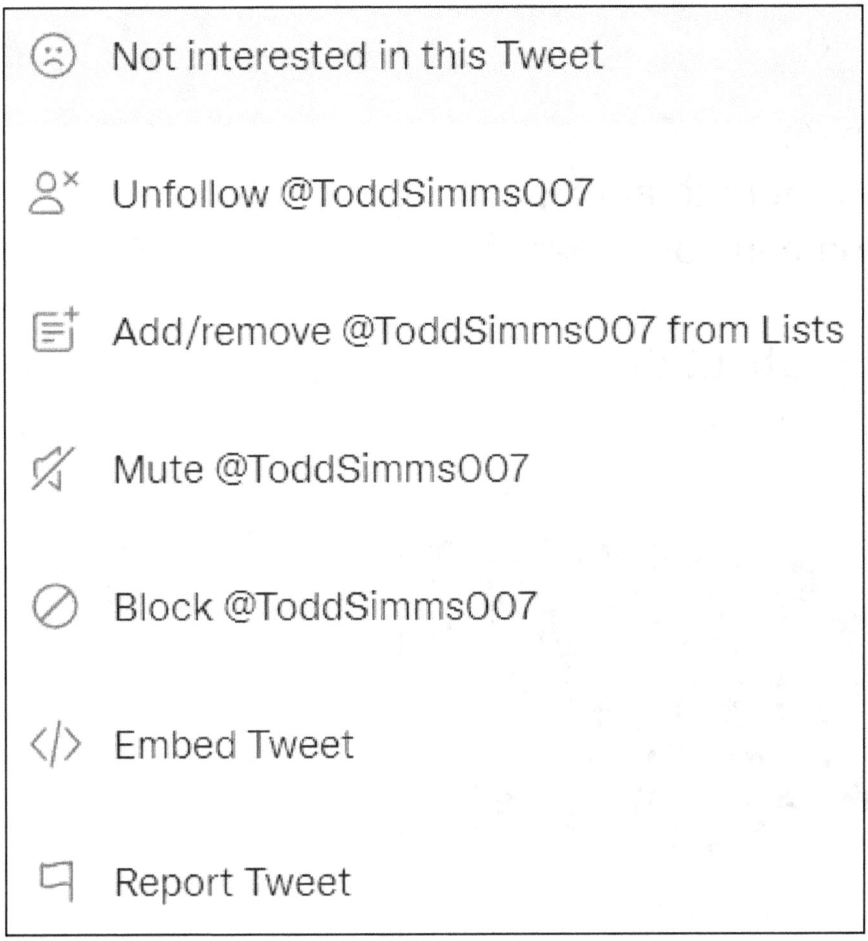

Chapter 4 – Twitter

```
☹  Not interested in this Tweet

☒  Unfollow @ToddSimms007

☱⁺ Add/remove @ToddSimms007 from Lists

🔇  Mute @ToddSimms007

⊘  Block @ToddSimms007

</>  Embed Tweet

⚑  Report Tweet
```
Figure 4.21

Liking, Commenting and Sharing Tweets
Once you start following people you may find yourself wanting to participate in the topic that is being discussed or at least show that you approve of what the person you are following is saying.

When you view a Tweet, you have several actions you can take on that message (figure 4.22).

Chapter 4 – Twitter

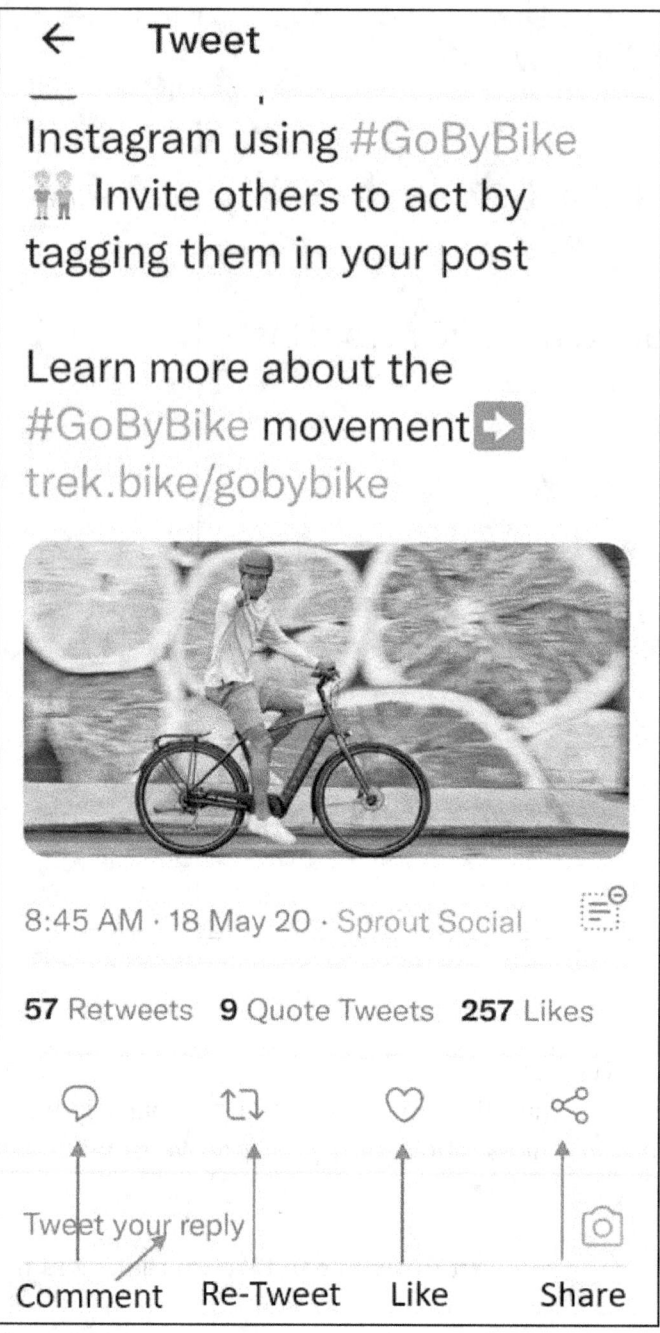

Figure 4.22

- **Comment** - You can make a comment on the Tweet by tapping or clicking on the comment icon or by typing your comment in the reply box.

- **Re-Tweet** – If you want to repost a particular Tweet to your Twitter feed so your followers see it then use this option.

Chapter 4 – Twitter

- **Like** – Tapping or clicking on this will show that you like this particular Tweet.

- **Share** – If you want to share a Tweet with someone else via an email, text message, chat box etc., you can do so from here. The sharing choices you have will vary on what other apps you have installed on your device.

Another thing you might have noticed in figure 4.22 is that you can see how many other people commented, re-Tweeted and liked a particular post.

Notifications
Since you are following people on Twitter to find out what they have to say about various topics, it makes sense that the app will notify you when someone Tweets something new. But you might not want to get notified about every little thing or from everyone you are following. Notifications will show up at the bottom of the app next to the notification bell icon.

Figure 4.23

To change these types of settings, you can go to the notifications section, then settings, and make adjustments as needed (figure 4.24). The process to get to your notification settings from your PC will be the same.

Chapter 4 – Twitter

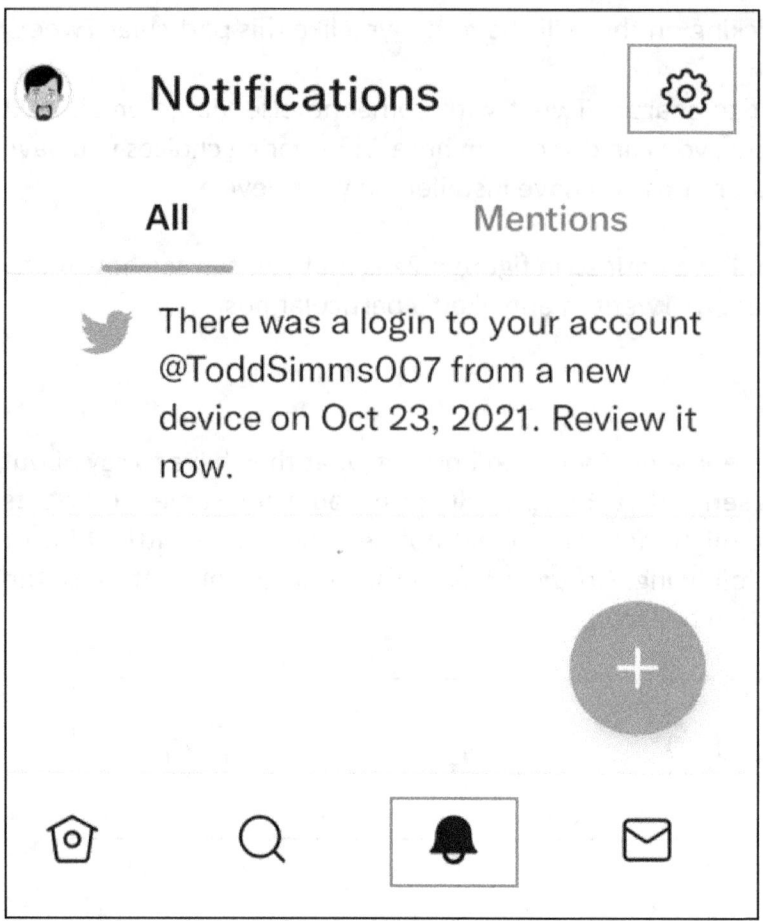

Figure 4.24

You can then choose to set notification *filters* or *preferences*. Filters will allow you to filter out content you don't want to see such as Tweets from people you don't follow or anything that has a specific word you find offensive.

Chapter 4 – Twitter

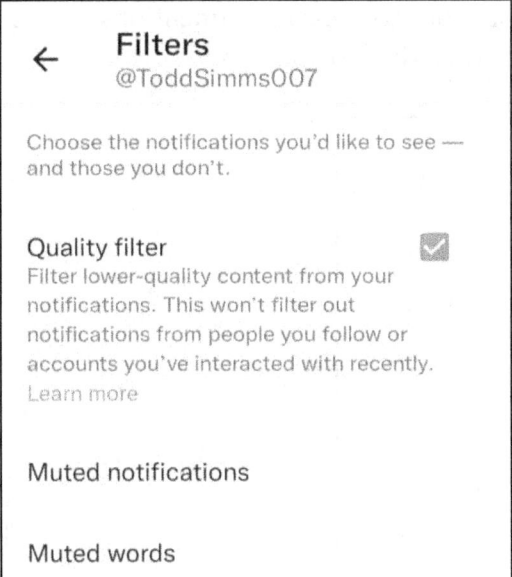

Figure 4.25

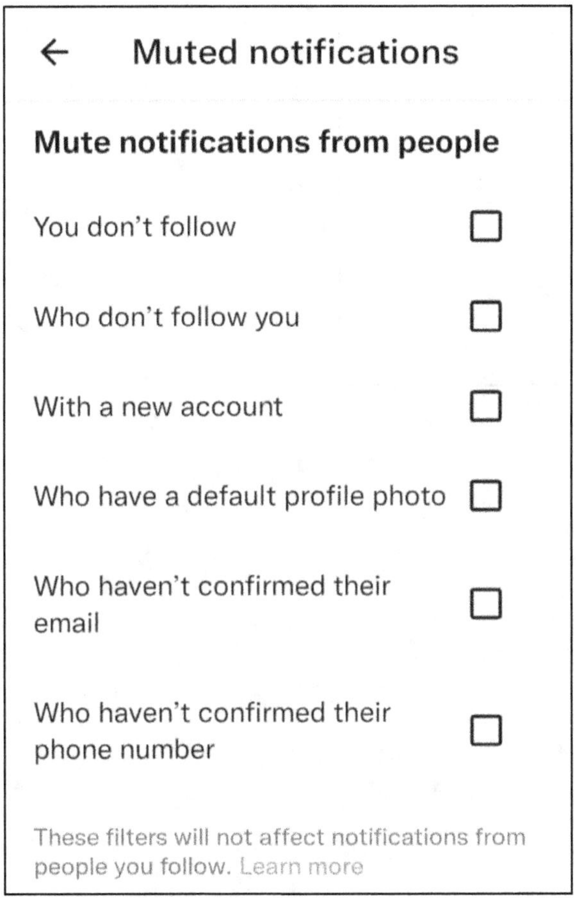

Figure 4.26

Chapter 4 – Twitter

Preferences are used to tell Twitter how you want to receive notifications such as receiving text messages, emails or popup notifications on your device.

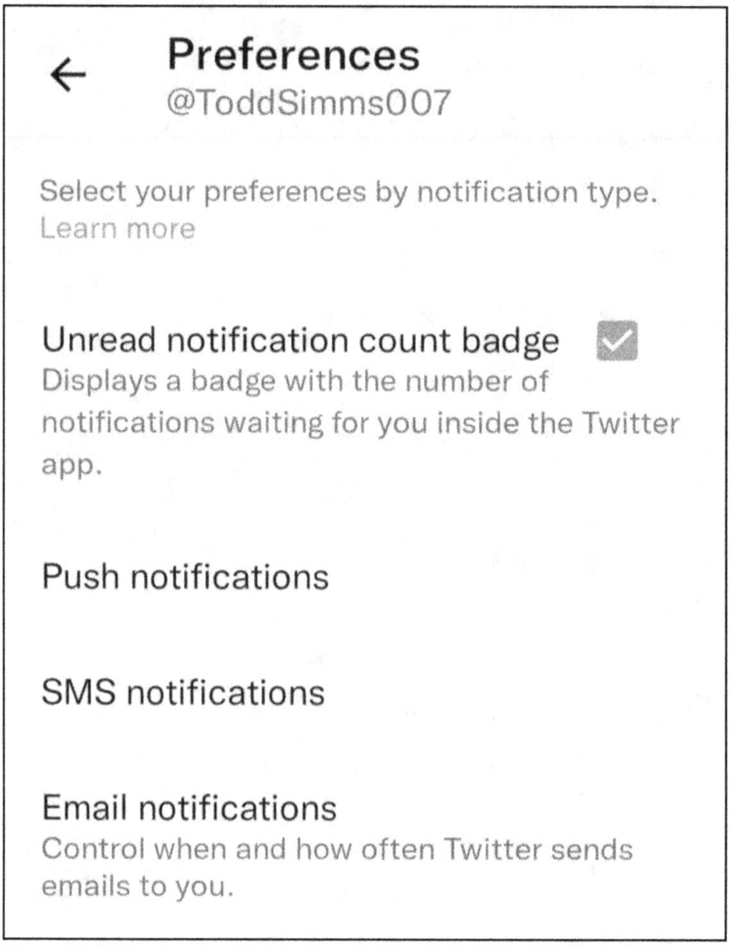

← **Preferences**
@ToddSimms007

Select your preferences by notification type. Learn more

Unread notification count badge
Displays a badge with the number of notifications waiting for you inside the Twitter app.

Push notifications

SMS notifications

Email notifications
Control when and how often Twitter sends emails to you.

Figure 4.27

Chapter 5 – Pinterest

If you are the type who likes to discover new ideas and interests, then Pinterest might be for you. You might have even noticed that it has interest in the name! Even though Pinterest counts as a social media platform, it's more of a low key way to see what others are up to.

Pinterest Overview
The idea behind Pinterest is to share your ideas, creations, videos, photos and so on with others for either fun or maybe to try and make a little bit of money. It's similar to Instagram but is structured differently and not as much of a social interface where you are receiving a lot of likes, comments and re-sharing.

Once you have a Pinterest account, you can then start creating what they call Pins which is a fancy name for a post. From there you can start sharing your ideas and maybe even get some followers at the same time. You can also create boards that consist of multiple Pins that cover the same topic. And if you find something you like, you can always share it with other people who you think might be interested in that particular Pin.

If you plan on using Pinterest to sell products or services, then you can even create a business account which gives you additional tools to help track how well your Pins are performing so you can make adjustments to try and get the most views as possible. You can also run advertisements with a business account.

As you can see, the Pinterest interface is made up of various Pins (posts) which will be related to your interests or activities from your account (figure 5.1). You can click on any one of them to get a better view and also to find out more information about that post.

Chapter 5 – Pinterest

Figure 5.1

Signing Up for an Account

To use Pinterest, you will need to sign up for an account. Both the personal and business accounts are free but if you want to perform certain functions like placing ads for your products on the site, then that will cost you money and will also require using a business account.

Once again, you have the option to sign up with your email address or connect your Facebook or Google account to log in that way, so the choice is up to you. If you choose this method, you will receive an email asking you to confirm your email address.

If you would like to learn more about the vast amount of Google apps that are available and free to use, then check out my book titled **Google Apps Made Easy**. https://www.amazon.com/dp/1798114992

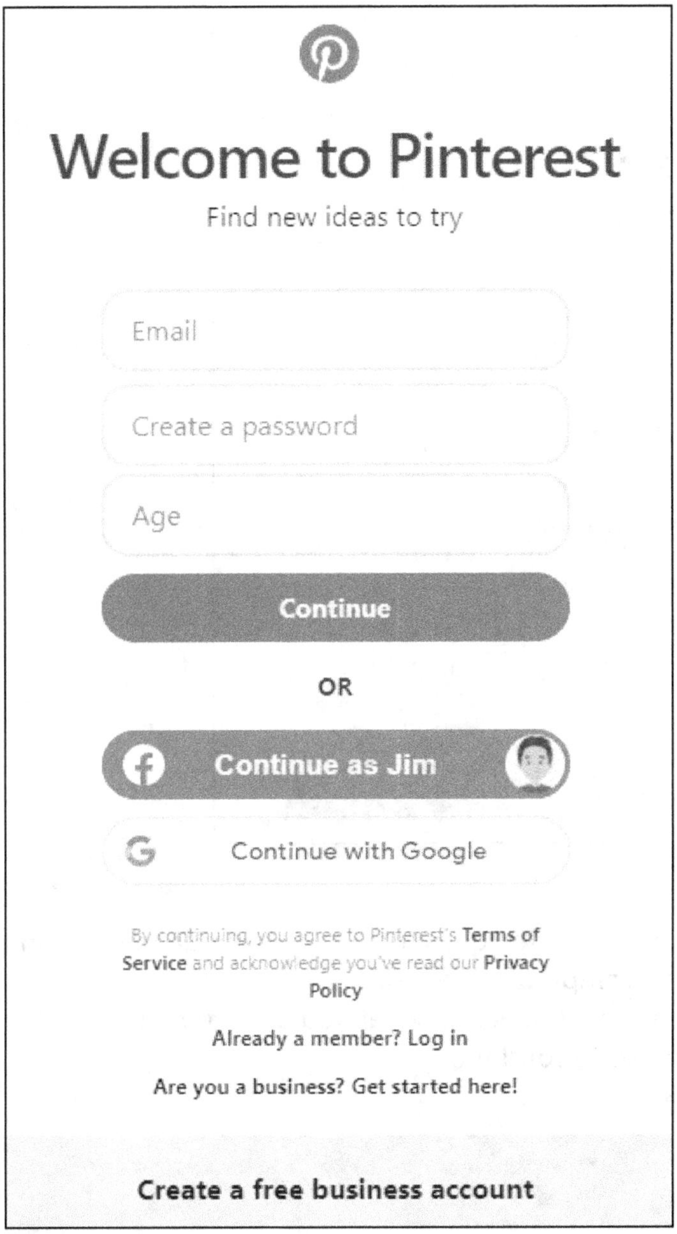

Chapter 5 – Pinterest

![Pinterest signup screen showing Welcome to Pinterest with email, password, age fields, Continue button, Continue as Jim, Continue with Google, and Create a free business account options]

Figure 5.2

For my example, I will sign up for a new account using my email address so I will fill in the fields for email, password and age and click the *Continue* button. As you can see in figure 5.3, it took the first part of my email address and used it for my name so I can then click the pencil icon to change this information.

Chapter 5 – Pinterest

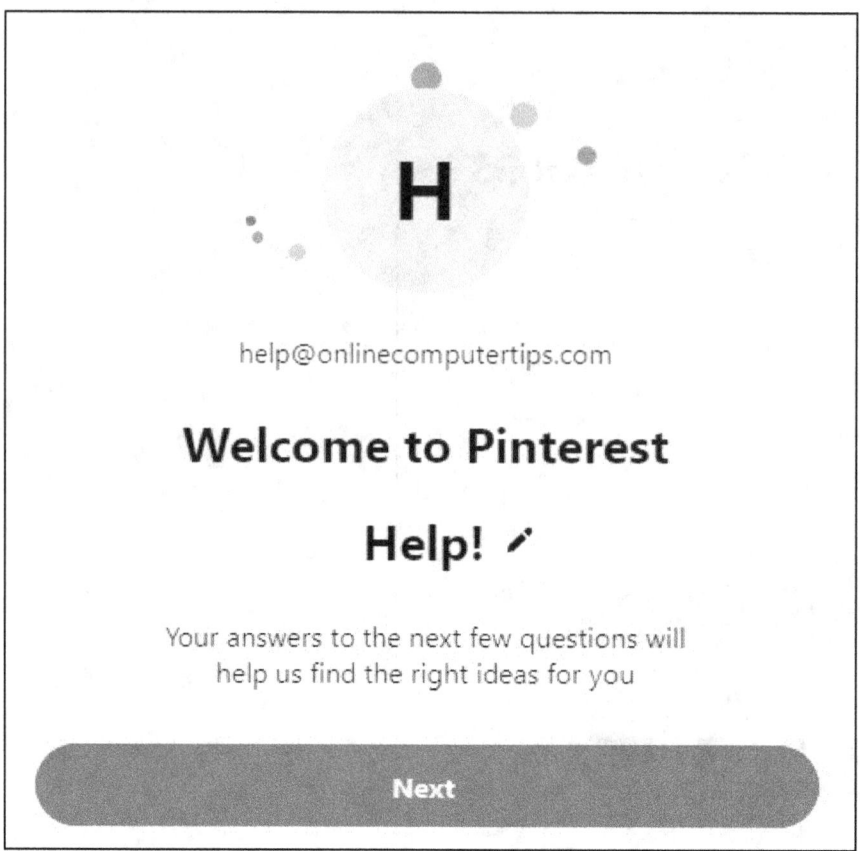

Figure 5.3

After that, you will be asked some other questions such as your gender and location and then you will be prompted to tell Pinterest about some of your interests so it can customize your experience to what you are interested in. You will need to select about 5 of these to continue.

Chapter 5 – Pinterest

Figure 5.4

Once you finish this step you should be taken into your new Pinterest account.

Editing Your Profile
If your goal is to make a presence for yourself or to even try and sell something on Pinterest then you might want to take a minute to make sure your profile is as informative as it can be.

To get to the profile settings, simply click on your profile icon at the top right of the page. It will most likely have the first letter of your first name inside of a circle. Then you can click on the *Edit Profile* button.

Chapter 5 – Pinterest

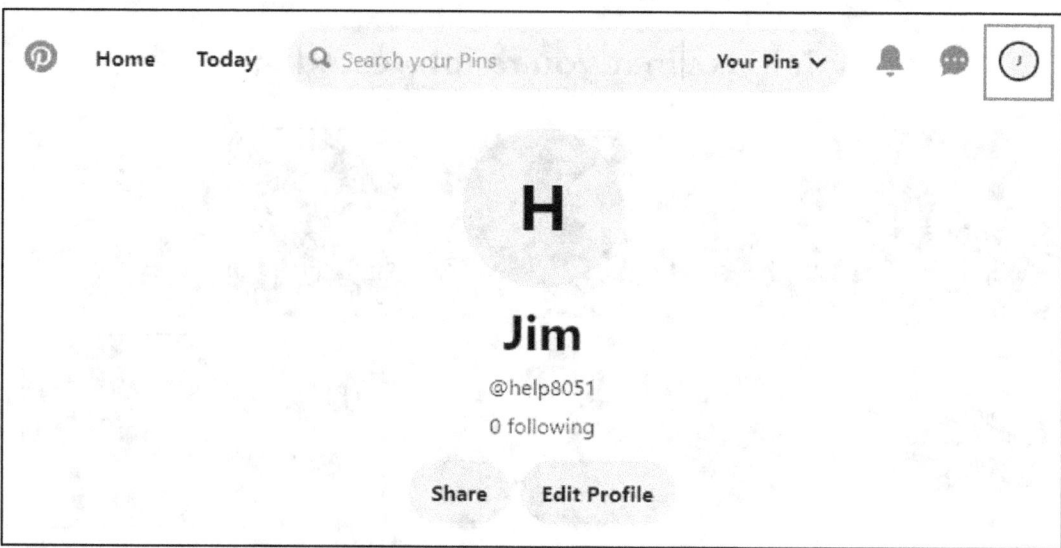

Figure 5.5

From here you can do things such as add your full name if you haven't already and set up a bio with a little information about yourself. If you have a website that is related to the content you are planning on adding to your Pinterest page, then you can add that as well.

If you take a look at figure 5.6, you will see that it gave me a username of @help8051 based on my email address. I don't think this username has a nice ring to it so I will change it to *MTBgeek* so it goes along with the theme of my Pins. MTB is short for mountain biking just in case you didn't know. I tried some other names first but since they were taken, I had to use whatever I could find that was available.

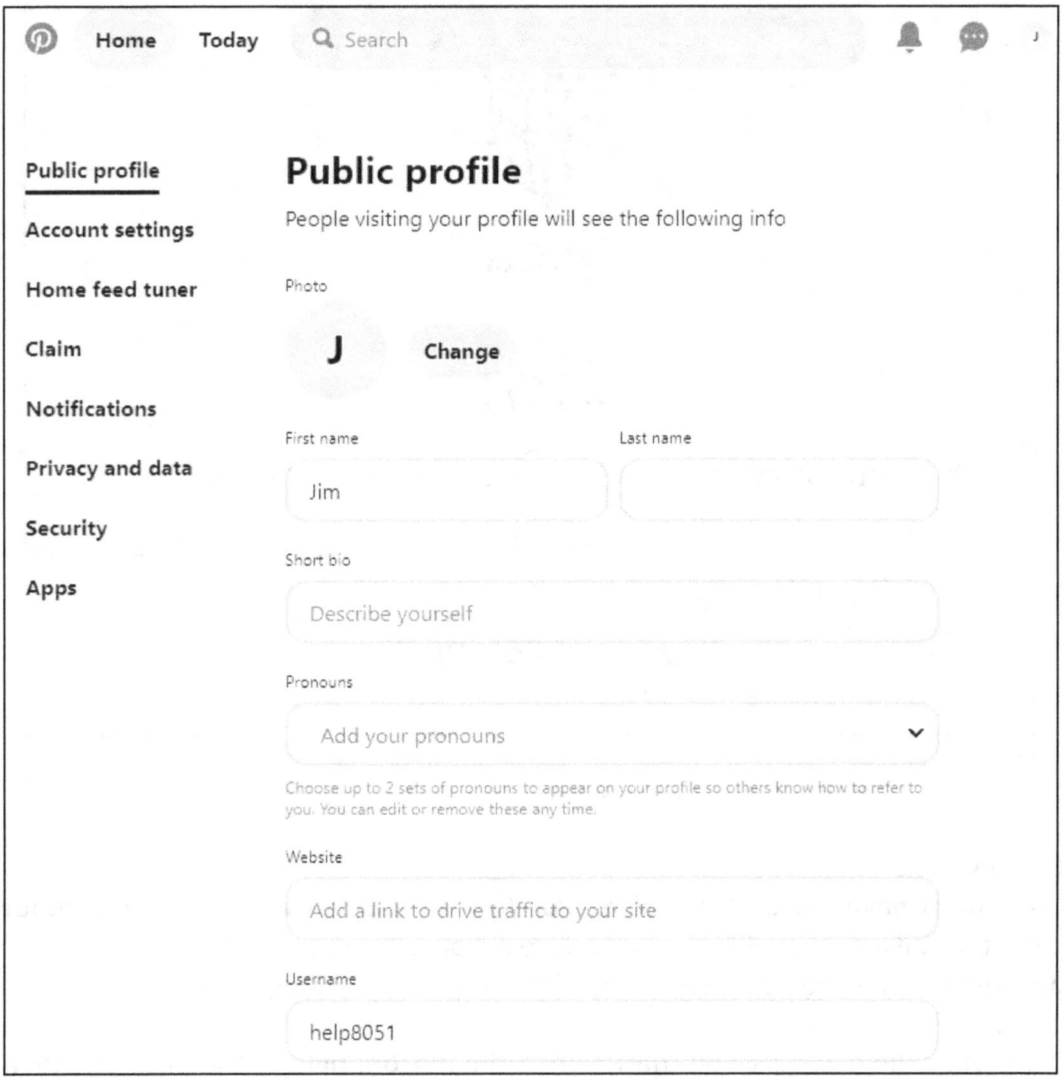

Chapter 5 – Pinterest

Figure 5.6

I will also change my profile picture and add the address for my mountain biking website while I am here by clicking on the *Change* button next to my current profile image. Figure 5.7 shows the results of my changes. Now my profile picture will show up when people visit my Pinterest page.

Chapter 5 – Pinterest

Figure 5.7

Creating Pins

Now that I have my profile looking good, I will start to add some Pins about mountain biking to build up my Pinterest page. I will start with some scenic pictures and then add some pictures of my bikes to mix things up a bit.

To create a Pin, I will click on the **+** sign at the bottom right of the page and then click on *Create a Pin*. Now I will be shown the new Pin page where I can add a picture from my computer. I can either drag and drop an image file from my computer into the grey box or click inside the grey box to browse to the folder on my computer where the picture is stored.

Chapter 5 – Pinterest

Figure 5.8

Chapter 5 – Pinterest

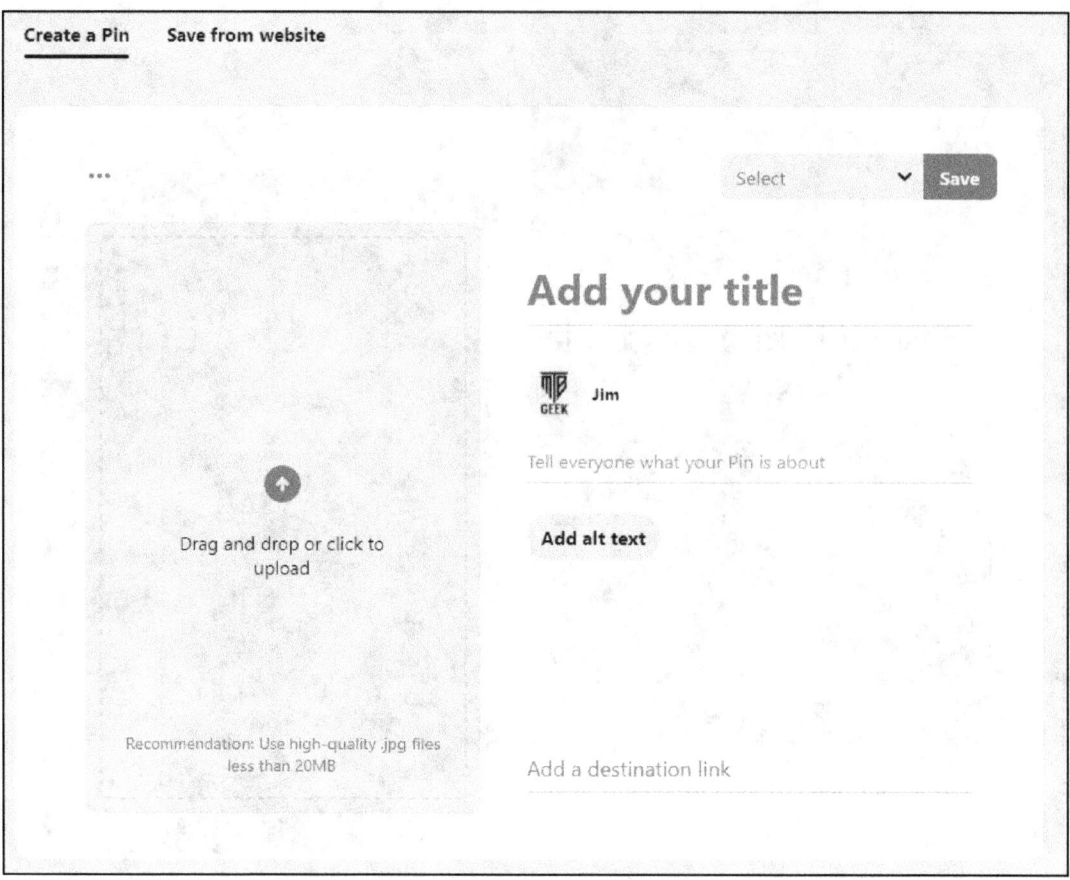

Figure 5.9

Once I find the picture on my hard drive, I can simply click on *Open* to have the picture added to my Pin.

Chapter 5 – Pinterest

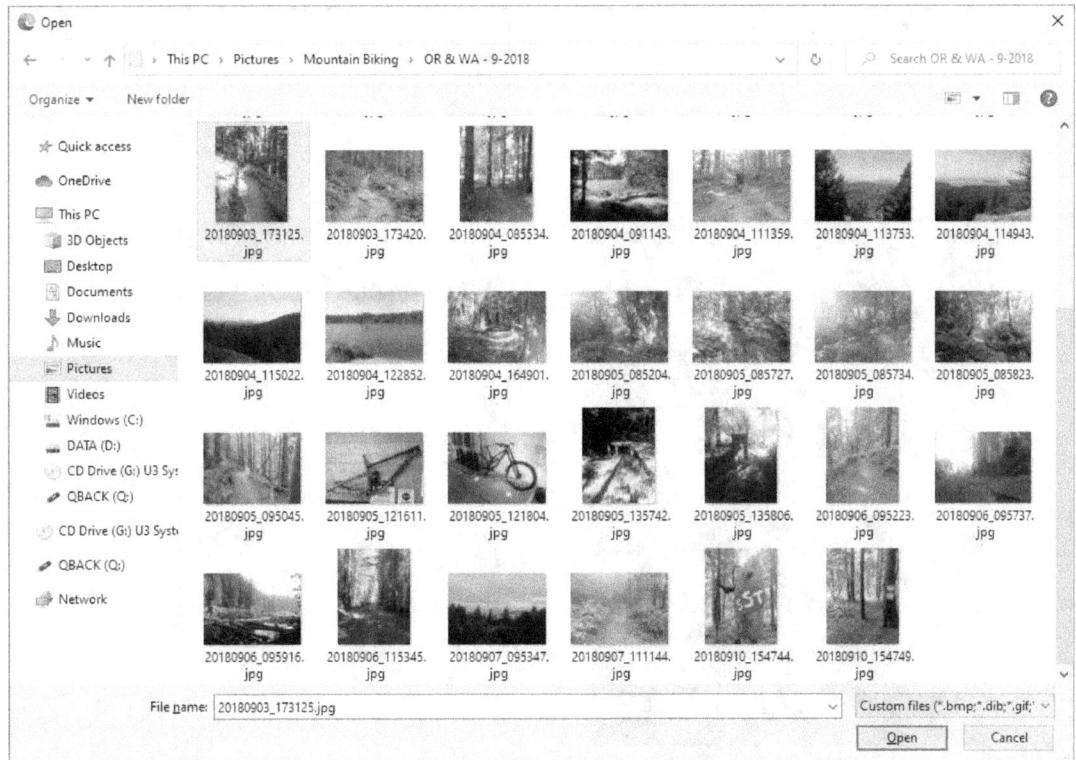

Figure 5.10

After adding the photo, I will add a title and description for my pin (figure 5.11). Since I want people who view this Pin to go to my mountain biking website, I will add a destination link to the page on my site that is about Blanchard Mountain. The alt text option is there to add text to describe your image in case it doesn't appear on the page or for the vision impaired. Alt text can also be used by Internet search engines to help find your image when certain words are searched for. If you want to create a video Pin, you will need to convert your account to a business account first.

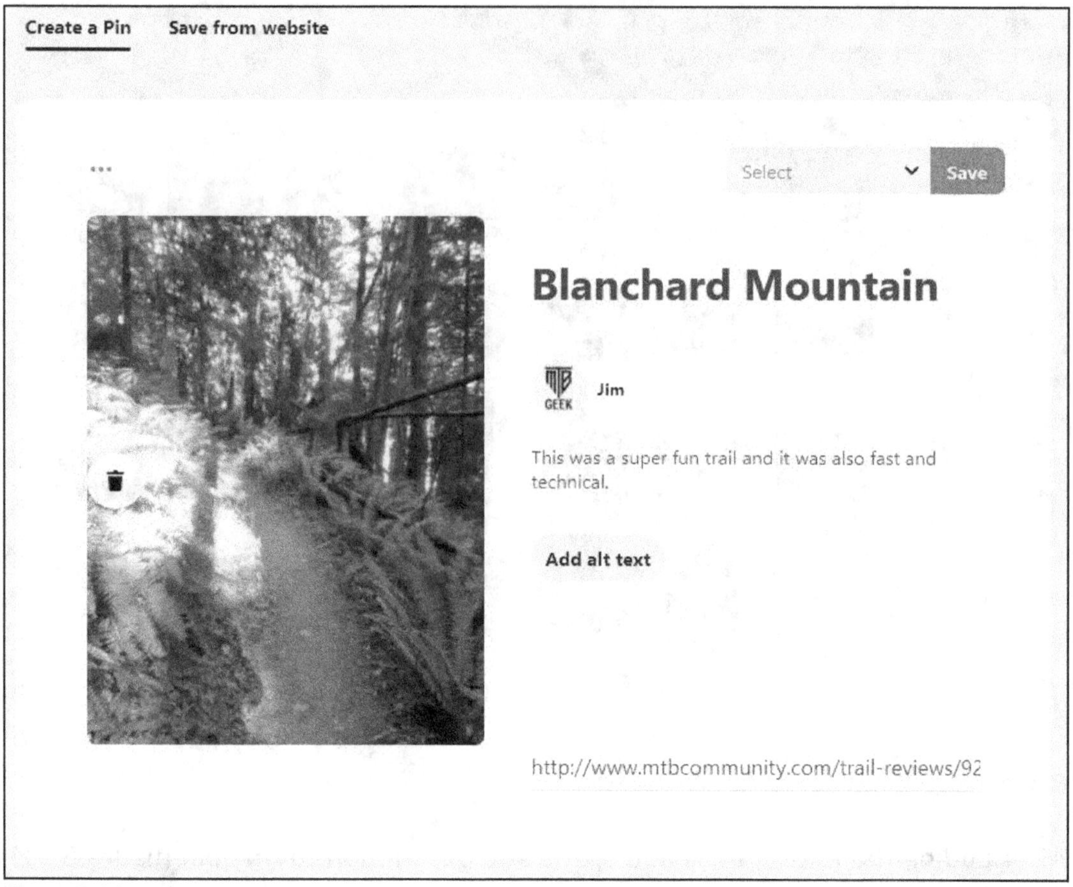

Chapter 5 – Pinterest

Figure 5.11

 If you add a picture and realize you added the wrong one by mistake or changed your mind, you can click on the trash can icon to have the picture removed from your Pin and then you can add a different one.

If everything looks good, I can click on the *Save* button to have my Pin posted on my page. The *Select* drop down menu is used to post your Pins on a certain board which I will be discussing in the next section. But since I don't have any boards, Pinterest will make me create one before continuing. I will create a board called **Bike Trails** and click on the *Create* button. Then I will be able to save my new Pin and choose my new Bike Trails board.

138

Chapter 5 – Pinterest

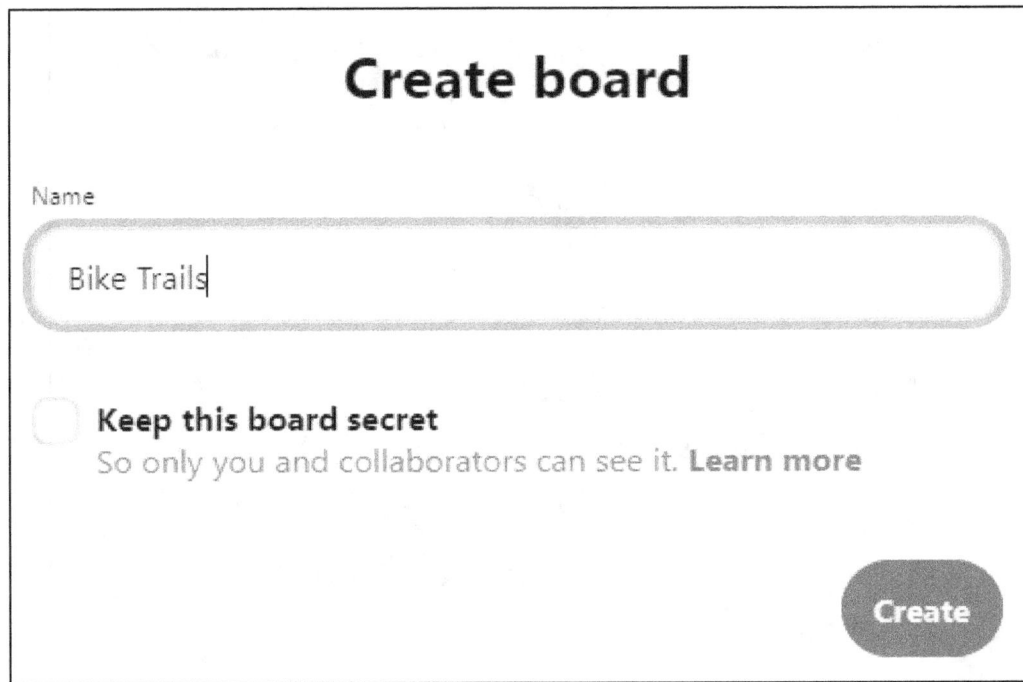

Figure 5.12

Now if I click on my profile, I will be shown my one Pin that was created on my one board.

Chapter 5 – Pinterest

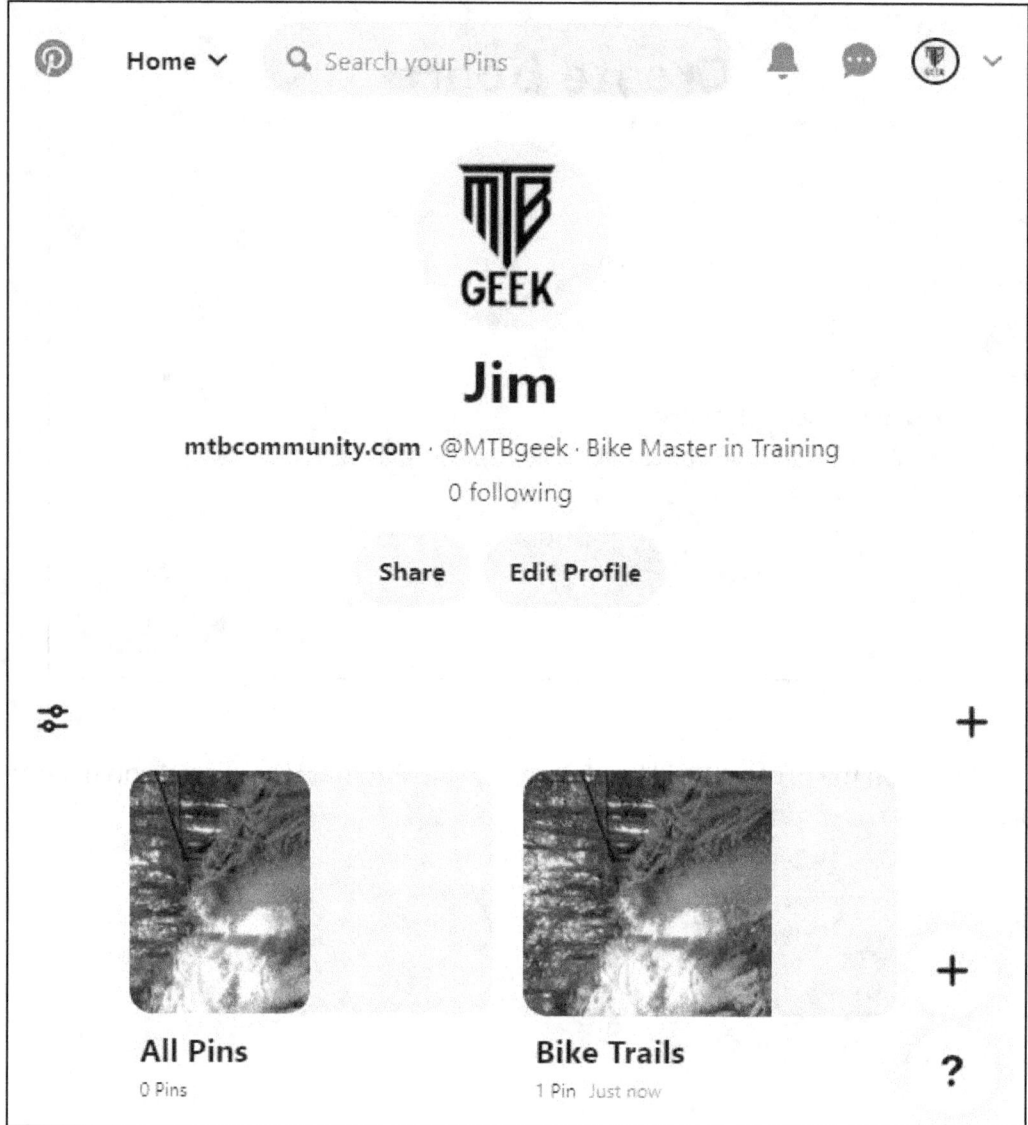

Figure 5.13

If I were to click on my *Pin to* open it and then hover my mouse over the Pin, I would see that I have options to save, edit and share it. Clicking on *Save* will save it to my profile making it easier to find later. Normally you would do this with other Pinterest users posts rather than your own.

Chapter 5 – Pinterest

Figure 5.14

The pencil icon will open the edit menu where you can make changes to the information you added when creating the pin. You can also enable or disable allowing comments or shopping recommendations based on your Pin.

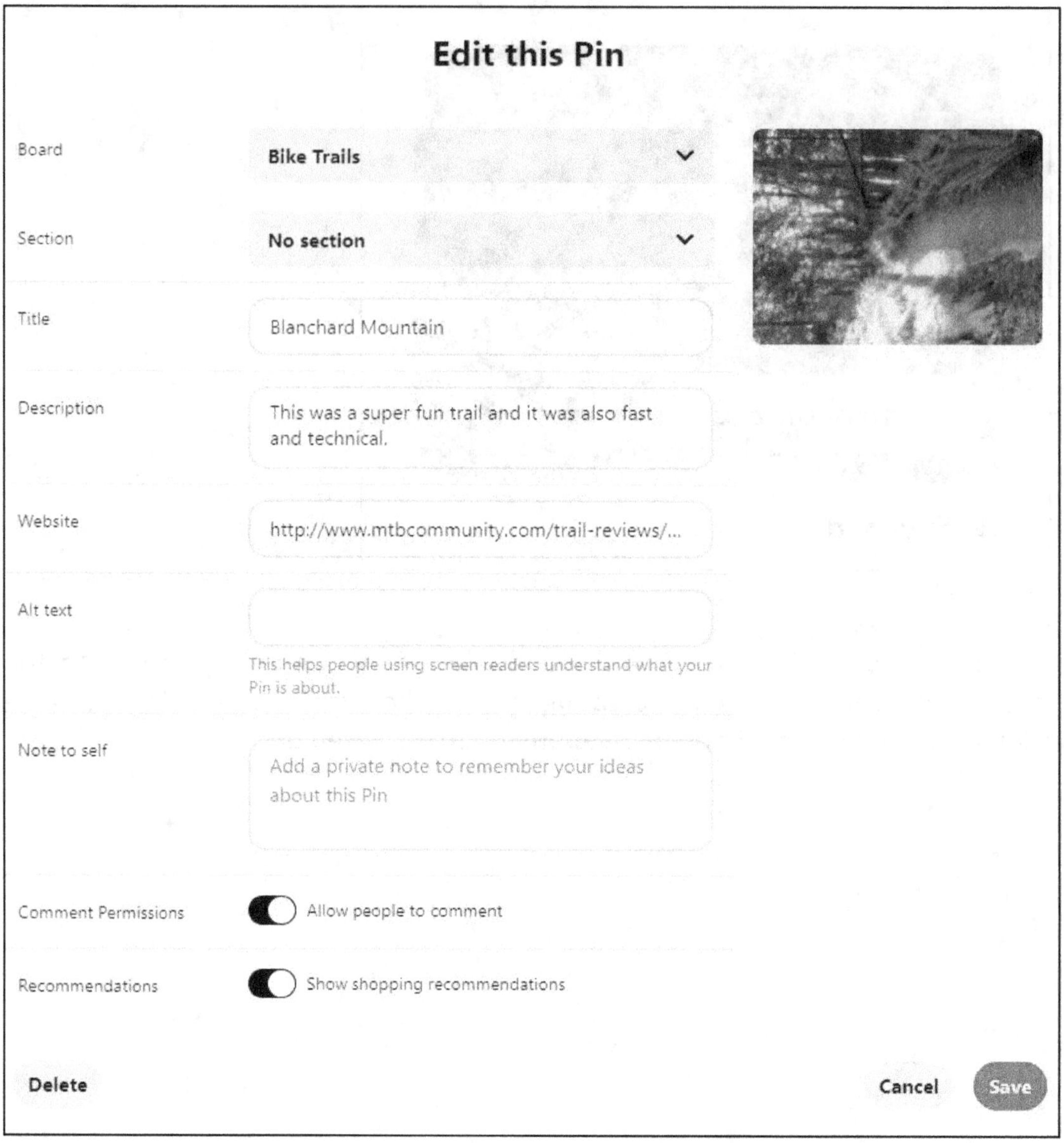

Chapter 5 – Pinterest

Figure 5.15

If you have a Pin of yours or found a Pin belonging to someone else and want to share it then you can click on the share icon. Then you will be able to share it via different apps such as Facebook or Twitter. You can also use the *Copy link* button to create a link to the Pin that you can paste into an email or chat box etc.

Chapter 5 – Pinterest

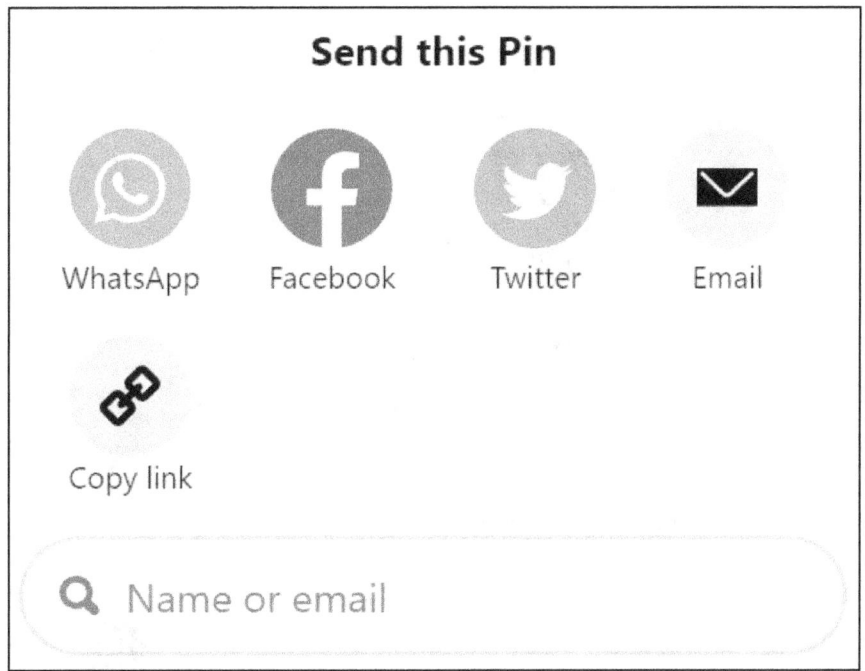

Figure 5.16

Creating Boards
Before I get into creating any more pins, I want to discuss Pinterest boards and create a few of them so things will make a little more sense. If you recall from our discussion on creating Pins, you need at least one board in order to do so.

Boards make it easier to organize your Pins and therefore your ideas, products, pictures etc. boards are easy to create and it's also easy to move your Pins from board to board as needed.

Going back to my profile, you can see that I still have the one board named Bike Trails that I created when I made my first Pin, and my first Pin is part of that board. If I were to click on the lower add + button, I would be able to create a new Pin but if I click the upper + button, I can then create either a Pin or a board.

Chapter 5 – Pinterest

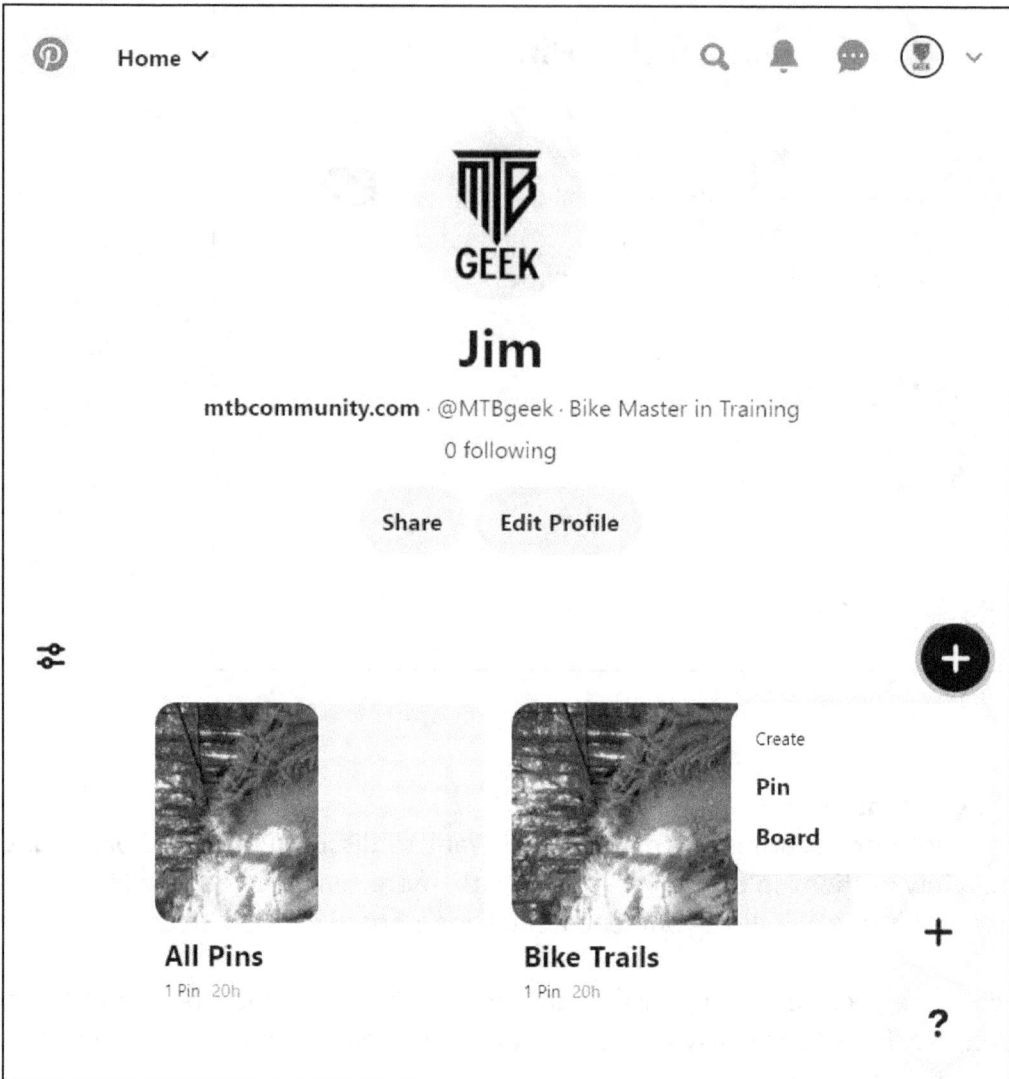

Figure 5.17

Now I will create a new board and call it Bike Accessories for my make believe bike store (figure 5.18). After I click on create, Pinterest will suggest some Pins that I add to my board based on its name. I will not add any of their suggestions at this time.

Chapter 5 – Pinterest

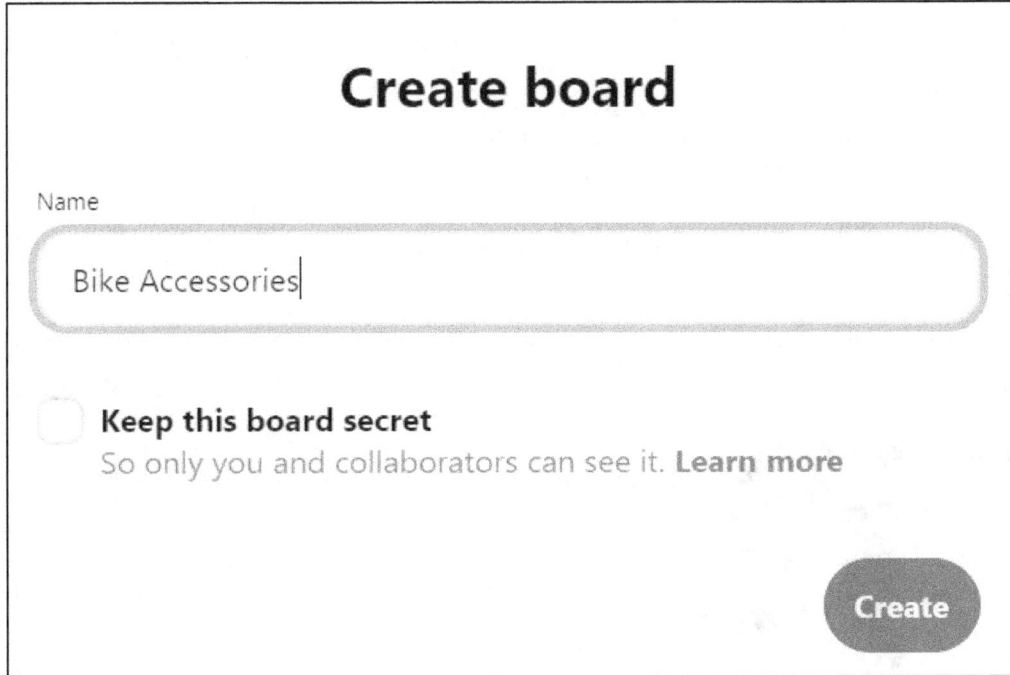

Figure 5.18

Now my new Bike Accessories board shows up in my profile with my original one. If I need to edit the name of the board, I can click the pencil icon on the board itself to do so.

Chapter 5 – Pinterest

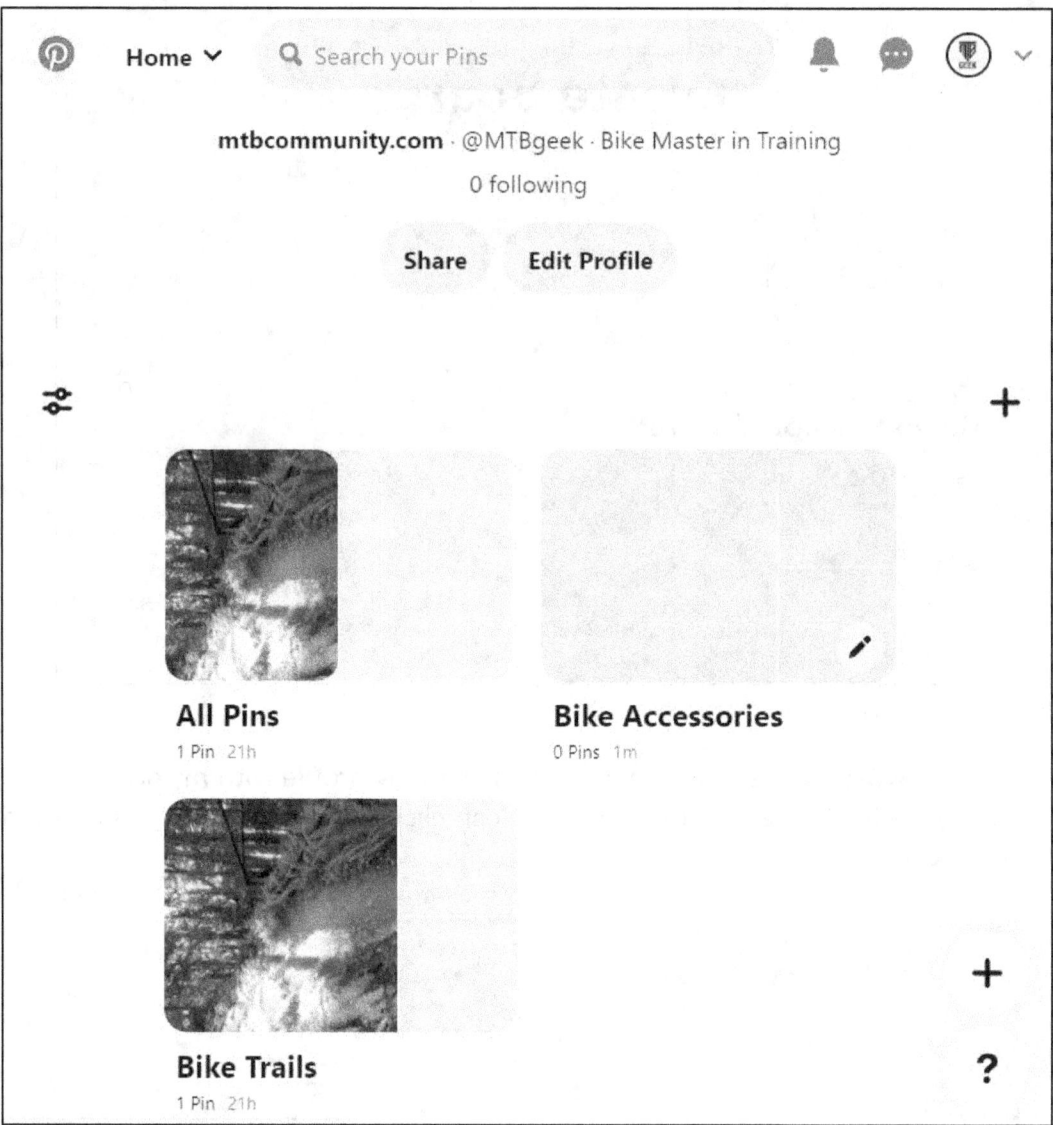

Figure 5.19

Now when I add new Pins, I can select from either one of my two boards to place them on.

Chapter 5 – Pinterest

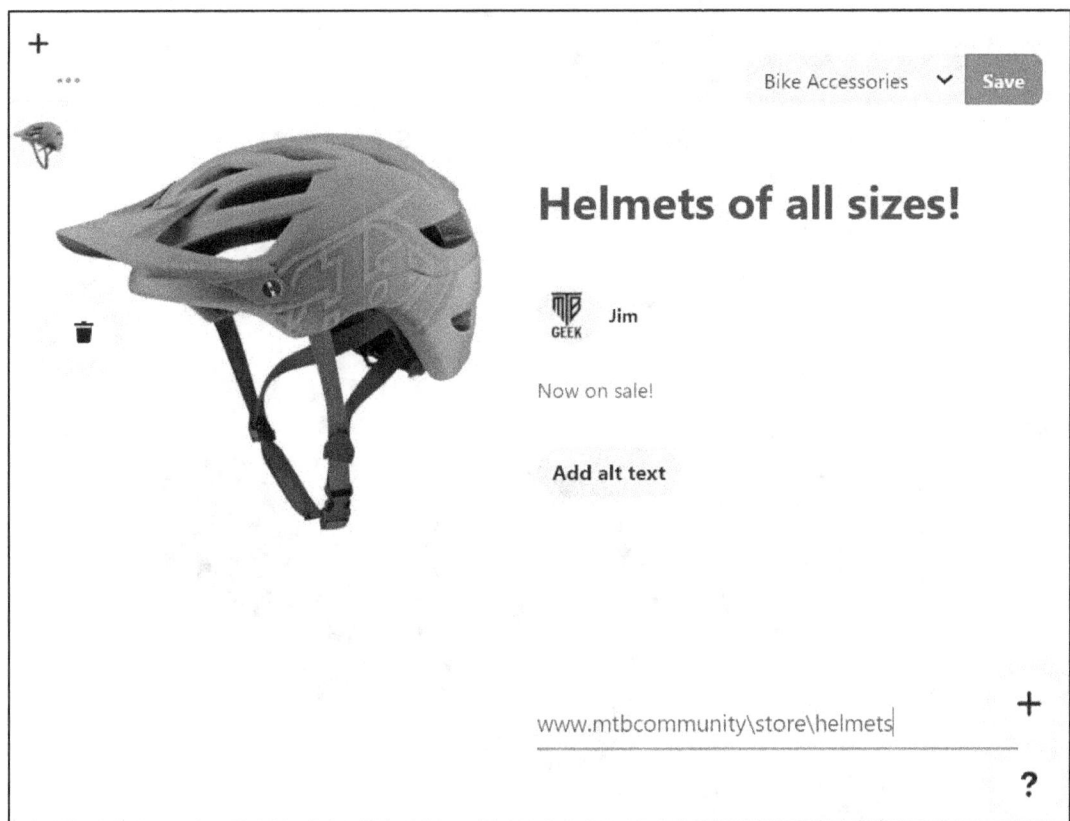

Figure 5.20

Now that I have added some Pins to my board, you can see that things are starting to look organized. I can click on any one of them to get more details about that Pin or to edit it if needed.

Chapter 5 – Pinterest

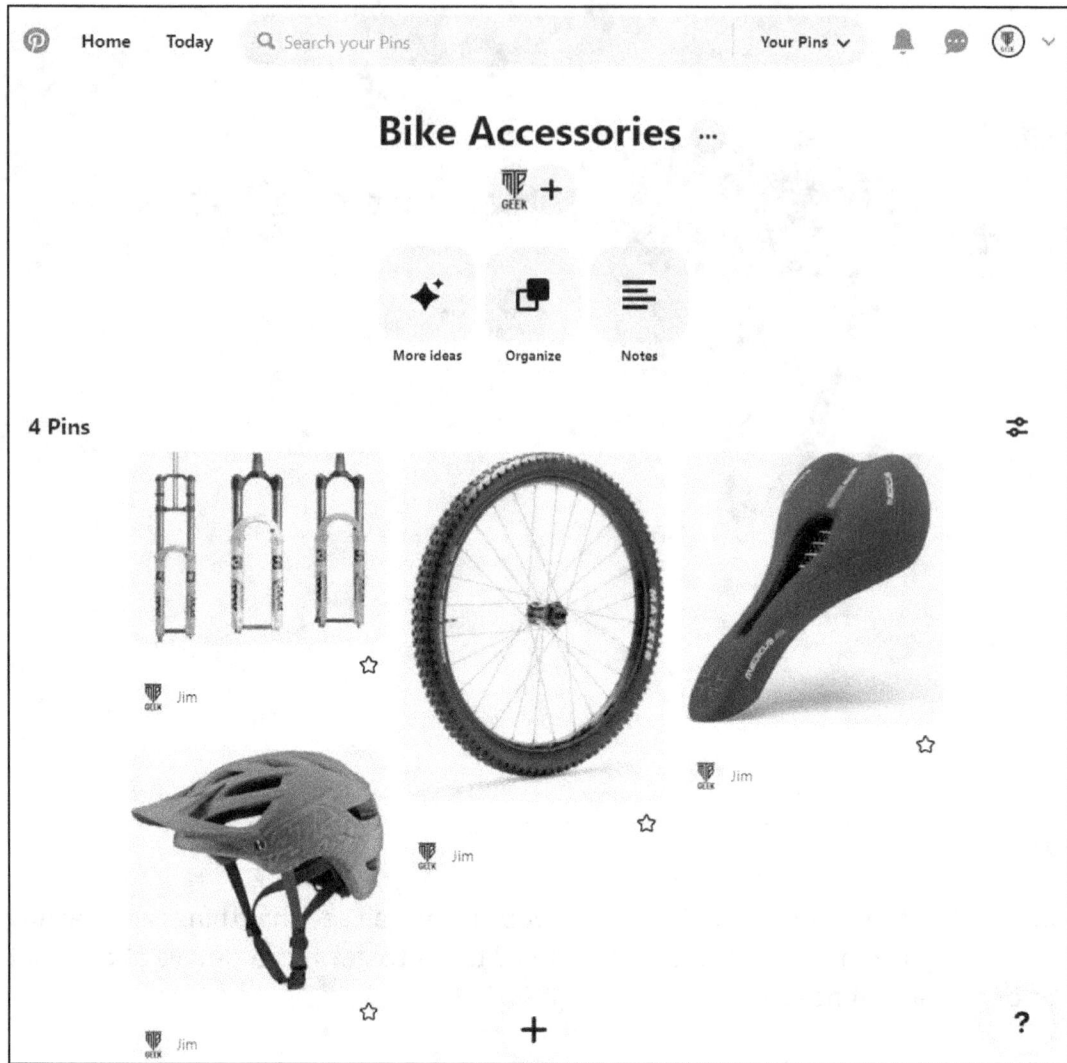

Figure 5.21

If you look at the top of figure 5.21, you will see that I have some options for this board that I can click on.

- **More ideas** – If I want to see other Pins related to this one, then I can choose this option and add them to my board if I like.

- **Organize** – This can be used to rearrange the order of the Pins on the board.

- **Notes** – This is used to make private notes to yourself about the board and can be used as a place to add reminders of things you need to do with this board. You can also add notes within individual Pins.

Chapter 5 – Pinterest

Clicking on the ellipsis at the top right will give me some additional options.

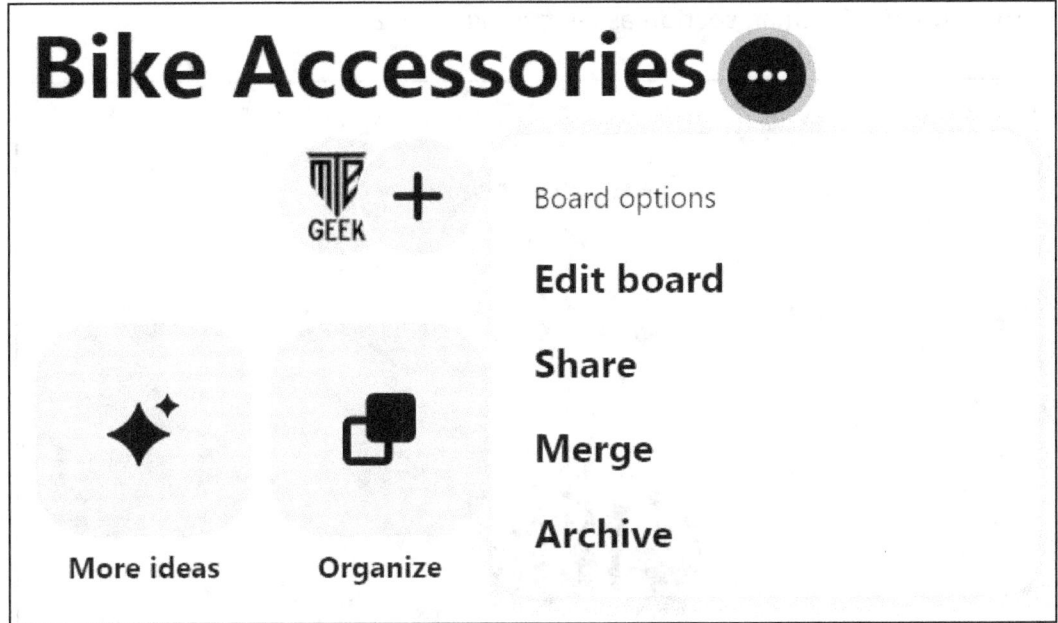

Figure 5.22

- **Edit board** – Here you can do things such as rename the board, make it secret, add a description and even delete it.

- **Share** – You can share your board with others from here. I will be going over sharing in more detail later in this chapter.

- **Merge** – If you have two boards that you want to merge into one, you can do so from here. Just keep in mind that the board you perform this action with will be deleted and its Pins added to the board you choose during the merge process.

- **Archive** – This will let you archive a board meaning it will still be there, but you won't be able to save Pins to it and it will be hidden from your profile.

I also wanted to mention the + sign button next to my profile icon in figure 5.22. This is the collaborate button and will allow you to invite other Pinterest members to add, move or delete Pins and sections from this board as well as comment and react.

Chapter 5 – Pinterest

Speaking of sections, when you are in one of your boards, you can create a section that will let you further organize your ideas or products. For my Bike Accessories board, I added a Clothing section as seen in figure 5.23.

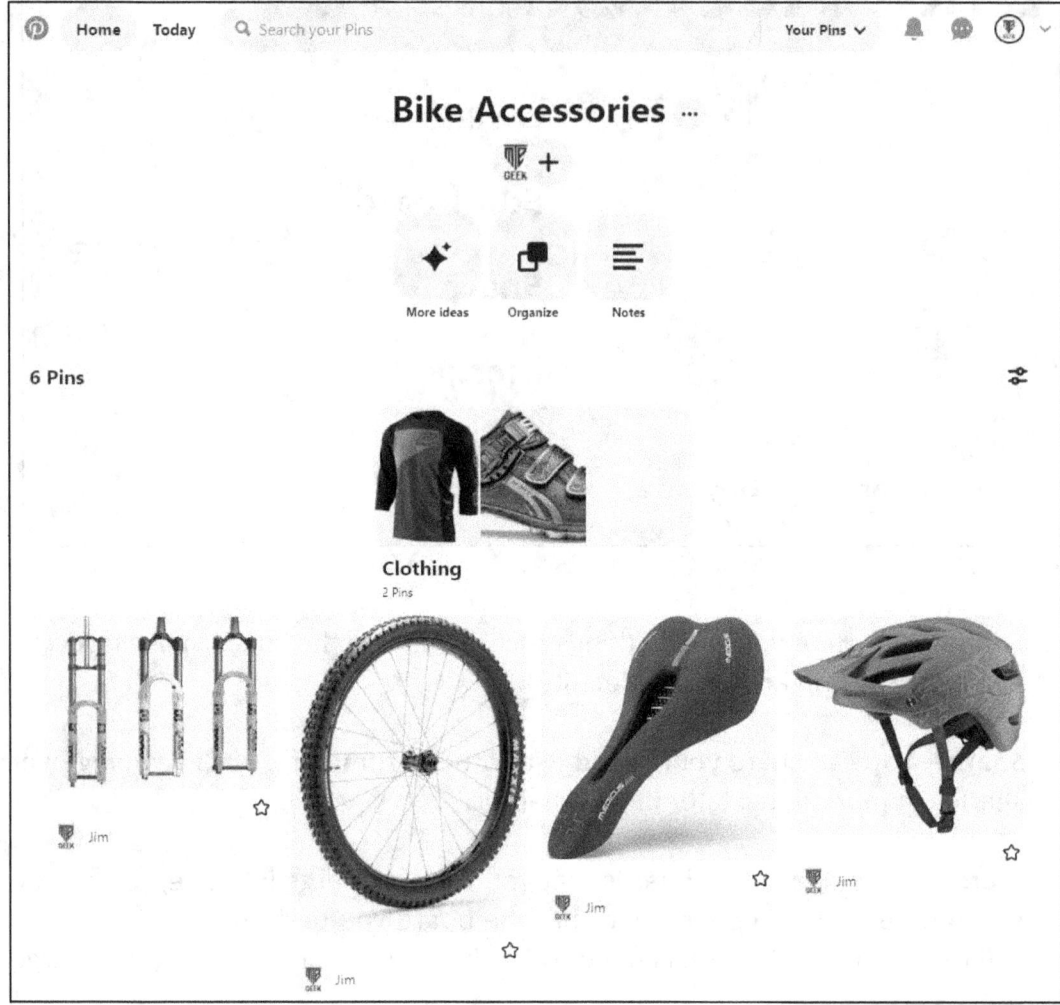

Figure 5.23

Sharing Pins and Boards

Just like with most other social media platforms, sharing is a key part of using Pinterest and without it, it would be much harder to get your ideas or products out to the rest of the world. Or at least to your friends and family!

It is possible to share an individual Pin, or an entire board and the process works the same for either one. Figure 5.22 shows you where to click to save a board and figure 5.24 shows you where to click to share a Pin.

Chapter 5 – Pinterest

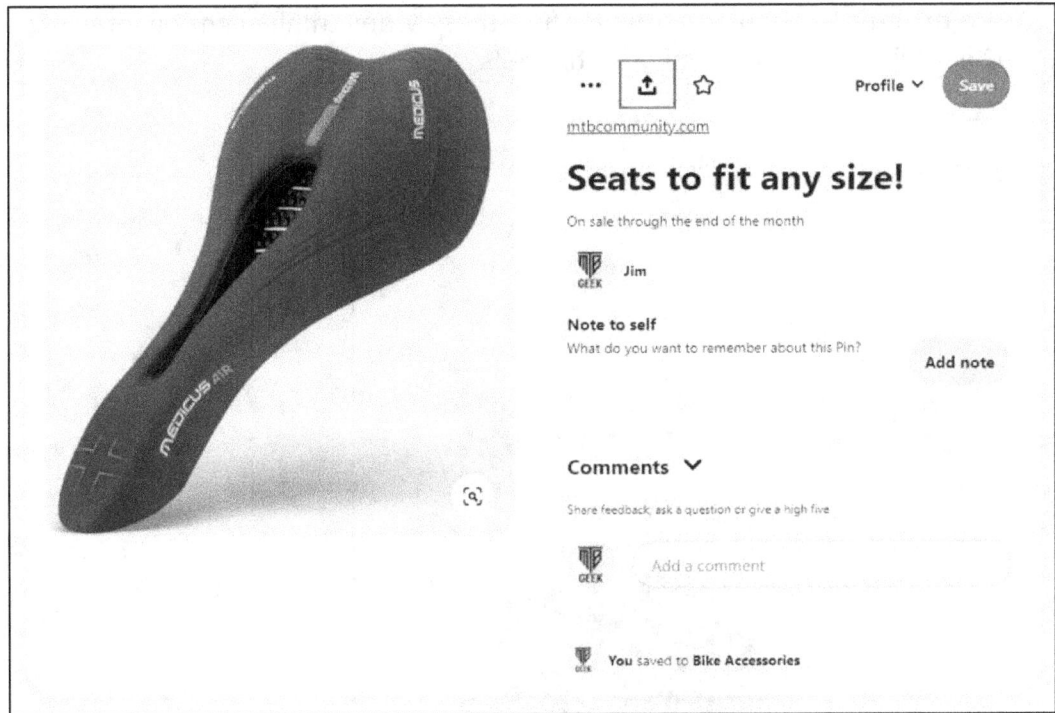

Figure 5.24

Once you click the share button, you will have the option to share your Pin or board via WhatsApp, Facebook, Twitter, Email or by copying a link to your Pin or board that you can then paste into whichever platform you like to share it. The *name or email* section can be used to share with another Pinterest user if you know their username which will begin with the @ symbol.

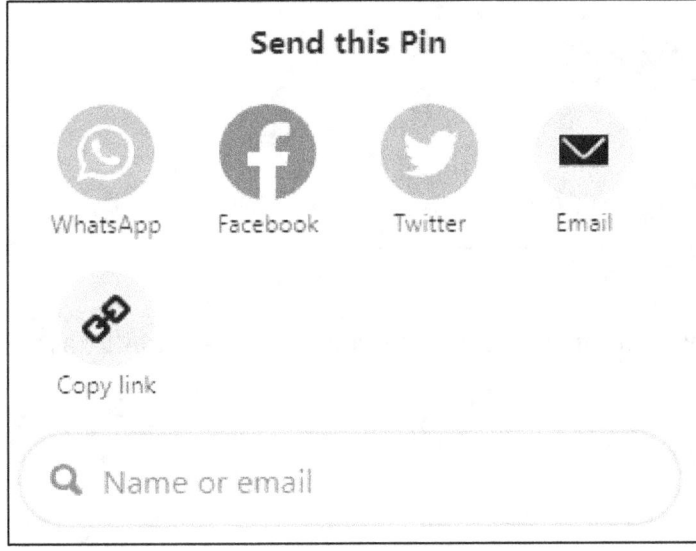

Figure 5.25

151

Chapter 5 – Pinterest

I will use the email option and send it off to those who I think might be interested in it. They will get an email similar to figure 5.26.

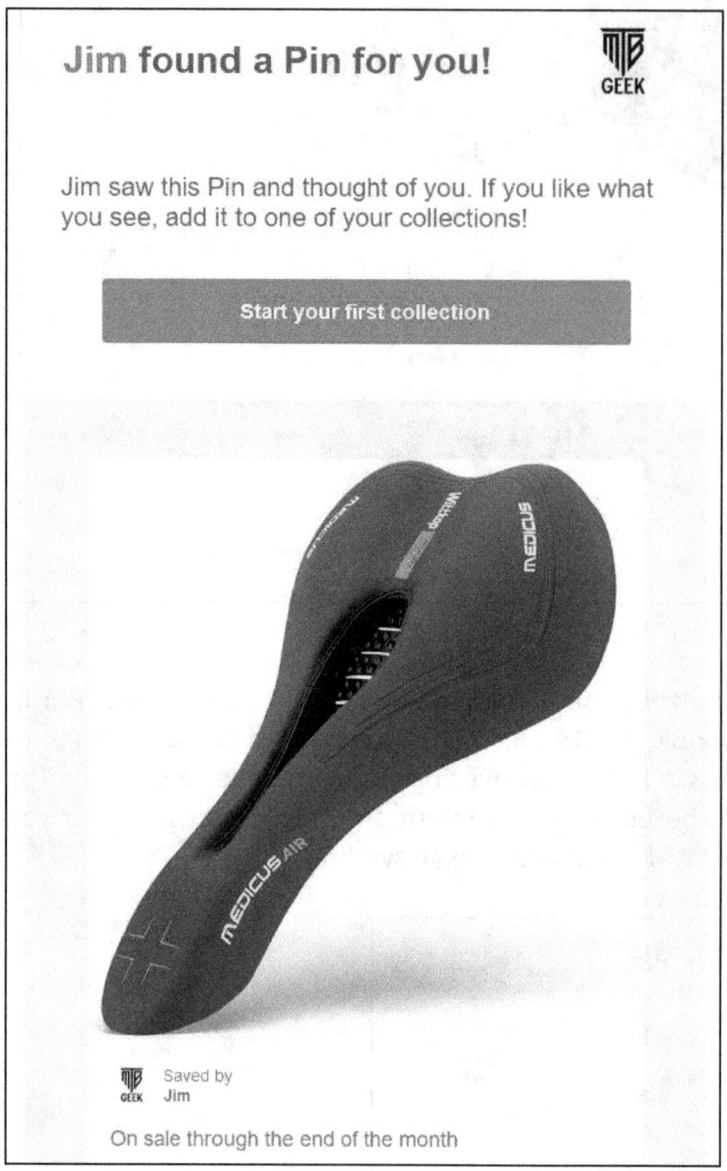

Figure 5.26

Then the person I sent it to will be able to see my Pin even if they don't have a Pinterest account.

Chapter 6 – YouTube

If you are the type that likes to spend your time watching videos that are most likely a waste of your time, then YouTube is for you! Actually there are some very interesting and helpful videos on YouTube but there are many that really shouldn't be seen by anyone because they are completely pointless. Once you start using YouTube, you will see exactly what I mean.

YouTube Overview
YouTube was created back in 2005 with the idea that people would enjoy sharing their home videos with other people on the internet. Now YouTube currently has over 1 billion visitors per month and these visitors watch over 1 billion hours of videos each day. Search engine giant Google purchased YouTube for $1.65 billion in stock in November 2006 and has owned it ever since.

The idea behind YouTube is simple. You upload videos on whatever subject you like, make them viewable to the public and see if anyone else watches them. Of course you can't upload anything too inappropriate or copyrighted otherwise it will get removed and your account might also get canceled.

You also have the choice of making your videos private so only you can watch them or anyone you happen to send a link to. Otherwise, if they are public, they will come up in search results and be viewable by anyone around the world. Plus you will be able to see how many people have watched your video, so you know how popular it is.

When you start your YouTube channel as it is called, you will then be able to manage all of your videos from a single location and do things such as edit the title, description, tags and even make it private or delete it altogether.

Signing Up for an Account
Since YouTube is owned by Google, you will need a Google account in order to upload videos to YouTube. You don't need a Google account to watch videos on YouTube unless you want to watch one that is intended for mature audiences and then YouTube will use your Google account to verify your age otherwise you won't be able to watch the video.

Chapter 6 – YouTube

If you have a Gmail email address, then you already have a Google account. If you have an Android smartphone or tablet, then you most likely already have a Google account as well.

To create a Google account simply to go **www.google.com** and click on the *Sign In* button. If you don't already have an account, then you will be prompted to create one (as seen in figure 6.1).

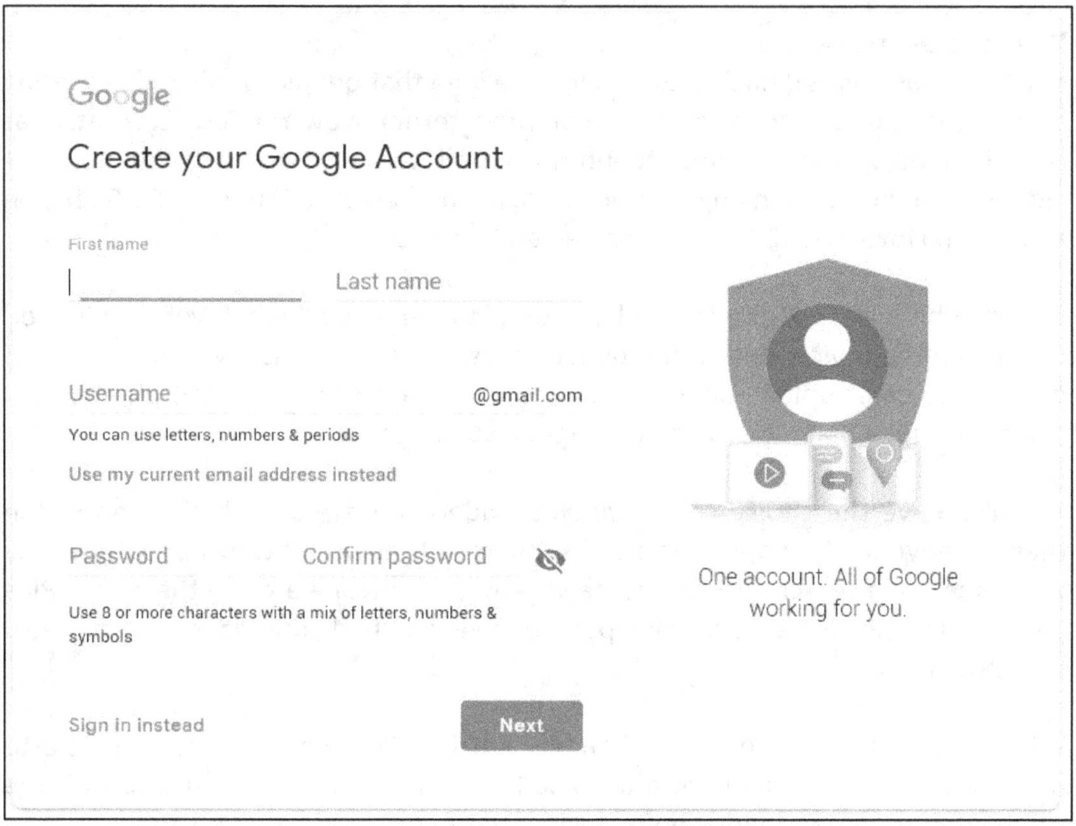

Figure 6.1

Simply enter your first and last name and choose a username, which will also be used for your Gmail email account ending in @gmail.com. If the username has already been taken, then you will be prompted to enter a new one. Notice that there is an option that says Use my current email address instead. This can be done if you do not want a Gmail email address, but still want to create a Google account with your current email address. (I would suggest creating a Gmail email address just to make things easier if you plan on using other Google Apps.)

Chapter 6 – YouTube

Then you will need to come up with a password that has 8 or more characters and uses letters, numbers, and symbols (such as ! or # for example) and click on *Next*.

After that, you will need to enter your phone number so Google can verify it is really you. It will send you a six digit number via text message that you will have to enter in the next step. Doing this will also tie your phone number to your Google account, which comes in handy for things like password recovery if you forget your password. If you don't have a password, you can have Google call you with the code instead of texting it.

Next, you enter a recovery email address (which can also be used for password recovery), as well as your birth date information. The birth date information is used because some Google services have age requirements. The gender information it asks for is optional and is not shown to other Google users. You can also edit your Google account later if you wish to change or add anything.

You may be asked to add your phone number to your account to use for Google services. This is optional, but if you click on the *More options* link, you can specify exactly what you want or don't want your phone number to be used for.

Chapter 6 – YouTube

Choose what's right for you

○ Add my number for account security only

○ Add my number for account security and video calls, but don't use my number for other Google services like relevant ads

○ Yes, I'm in - add my number for use across Google services, including account security, video calls, and more relevant ads

You can always change your number, control how it's used, or remove it in your Google Account (account.google.com/phone).

Back   Done

Figure 6.2

If you don't want your number to be used at all, simply click on *Skip*, and you will be brought to the Privacy and Terms agreement, which you can read if you like. To continue, you will need to click on the *I agree* button. Finally, after clicking on I agree, your account will be created, and you will be logged in automatically. If you are on the Google home page, then you will see your first initial up in the right hand corner. You can go into your settings and edit your profile and add a picture if you like. Then you can access YouTube with your new account.

If you are interested in learning more about all the apps that Google has to offer such as Gmail, Docs, Calendar etc., then check out my book titles **Google Apps Made Easy**. https://www.amazon.com/dp/1798114992

Chapter 6 – YouTube

Searching for Videos

If the main reason you are going to visit YouTube is to watch videos, then it's a good idea to know how to search for them so you can find what you are looking for. You will search for videos the same way you would search for content in your web browser on your computer.

When you go to the YouTube website (youtube.com), you will be shown a bunch of suggested videos and also some search terms at the top that you can click on to take you to videos related to those terms. The first time you use YouTube, these videos and search terms will be completely random but as you start watching videos, YouTube will start suggesting other videos related to the videos you have been watching.

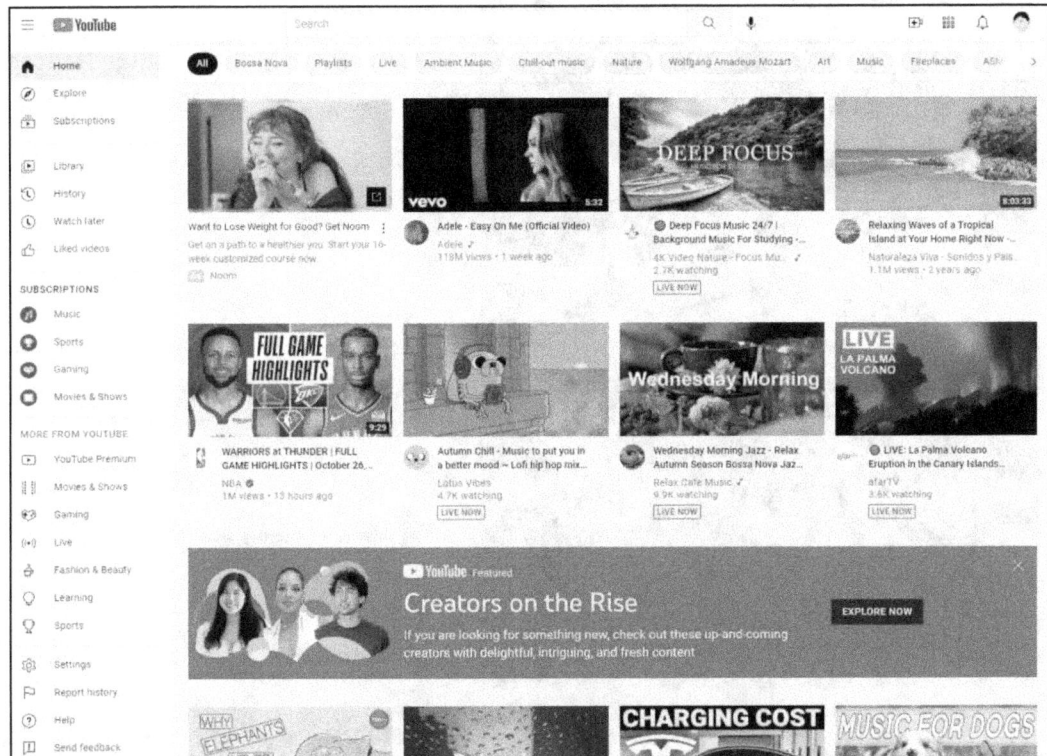

Figure 6.3

At the top of the window, you will see a search box where you can type in anything you wish to search for. You can use one word or type in an entire sentence. I am going to type in *mountain biking Washington state* to see what kind of biking videos I can find. Figure 6.4 shows the results of my search. YouTube will tend to put the more popular videos that have the most views and likes first.

Chapter 6 – YouTube

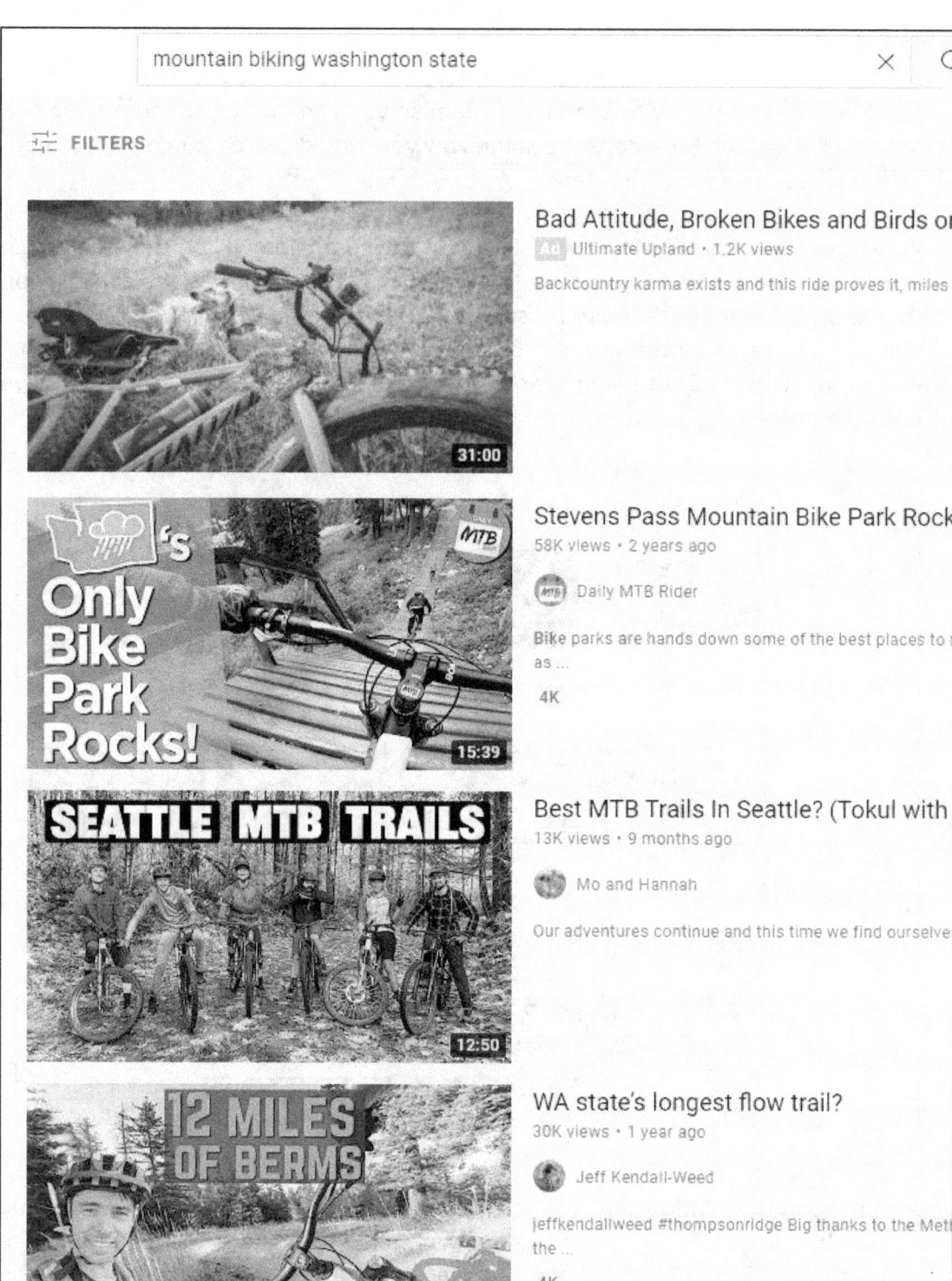

Figure 6.4

Chapter 6 – YouTube

If you want to sort out the search results, you can click on the word *Filter* at the top left of the page to sort by things such as the upload date, view count, duration and so on. If I wanted to see videos that were posted this week only, I would click on *This week* and would only be shown those results.

FILTERS				
UPLOAD DATE	TYPE	DURATION	FEATURES	SORT BY
Last hour	Video	Under 4 minutes	Live	Relevance
Today	Channel	4 - 20 minutes	4K	Upload date
This week	Playlist	Over 20 minutes	HD	View count
This month	Movie		Subtitles/CC	Rating
This year			Creative Commons	
			360°	
			VR180	
			3D	
			HDR	
			Location	
			Purchased	

Figure 6.5

Watching Videos

Once you find the video you are looking for, it's time to start watching it so you can enjoy the creator's hard work. Clicking on a video will make it start playing automatically.

When you hover your mouse over the video, you will see several control options at the bottom that you can use to control how the video plays and looks (figure 6.6).

Chapter 6 – YouTube

Figure 6.6

- **Pause\Play** – Use this button to play and pause the video. You can also click on the video itself to do the same thing.

- **Next Video** – Clicking on this will play the next video listed after the current video over to the right of the screen.

- **Volume** – Used to turn the volume up or down. You can also mute the volume.

- **Video Duration** – This shows how much of the video you have watched and its total length.

- **Auto Play** – If this is on, YouTube will play the next video in the list at the right side of the page automatically when the current video is finished playing.

- **Quality Settings** – Here you can choose the quality of the video playback. You always want to use the higher settings unless you are somewhere with a poor internet connection.

Chapter 6 – YouTube

- **Mini Player** – This will open the video in mini player at the lower corner of the screen. You can click the expand button at the top left to put the mode back to normal.

- **Theatre Mode** – This will play the video in a larger mode but still not full screen.

- **Full Screen** – This will make the video take up your entire screen. You can press the Esc key on your keyboard to get out of full screen mode.

I also want to show you what the other items that are listed at the bottom of the video are used for.

Figure 6.7

Most of these should be pretty self-explanatory and I will be going over liking, sharing and saving videos later in this chapter.

When watching videos on YouTube, you will be shown advertisements before and during certain videos, and the more popular the video, the greater the chances of you seeing advertisements.

Many times when you first play a video you will be shown an ad with a 5 second countdown at the right side of the video which will then turn into a *Skip Ads* button as shown in figure 6.8. When this happens, you can click the Skip Ads button to end the commercial and start your video. Some videos will make you watch an entire ad before starting the videos so be prepared for that.

Chapter 6 – YouTube

Figure 6.8

You will also see ads placed within the video as you are watching it. When this happens, you can click the X at the top right of the ad to close it.

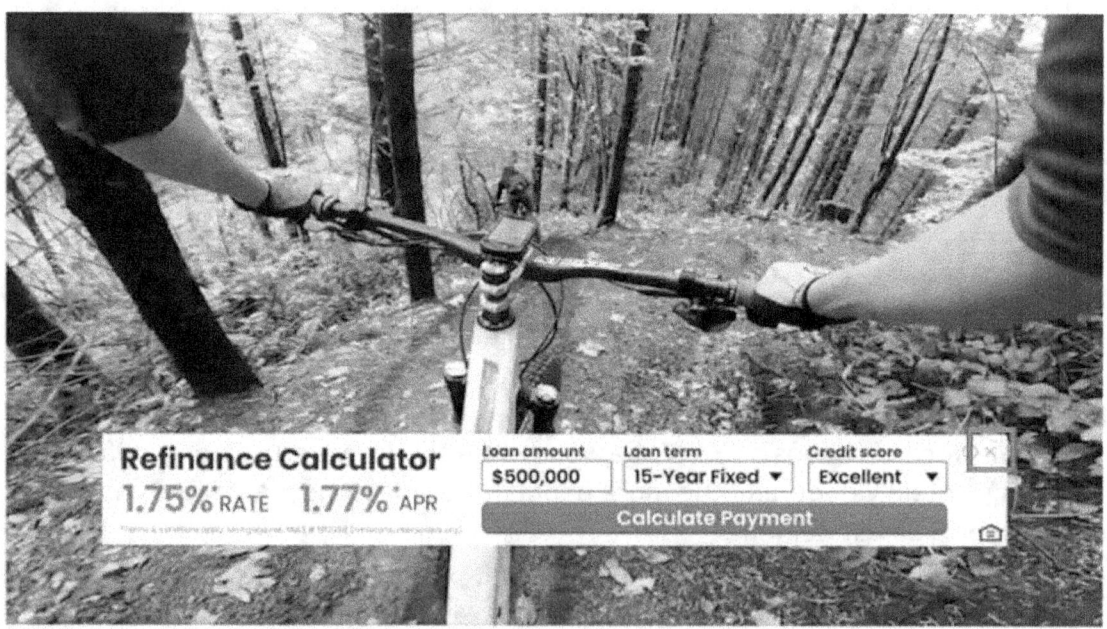

Figure 6.9

Another thing you will run across while watching and searching for videos are Playlists. A playlist is a listing of multiple videos on a single topic that you can

Chapter 6 – YouTube

watch one after the other. Figure 6.10 shows what a typical playlist looks like. The first playlist consists of 16 videos while the second has 33 videos.

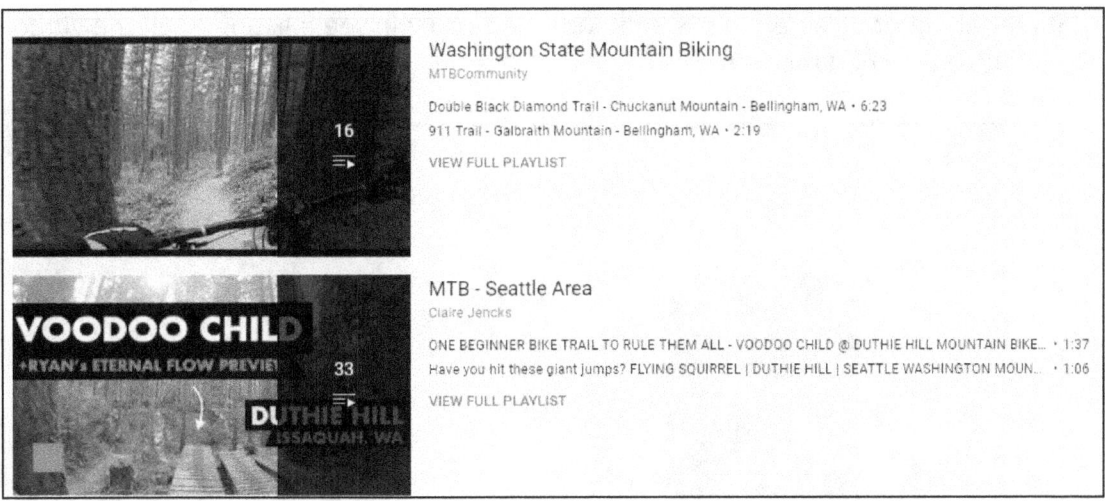

Figure 6.10

When you start a playlist, the first video will play and then you will see the upcoming videos over to the right in the order they will play. You can easily click on any video in the list to skip to it.

Figure 6.11

History and Watch Later
Just like with almost everything you do online, YouTube keeps a history of certain information about what videos you watch. There is a good chance that your watch history is disabled by default but that will depend on how your Google account is set up.

163

Chapter 6 – YouTube

This is very easy to check and enable or disable depending on your needs. If you click on the three vertical bars at the top left of the YouTube page, you will see many categories for various settings. If you go to the *History* setting you can see if it is enabled or disabled. If it's enabled, then you will see a listing of all the videos you have watched recently.

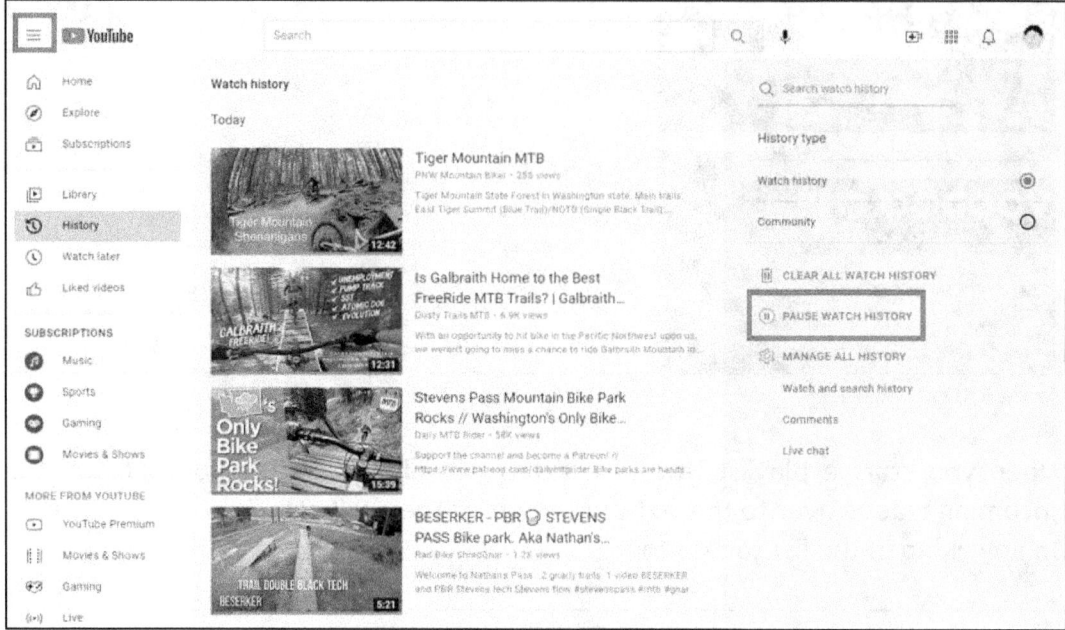

Figure 6.12

There are other options over to the right such as the ability to pause the history process or to clear your entire watch history.

While watching videos, you also have the option to save them for later and add them to your watchlist or make your own playlist from them as seen in figure 6.13.

Chapter 6 – YouTube

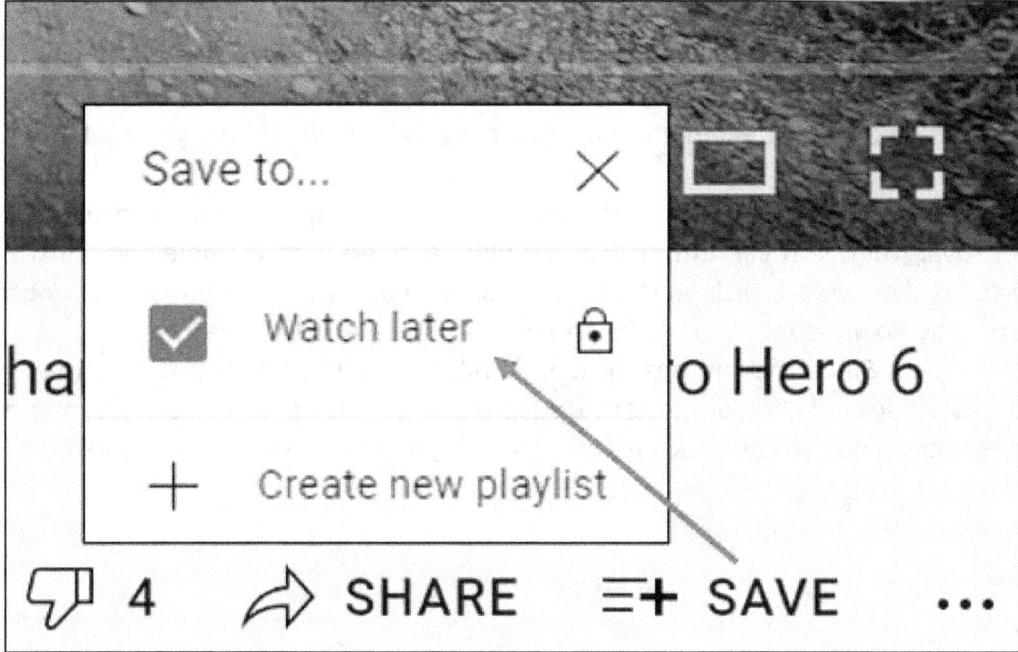

Figure 6.13

After you have chosen some videos to watch later, you can go to the *Watch later* section and see all of your saved videos and watch them whenever you like. You can even click on the ellipsis to add additional videos or remove them.

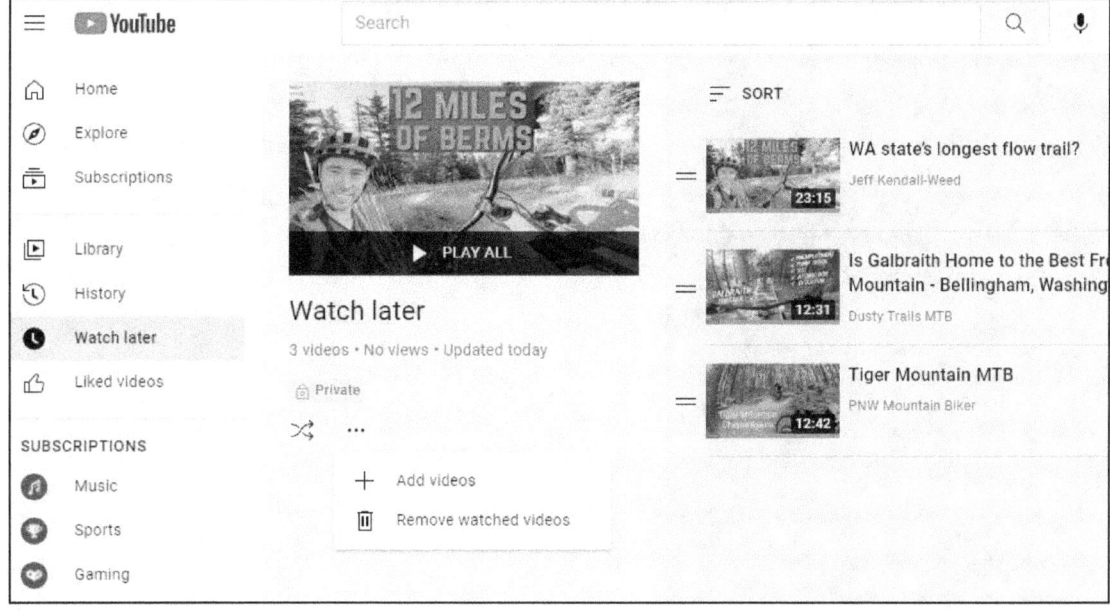

Figure 6.14

Chapter 6 – YouTube

Liking, Commenting, Subscribing and Sharing
Part of the social media experience is the ability to show how you feel about the work or comments that people make on all of these social media platforms. YouTube is no different when it comes to letting people know how you feel.

If you are watching a video and feel the need to show your approval or disapproval, then you can either like or unlike a video with a single click of the mouse. To like a video, click on the thumbs up icon and to dislike a video, click on the thumbs down icon. Figure 6.15 shows that there are 142 likes and 4 dislikes for this video. Since the thumbs up icon is filled in solid that means that I have liked this video and the count went up from 141 to 142. If you like a video and change your mind, simply click the thumbs up again to have your like removed.

Chapter 6 – YouTube

Figure 6.15

If you would like to give more than a thumbs up or down to a video then you can post a comment instead, or in addition to your thumbs up\down. As you can see in figure 6.16, the username of the person who posted this video is Dusty Trails MTB and he has 1400 subscribers to his channel (discussed later in this chapter). Under that is a description of the video and under that are 62 comments made by other YouTube members. You can even see that Dusty Trails MTB replied to the comment made by Johnny Corners.

Chapter 6 – YouTube

> # Is Galbraith Home to the Best FreeRide MTB Trails?
> 6,914 views • Sep 22, 2020
>
>  **Dusty Trails MTB**
> 1.4K subscribers
>
> With an opportunity to hit bike in the Pacific Northwest chance to ride Galbraith Mountain in Bellingham Wash Just a few ours outside of Seattle, this place is home t
>
> SHOW MORE
>
> 62 Comments   SORT BY
>
>
> Commenting publicly as Dan Edmunds
>
> **Johnny Corners** 11 months ago
> I am a Bellingham local and I just saw this video. I notic enough, it was me. How random?? Anyway, I hope you e
>
> 👍 8   👎   ❤️   REPLY
>
> ▼ View reply from Dusty Trails MTB
>
> **Aaron Brand** 9 months ago (edited)
> Fun to see your perspective on these trails. Most of then to get to Galbraith.) I'm glad you have the same experier

Figure 6.16

To make your own comment, simply type in the box where it says Commenting publicly as *your username*. Then you can type whatever you have to say and everyone else will be able to see your comment when they come to this video page. Other people besides the owner of the video can reply to your comment as

Chapter 6 – YouTube

well. The owner of the video can also delete your comment if they think its inappropriate.

If you find a channel that you really like, then you can subscribe to that channel and get notifications whenever that person posts a new video. You might have noticed the *Subscribe* button under the video. If you were to click on this button, then you would then be subscribed to that channel. I will be discussing channels in the next section. After you click on the Subscribe button, it will change to say Subscribed.

Figure 6.17

You can then go back to the YouTube options on the right and click on Subscriptions to see all the channels you have subscribed to. Then you can click on the bell icon to change what type of notifications you will receive from that channel (figure 6.18). You can also click on the *Subscribed* button to unsubscribe from that channel.

Chapter 6 – YouTube

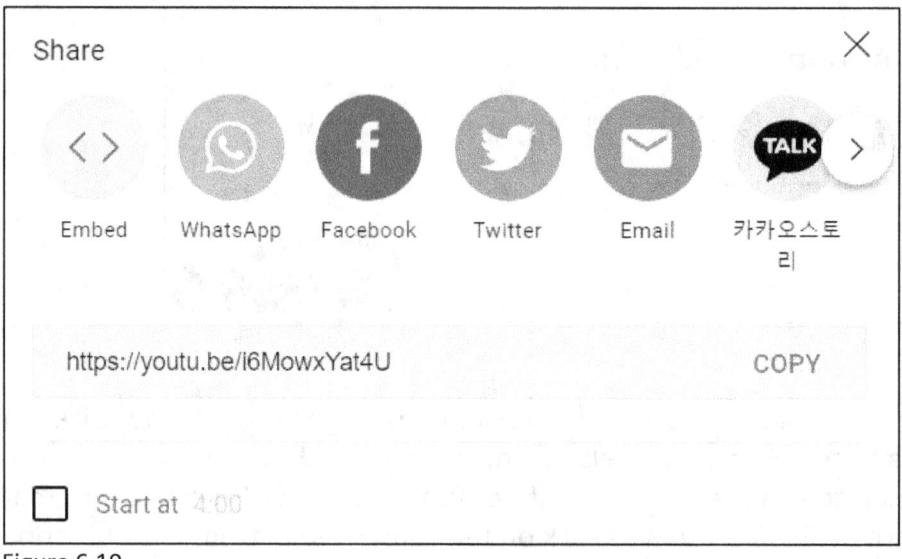
Figure 6.18

Another thing you might want to do if you find an interesting video or channel is share it with someone else who you think might want to check it out. While you are on the video you wish to share, you can click the word *Share* below that video to see what sharing options you have available to you. Figure 6.19 shows some of the available sharing methods such as sharing on Facebook, sharing via an Email or copying the link to paste into whichever sharing app you would like to use.

At the bottom of figure 6.19, you will see that there is a checkbox that says *Start at* with a time next to it. If you want to share a video but have it start at a specific time, then what you can do is click the Share button when the video is at the point where you want the other person to start watching and then check that box before choosing your share method. You can also manually type in a time here.

Figure 6.19

Chapter 6 – YouTube

Creating a Channel for Your Videos
If you decide you want to make a name for yourself in the YouTube world then you might want to consider making a channel for yourself. You can think of YouTube channels as channels on your TV except you get to decide what is playing.

It's very easy to make a channel and only involves a few steps to do so. To begin the process, you will need to click on your profile image at the top right of the screen and then click on *Create a channel*.

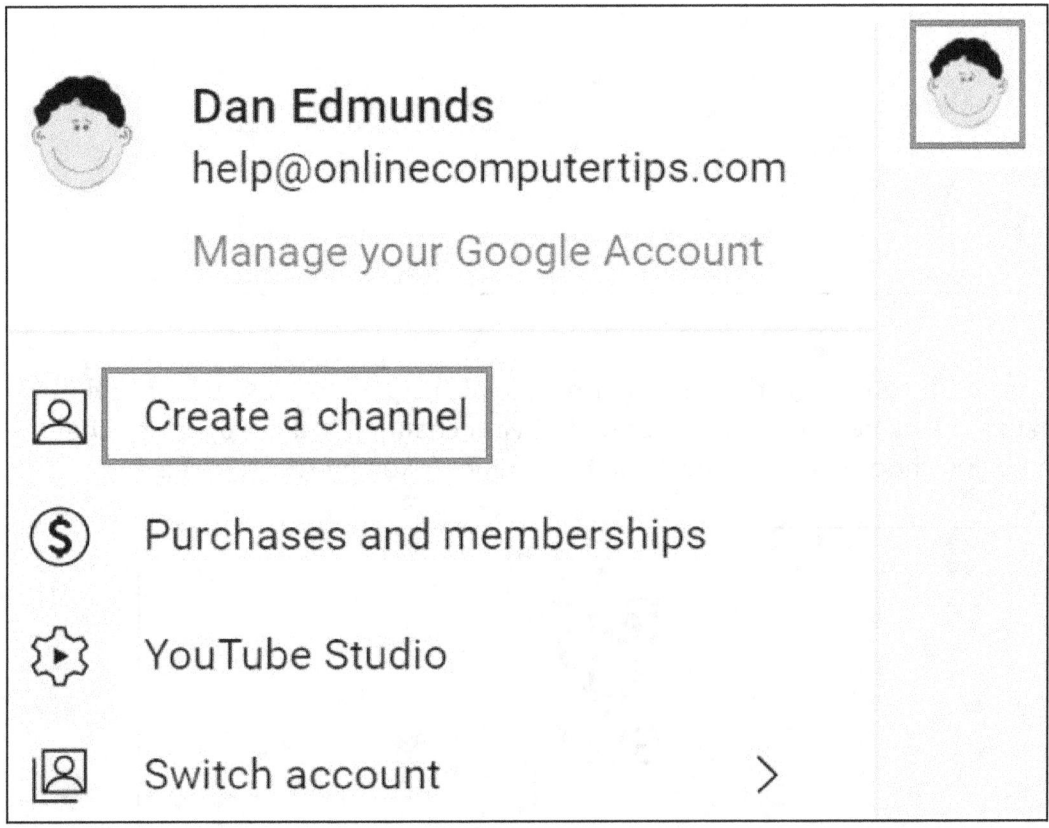
Figure 6.20

By default, YouTube will use your profile image (if you have one) and your name for your channel as seen in figure 6.21.

Chapter 6 – YouTube

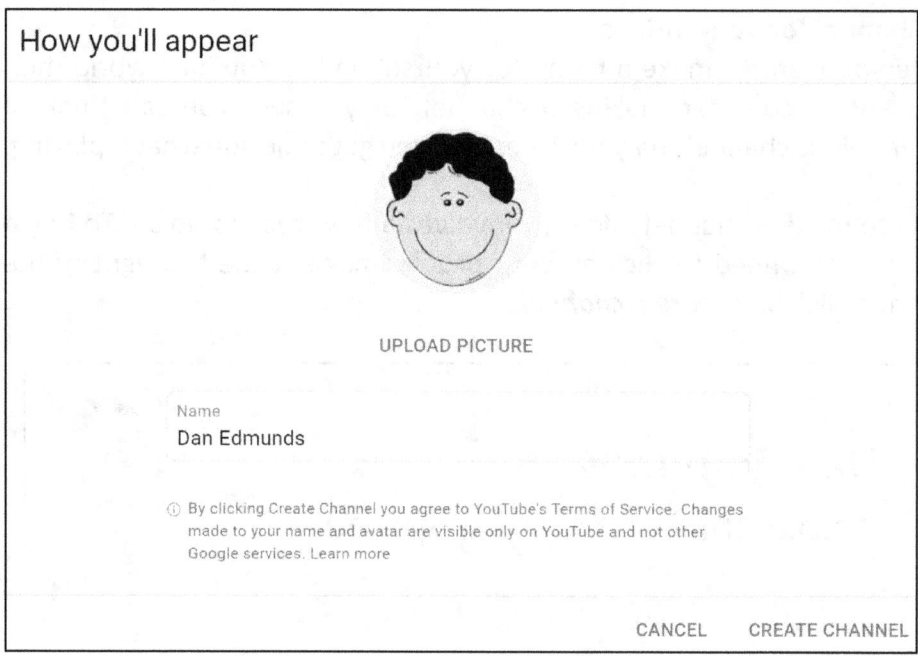

Figure 6.21

If you wish to change this information you can upload a new picture and also change the name to match the content of your channel. Just keep in mind that the name you choose needs to be available and not taken by someone else.

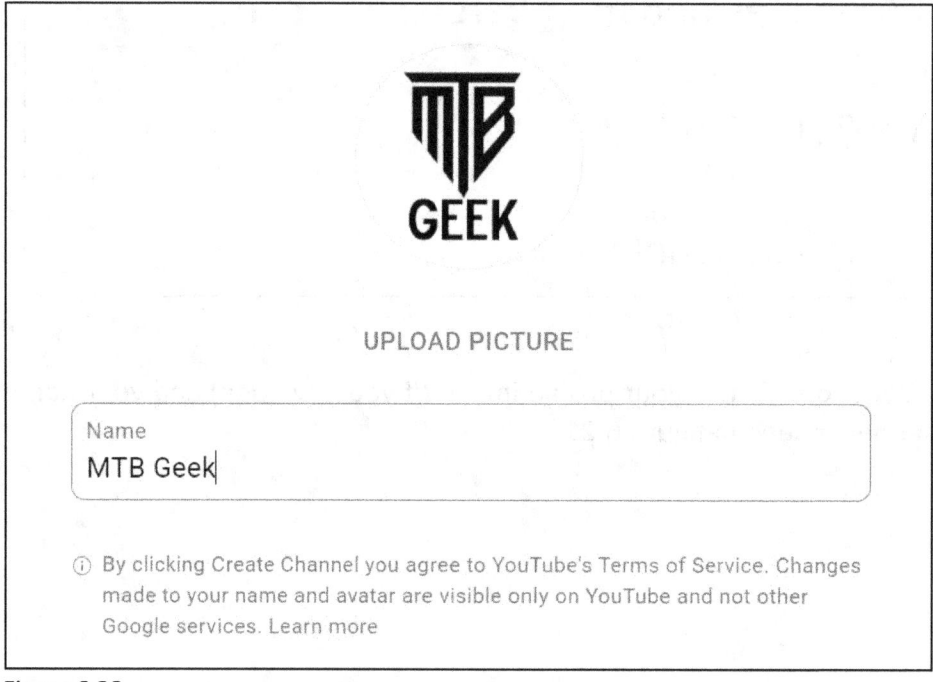

Figure 6.22

Chapter 6 – YouTube

After your channel is created you can then click on the *Customize Channel* button to make additional changes.

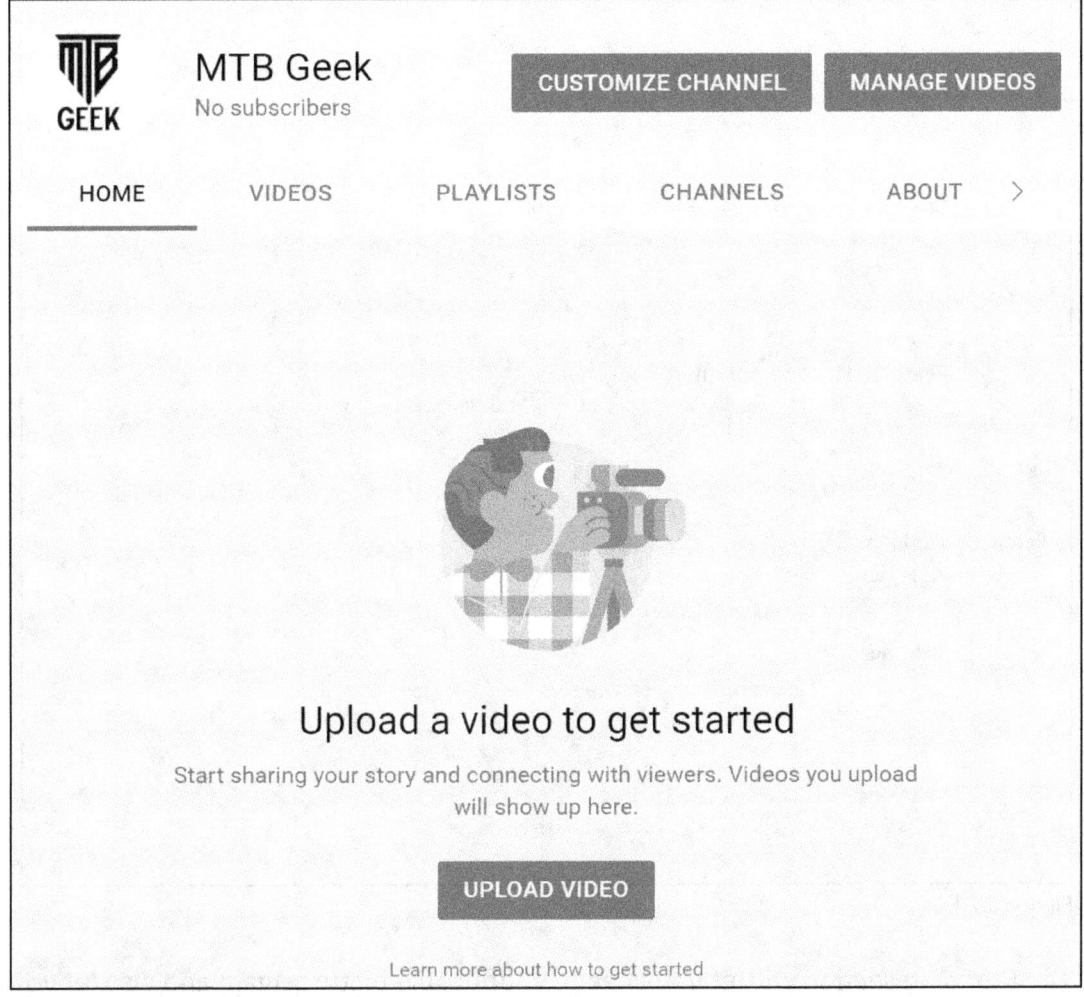
Figure 6.23

There are three main sections that you can go configure additional settings.

The *Layout* section will allow you to do things such as change the trailer for your channel which is the video that is shown when users go to your channel page. You can also configure what video is shown to people who have subscribed to your channel when they arrive there.

Chapter 6 – YouTube

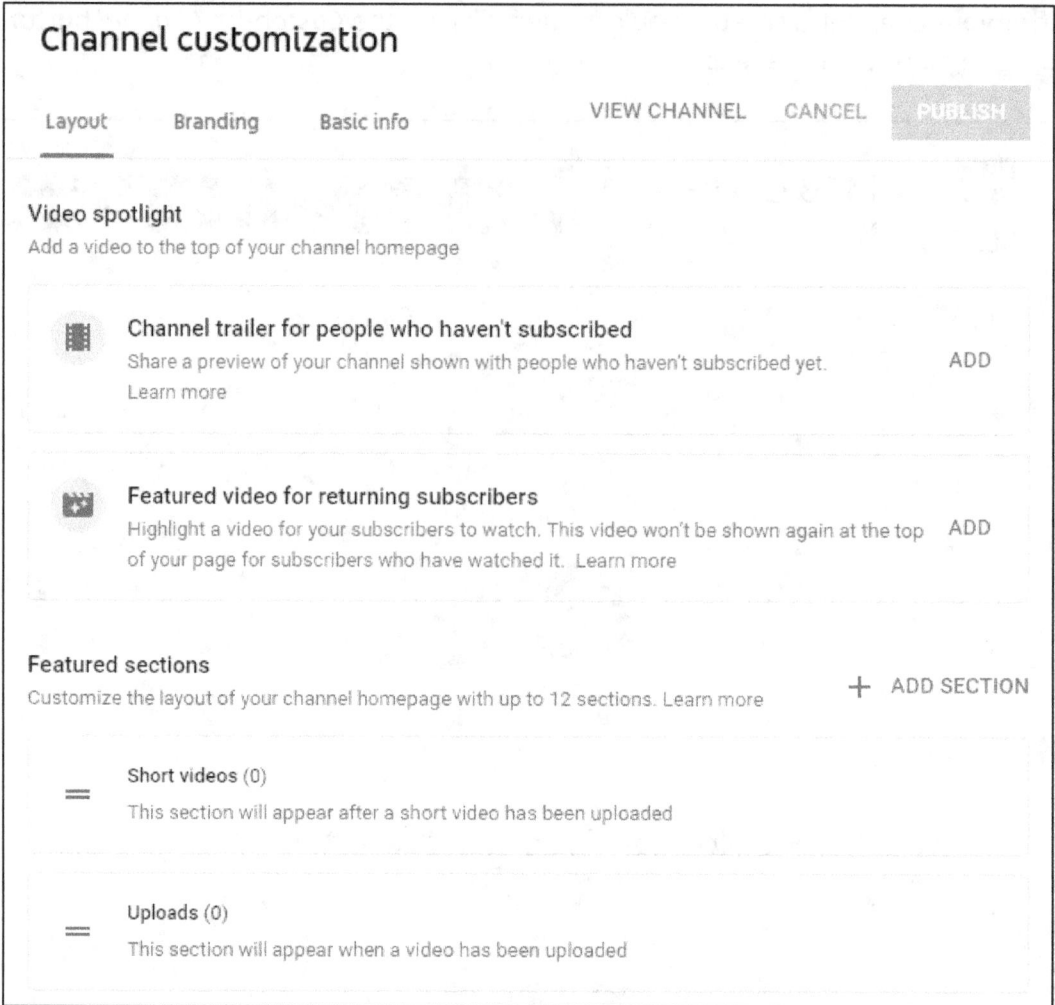

Figure 6.24

The *Branding* section will let you change your profile picture again and also let you upload a banner image that will be displayed at the top of your channel. You just need to make sure you use the right image size otherwise it won't look right. The watermark option will let you place a logo image etc. at the bottom right of your video to mark it as your own.

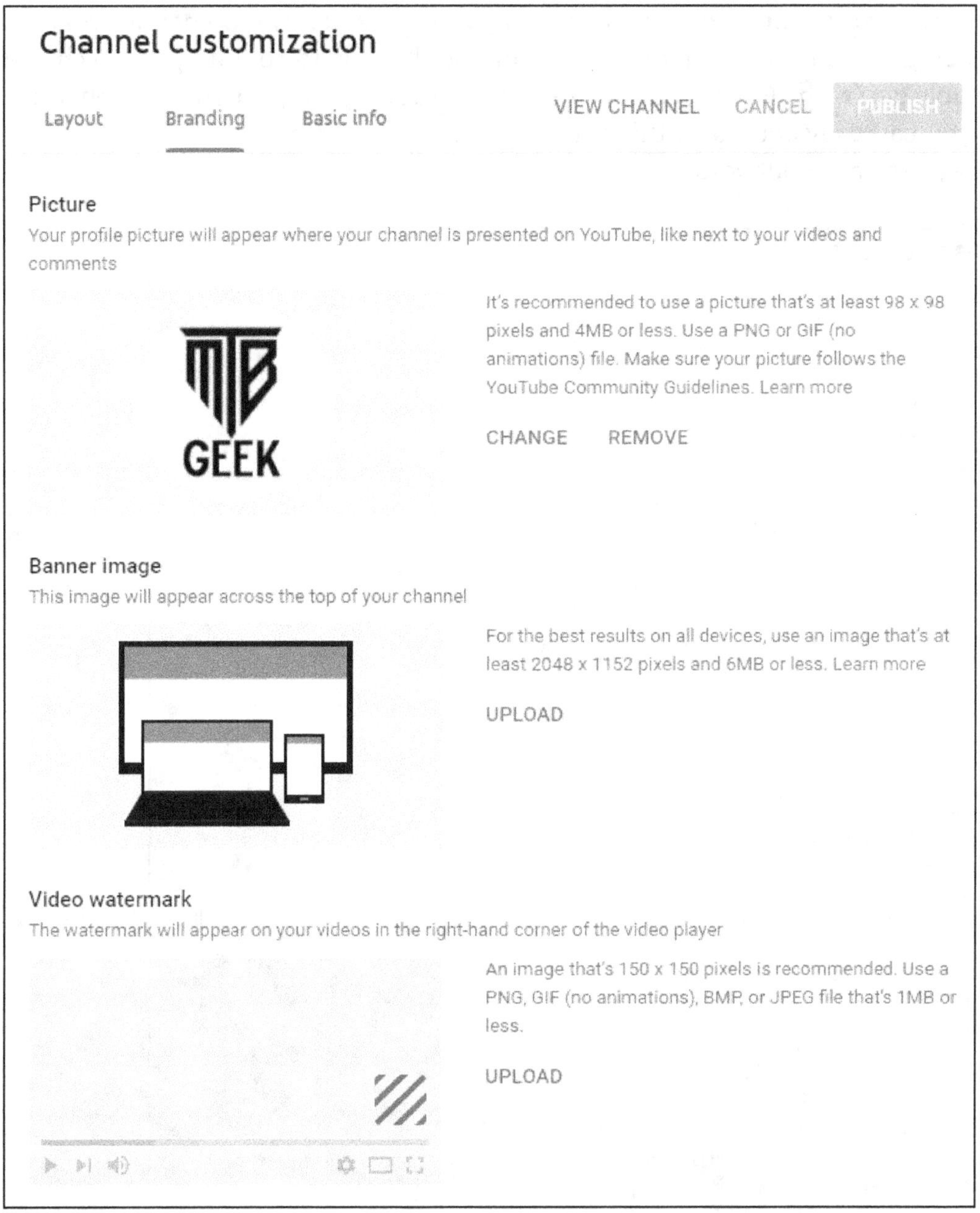

Chapter 6 – YouTube

Figure 6.25

 If you plan on changing your profile picture and especially if you are planning on adding a banner image, it might be a good idea to get some help from someone who knows how to edit photos to be able to make them the correct size otherwise they probably won't look right on your channel.

Chapter 6 – YouTube

The *Basic info* section is where you would go to add a description of your channel and add an email address if you want people to be able to contact you which you probably don't. The Channel URL box shows the address to your YouTube channel, and you can copy and paste this address in an email etc. to send to other people so they can check out your videos.

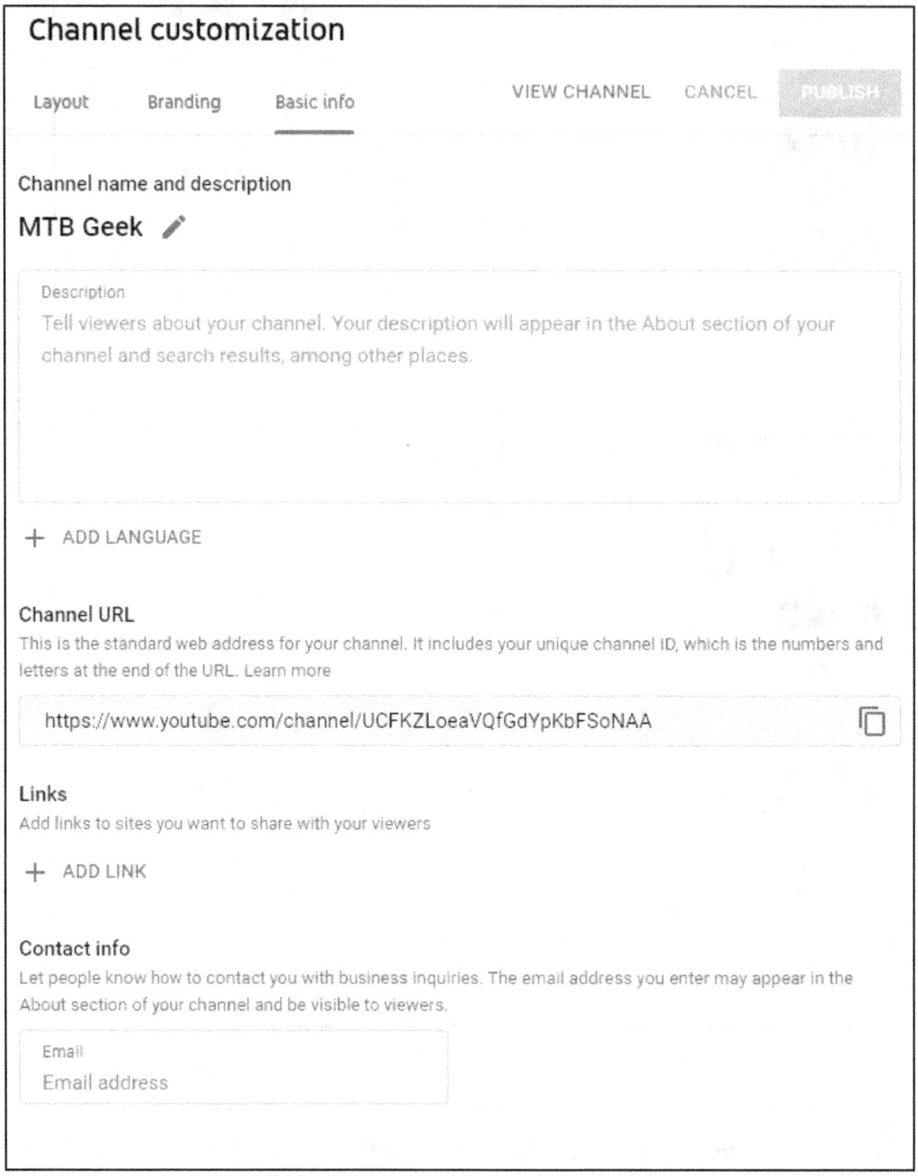

Figure 6.26

After you make any changes, you will need to click on the *Publish* button at the top right of the screen and then you can go to your channel to see how it will look.

Chapter 6 – YouTube

Figure 6.27

Uploading Videos
Now that you have your channel looking professional (hopefully), it's time to start adding some videos so other people on YouTube can see how exciting your life really is.

To upload a video, you will need to click on the video camera icon and then choose *Upload video*.

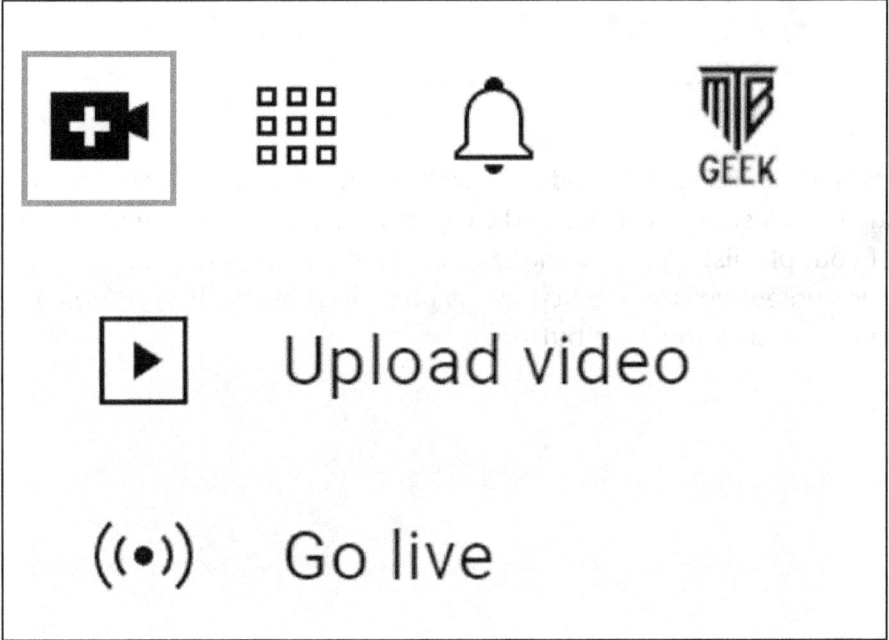

Figure 6.28

Chapter 6 – YouTube

Then you can either drag the video file into your web browser or click on the *Select Files* button to browse your computer to find your video.

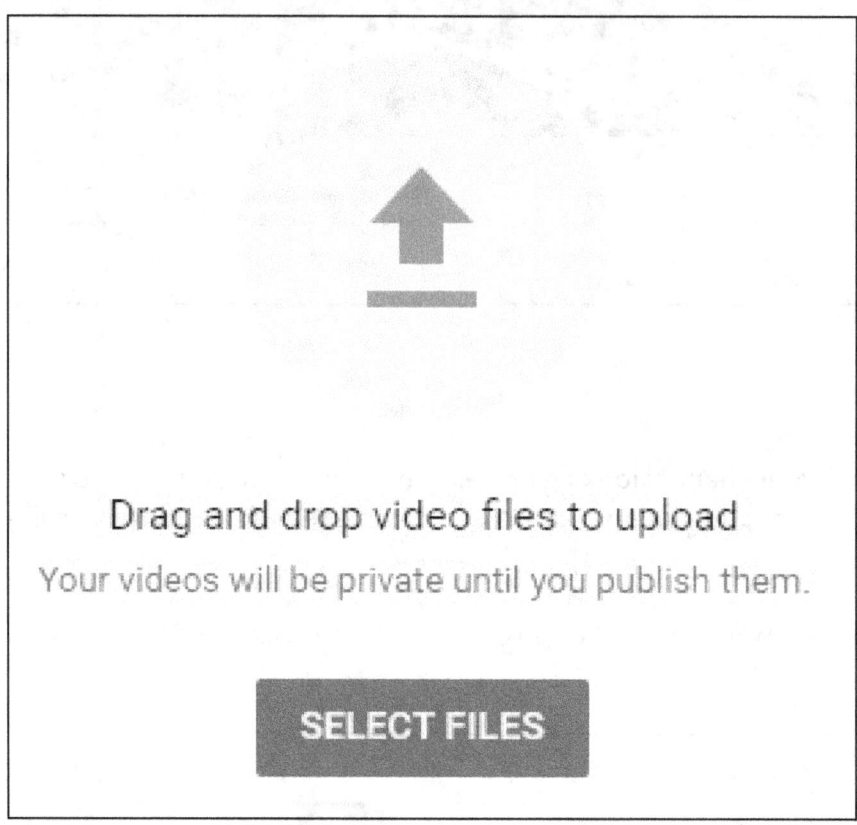

Figure 6.29

Next, you will type in a name for the video as well as a description. If your channel had playlists such as Washington Trails and Oregon Trails, you could then add this video to one of your playlists. You also need to check the button that says *No, it's not made for kids* unless your video actually is intended for children. When you are ready to continue, click the *Next* button.

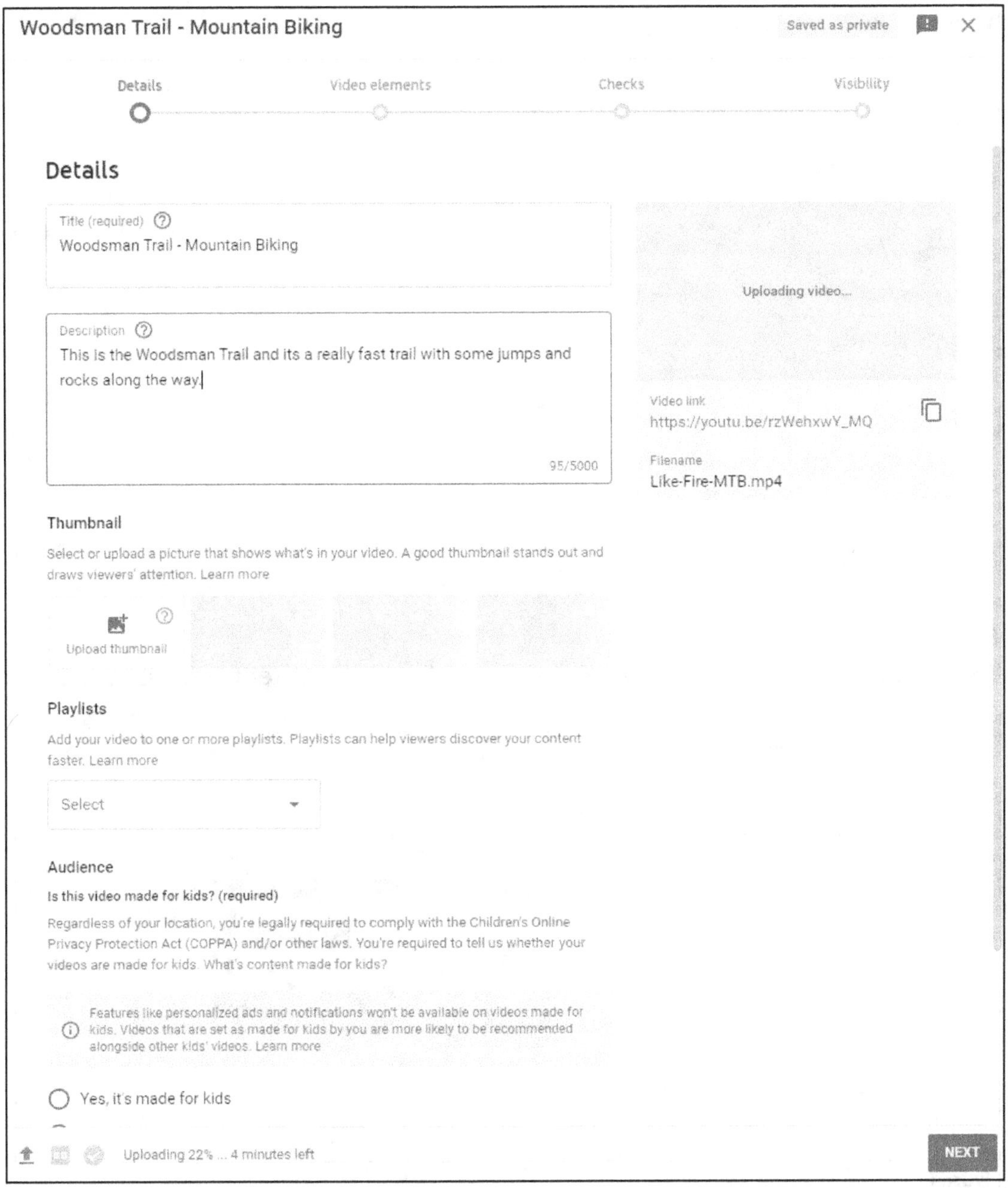

Chapter 6 – YouTube

Figure 6.30

The *Video elements* section is optional and is used to promote some of your other videos by adding suggested videos at the end of your video from the *Add an end screen* section. The *Add cards* features is also used to add a small popup on your video that viewers can click on to be taken to another one of your videos or one of your playlists. You might want to bypass this section for now and come back to it later once you get used to posting videos.

Chapter 6 – YouTube

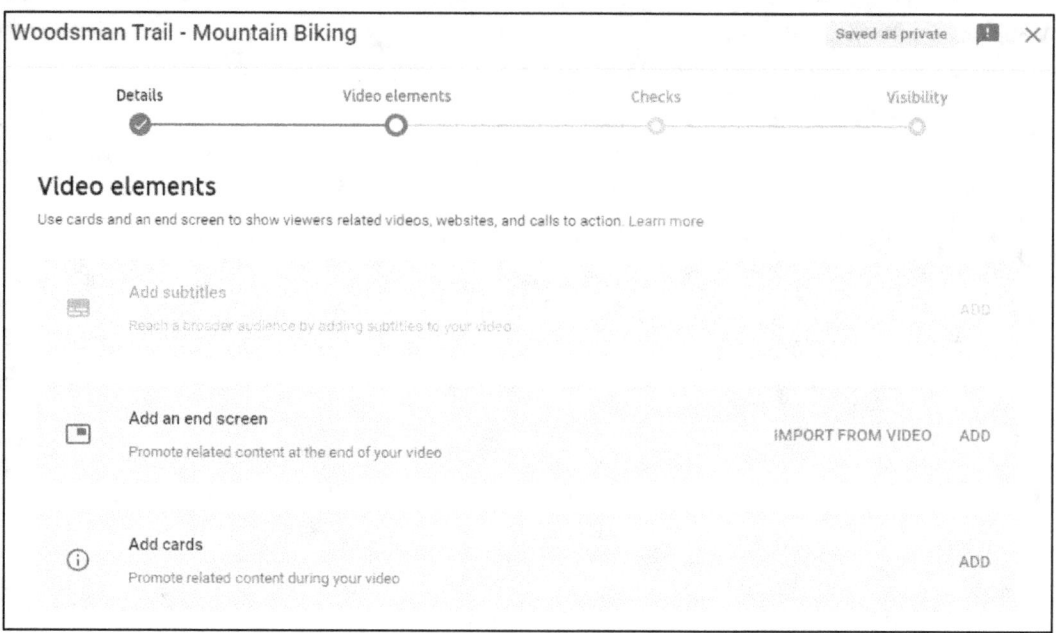

Figure 6.31

YouTube will then check your video for any unlicensed content such as music.

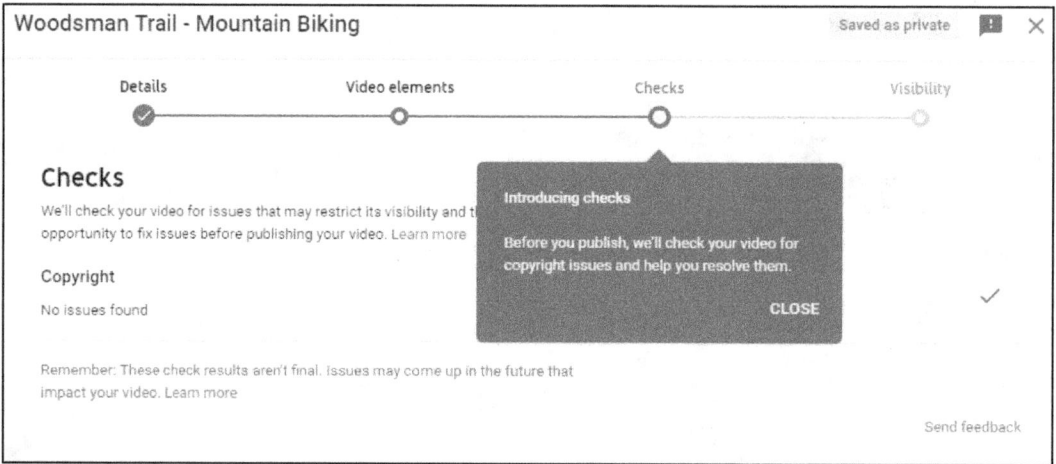

Figure 6.32

Finally, you can decide if you want your video to be private, unlisted or public. You can also schedule when your video will go live. Once everything looks good, click on the *Publish* button to have your video go live, unless you scheduled it of course. If you made it private, then you will need to email the video link to people to allow them to watch it.

Chapter 6 – YouTube

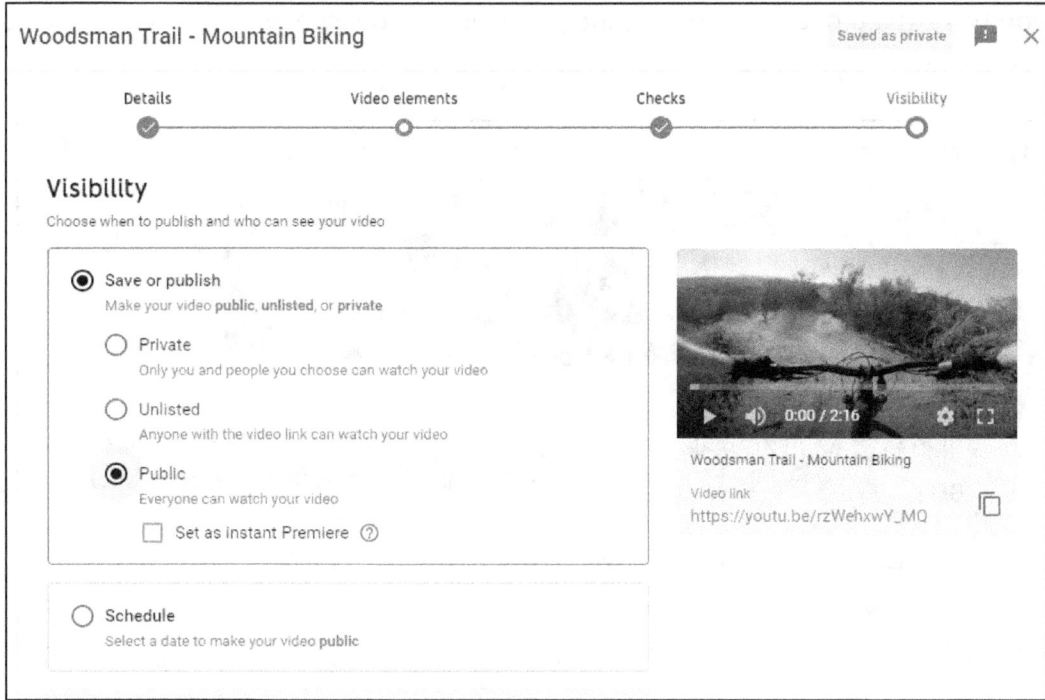

Figure 6.33

You will then be asked if you want to share your video now that it is live on YouTube. If not, then you can click on *close* and can always share it later.

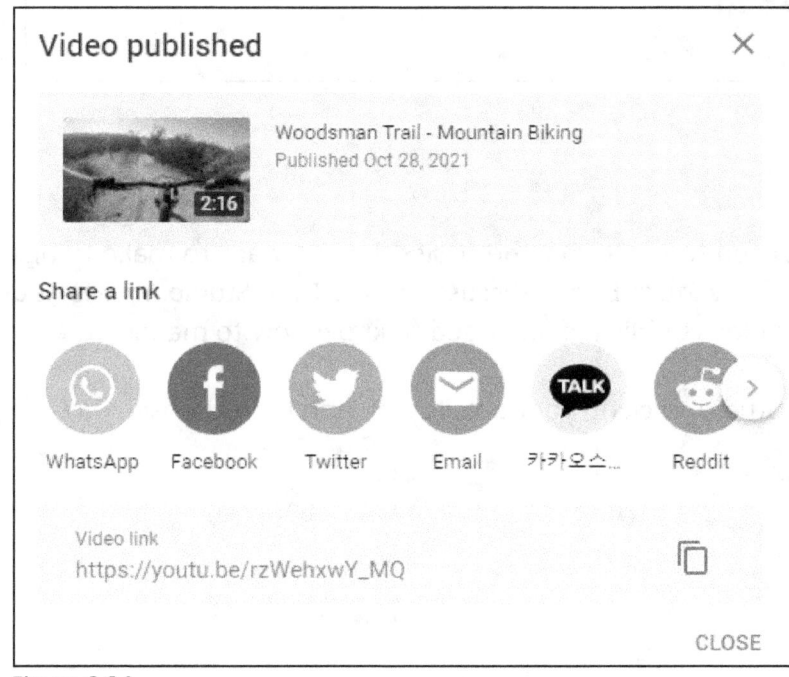

Figure 6.34

Chapter 6 – YouTube

If you were to go back to your channel, you would now see your new video listed there.

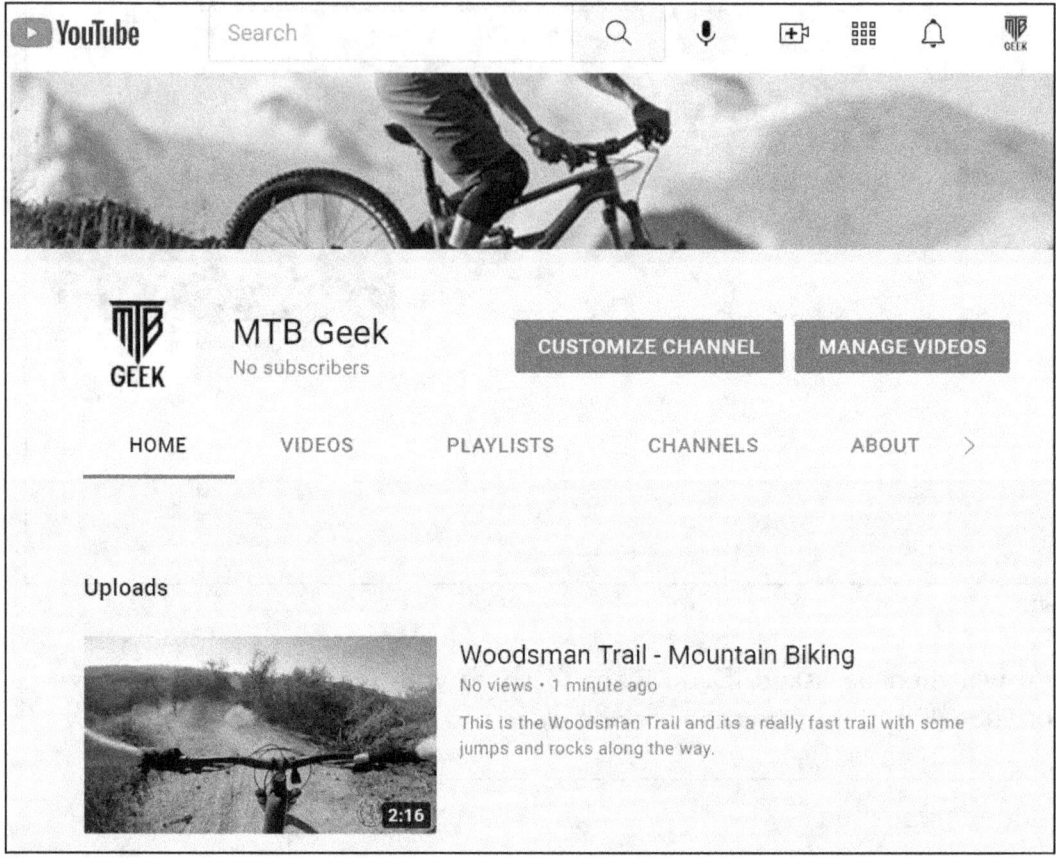

Figure 6.35

YouTube Studio
Since this book is supposed to just cover the basics, I don't want to make things too complicated, but I did want to briefly discuss the YouTube Studio in case you plan on having a lot of videos published and need to know how to manage them.

To get to the YouTube Studio, click on your profile icon and then choose *YouTube Studio*.

Chapter 6 – YouTube

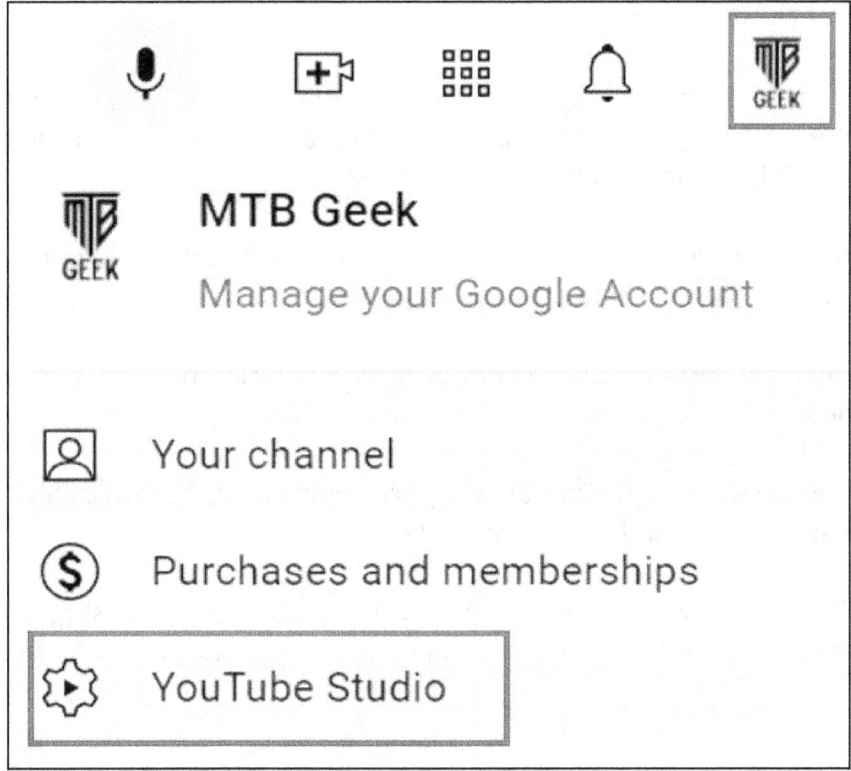

Figure 6.36

As you can see from figure 6.37, YouTube Studio has a variety of sections that you can use to configure and analyze your video's performance.

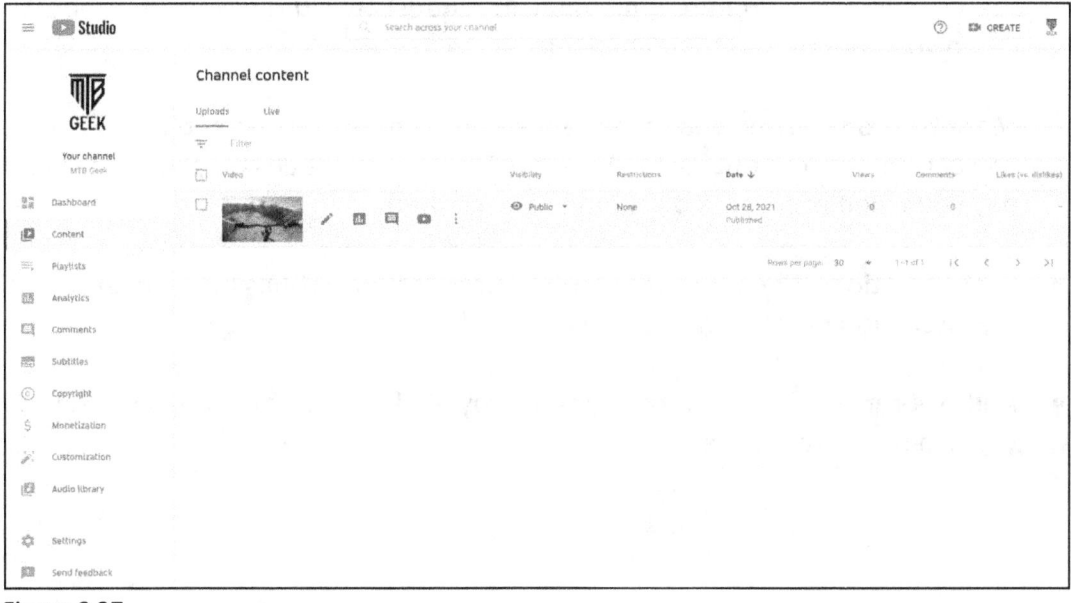

Figure 6.37

Chapter 6 – YouTube

Here is what each of these sections will allow you to do.

- **Dashboard** – This is the main area of the YouTube Studio which will give you an overview of what's on your channel and what kind of views you are getting on your videos and how many subscribers you have.

- **Content** – Here you will find a listing of your uploaded videos and can do things such as edit, play and delete them etc.

- **Playlists** – If you have created any playlists, you can find them here as well as create new ones.

- **Analytics** – Here you will find performance reports on your videos such as how many views they have had and where those views came from.

- **Comments** – When people comment on your videos, you can see a listing of those comments here and also manage any comments that are held for review.

- **Subtitles** – If your videos contain dialog and you would like to enable them to show subtitles, then you can configure this here.

- **Copyright** – Many YouTubers have a problem where other users post their videos on their channel as their own. If YouTube finds any duplicate content, then it will be shown here, and you can request that the offending user take down your video from their channel.

- **Monetization** – When your channel gets enough subscribers and watch hours, you can enable monetization where YouTube will place ads on your videos and pay you when users click on them or watch them.

- **Customization** – These are the same customization settings I went over during my discussion on creating a channel.

- **Audio library** – If you want to add some royalty free music to your videos, then you can do so from here.

Chapter 6 – YouTube

 Try not to use other peoples copyrighted music in your videos because YouTube will most likely remove all the audio from your video or remove the video itself. And if you get too many "strikes', they might also remove your account.

Chapter 7 - WhatsApp

Ever since the internet took over our lives, the world is more connected than it has ever been. Back in the old days, if you wanted to call someone in a different state, you dreaded receiving the phone bill because you knew it was going to be more than you wanted to pay.

Now that everyone has either a computer, tablet, smartphone, or all of the above, it's easy to reach anyone in the world without much effort. But of course, talking with friends and family in your own country is usually a bit easier than chatting with those in different countries. This is where apps such as WhatsApp come into play.

WhatsApp Overview
WhatsApp is a free app that you can use on your smartphone or tablet that allows you to communicate with other WhatsApp users via the internet connection on your device. Therefore, you are not using your cellular service for calls and text messages which can save you money if you do not have unlimited calling and texting on your phone. But if you are using the app on the road with now Wi-Fi connection, you will be using some of your data plan allocation.

The app allows you to text other WhatsApp users and attach items such as photos, videos and documents. You can also make voice calls using your internet connection and not use the minutes from your calling plan. Plus, if you like to see the person you are talking to, you have the option to make video calls.

If you are the type of person who prefers to use their desktop computer or laptop for things rather than having to look at the smaller screen on your mobile device, then WhatsApp also has a desktop app that you can use with your computer.

Installing and Configuring the Mobile App
Once again, when downloading and installing the mobile app on your tablet or smartphone, make sure it's from the right developer and not a third party app that is trying to make you think you are actually downloading WhatsApp. And once again you can find the app in the Play Store (Android devices) and App Store (iPhones and iPads).

Chapter 7 - WhatsApp

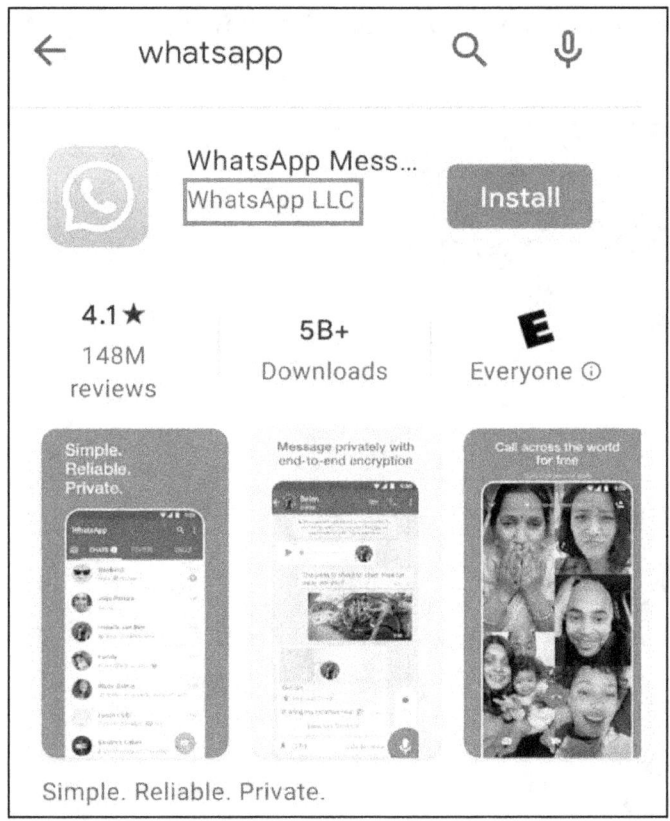

Figure 7.1

After you install the app and open it, you will most likely need to agree to the terms of service by tapping on the agree button.

Next, you will be asked to enter your phone number with the area code so it can be used with the app. You will then receive a text message with a verification code to make sure you added the right number.

If you are using an Android device, you may be prompted to restore a WhatsApp backup from Google Drive and you would most likely tap on *Not Now* unless for some reason you have an old WhatsApp backup.

Then you will enter your name and add a picture for your profile if you have one on your device that you wish to use. You also have the option to use your camera to take a picture on the spot that you can then use for your profile picture.

Next, you will be asked if you want WhatsApp to access your contacts to see who else you know is using the app. This is usually a good idea if you plan on using the

Chapter 7 - WhatsApp

app with people that you have as contacts on your phone. To configure the app to use your contacts tap on the *Settings* button.

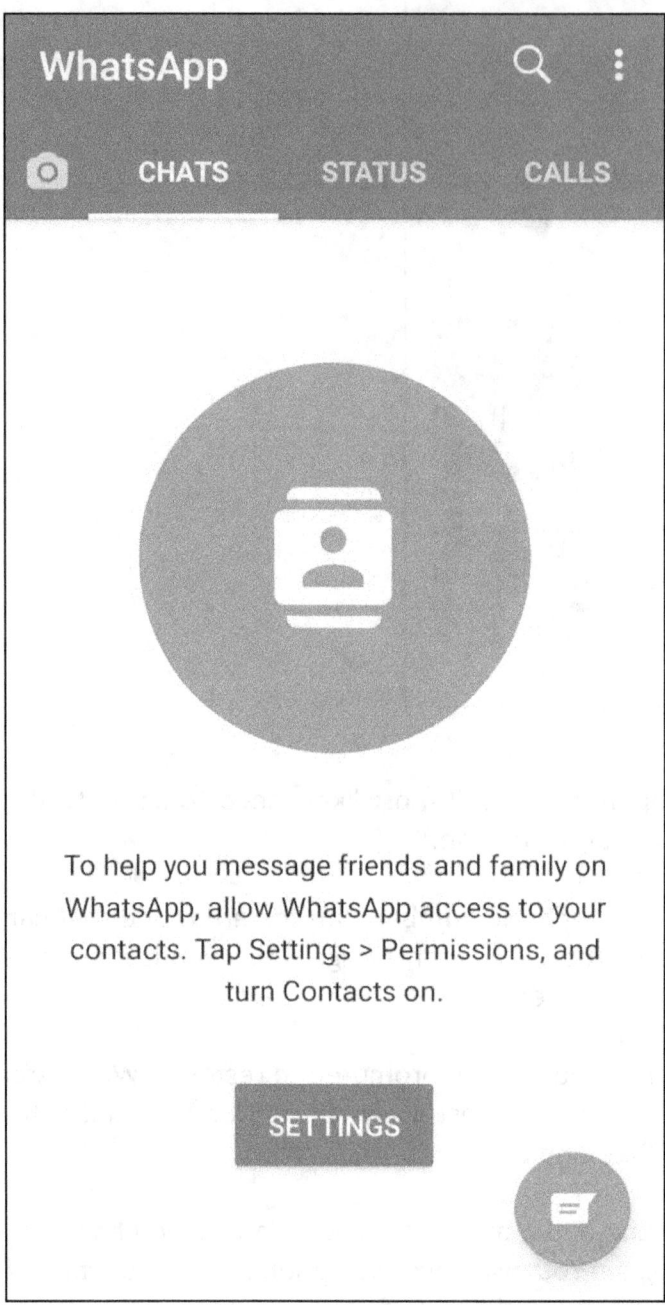

Figure 7.2

The steps to allow WhatsApp to access your contacts will vary from device to device but this is how you do it on a current model Android smartphone.

Chapter 7 - WhatsApp

After you tap on the Settings button you will then look for the apps permissions setting.

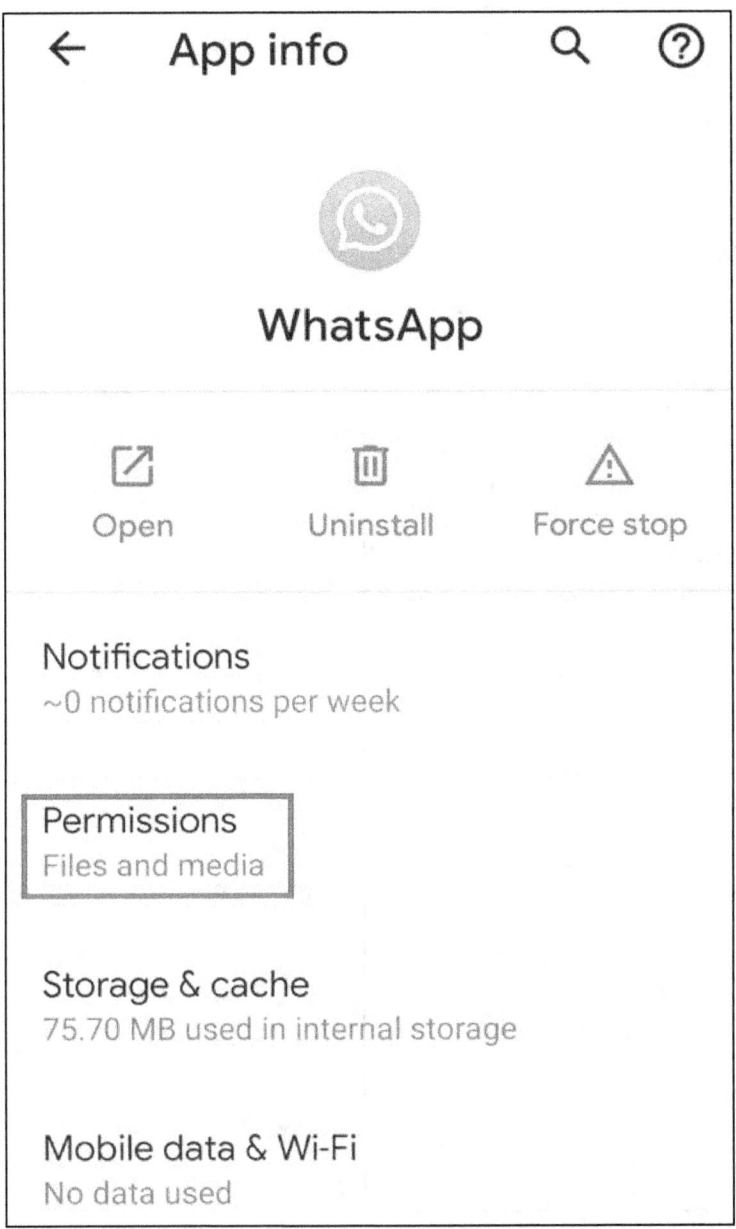

Figure 7.3

Chapter 7 - WhatsApp

Then you will look for something that says contacts.

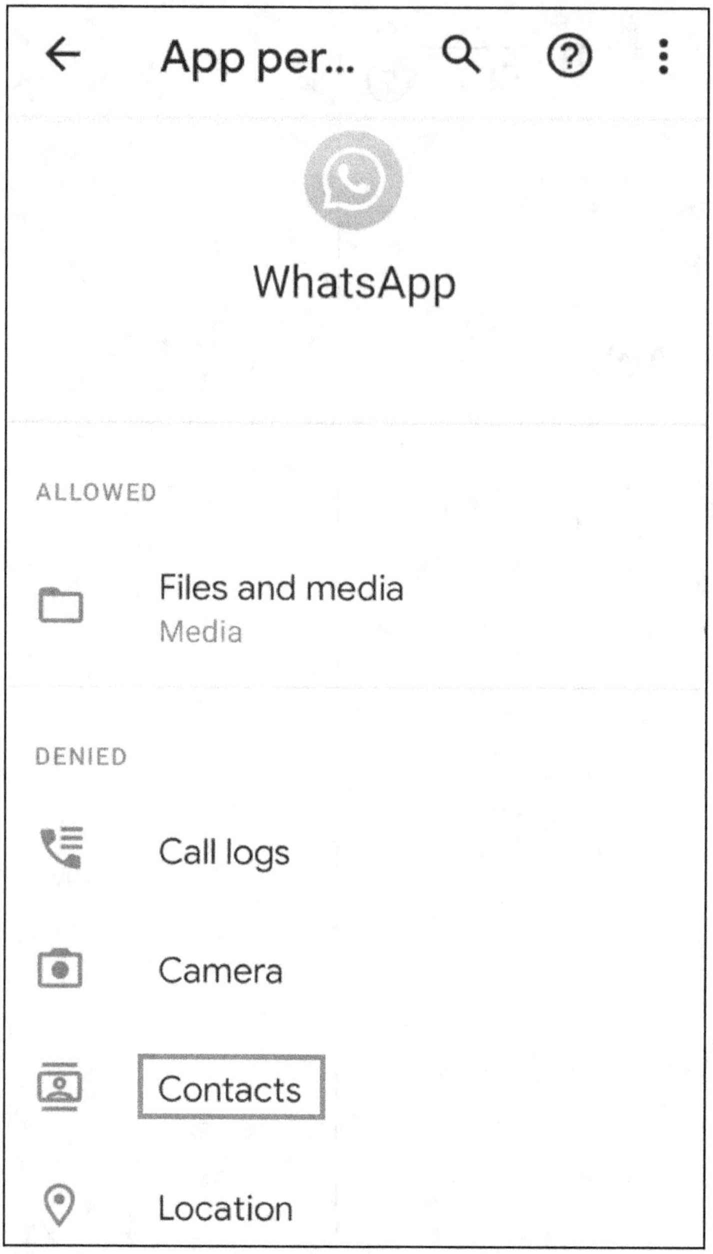

Figure 7.4

Chapter 7 - WhatsApp

Finally, you will change the setting from deny to allow and you should be all set.

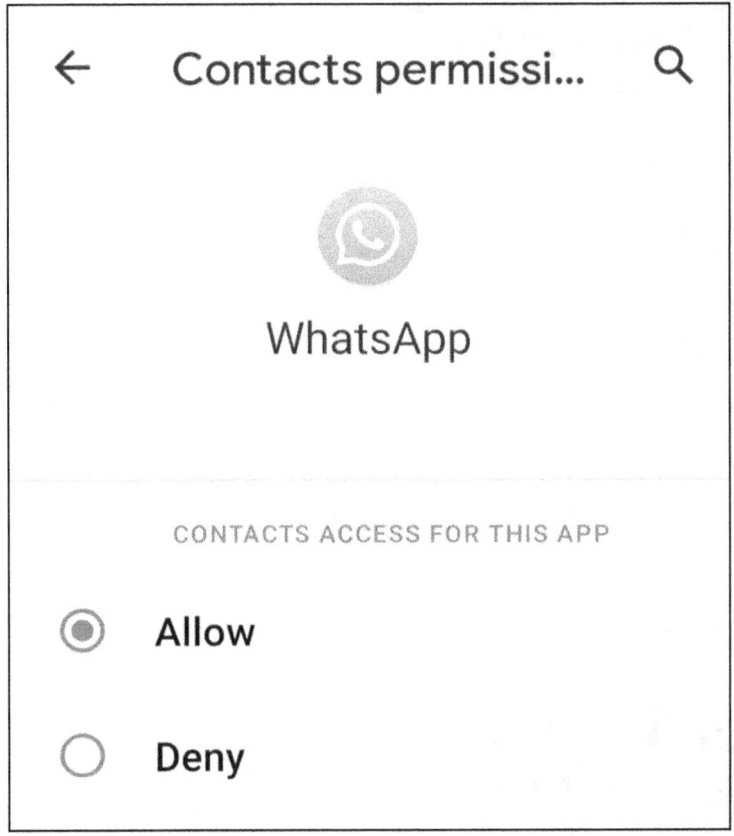

Figure 7.5

If your phone contacts contain people that are using WhatsApp, you will be shown these people. If not, then you will see an option to invite a friend to use WhatsApp.

To find contacts that are also using WhatsApp, simply tap on the message icon as seen in the lower right hand corner of figure 7.6 or the call icon as seen in figure 7.7. As you can see in figure 7.6, WhatsApp found contacts on my phone who have a WhatsApp account and will actually show me which ones I can communicate with via the app. If you want to use WhatsApp with someone who is in your contacts but not using the app, they will need to install it on their device first.

Chapter 7 - WhatsApp

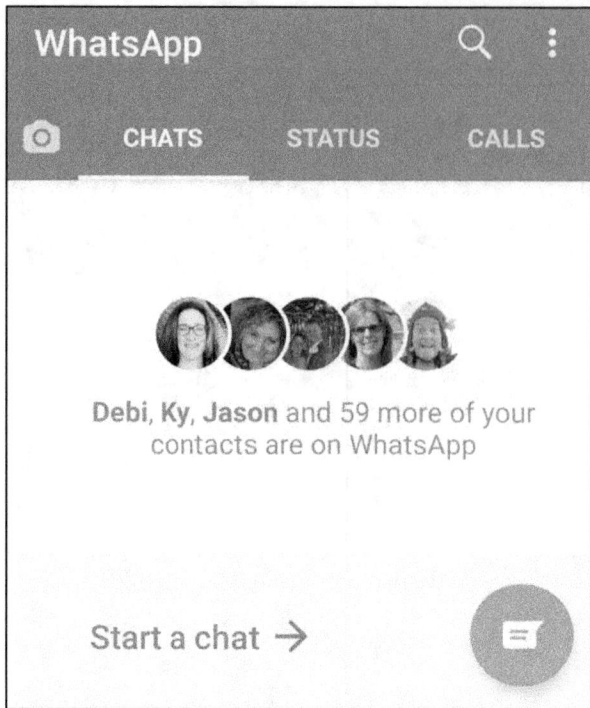

Figure 7.6

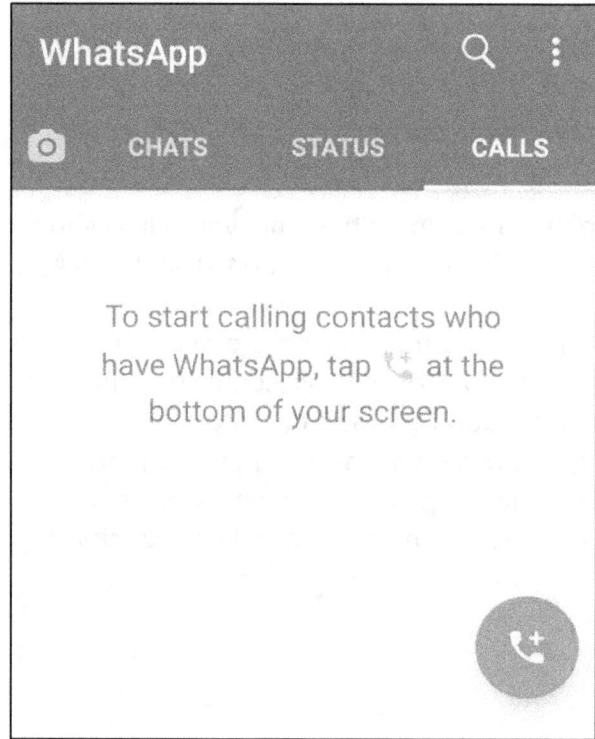

Figure 7.7

Chapter 7 - WhatsApp

Sending Text and Voice Messages
One of the main reasons for using WhatsApp is the ability to send messages to your friend and family anywhere in the world who are also using the app. As long as both of you have an internet connection, you should be able to send messages back and forth without any problems.

WhatsApp has the ability to send standard text messages that you are most likely used to doing on your smartphone. Once you go to the *Chats* section in the app and tap *Start a chat*, you will see all of your contacts that also have WhatsApp installed on their smartphone or tablet. You will also see their status which might say *Available*, meaning they are online or *Hey there! I am using WhatsApp* meaning they have it installed on their phone but are not currently online.

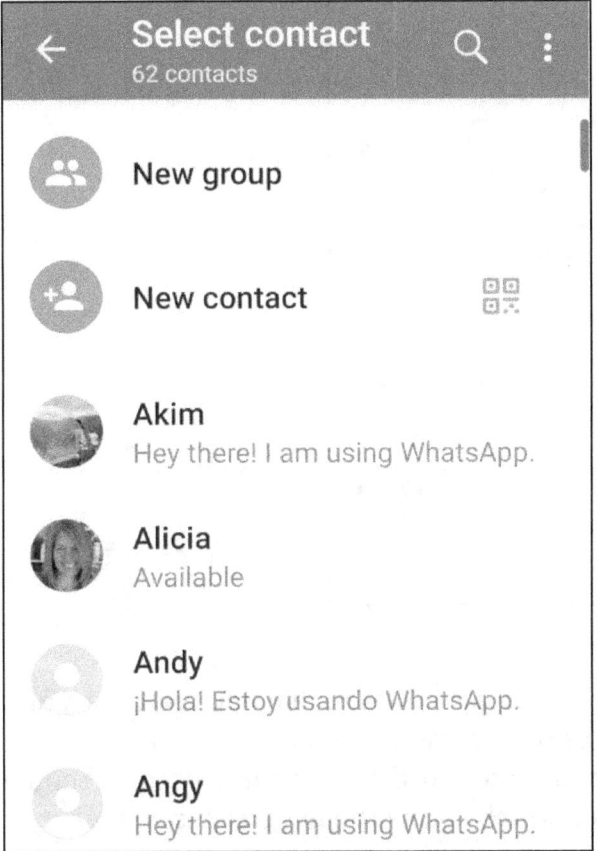

Figure 7.8

Then all you need to do is tap on a name to bring up a new screen with a *Message* box where you can start typing what you want to say just like you would when texting on your smartphone using your text messaging app.

Chapter 7 - WhatsApp

Figure 7.9

If you look at the Message box in figure 7.9, you will see that you can attach files using the paperclip icon or photos using the camera icon. If you start typing a message, the photo icon will disappear and that is because it is used to send a photo by itself. You can still attach a photo by using the paperclip icon as seen in figure 7.10.

Chapter 7 - WhatsApp

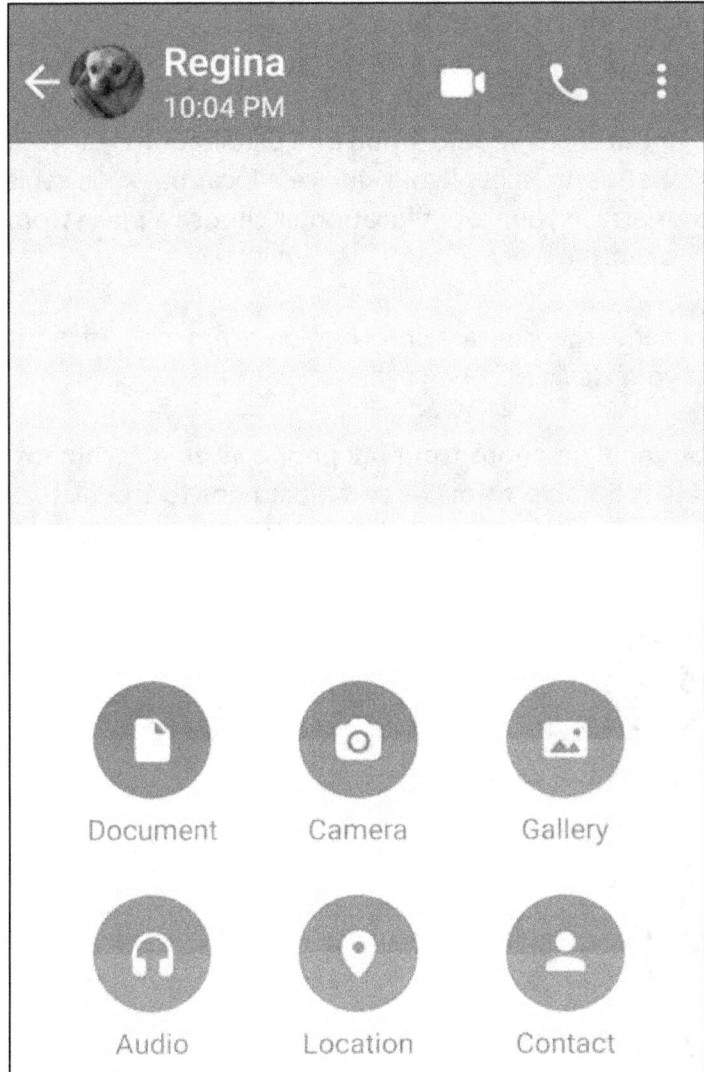

Figure 7.10

Here is what each of these choices will do.

- **Document** – Lets you attach a document such as a PDF or Word document that you have stored on your device.

- **Camera** – This will open your camera allowing you to take a picture on the spot and then attach it.

- **Gallery** – Use this option to attach a photo you already have on your device.

Chapter 7 - WhatsApp

- **Audio** – If you have any audio files such as MP3 music files, you can attach them with this choice.

- **Location** – This will allow you to share your location or a destination near you. You will need to allow WhatsApp to access your device's location to use this feature. Then you can either attach your exact location or choose a place from the map that you will be shown.

- **Contact** – Here you can send the contact information from one of your contacts that you have on your device.

I will now send a message containing a photo from my phone as an attachment. When I add the photo, I will first be able to make an adjustment to the picture such as cropping or rotating it, adjusting the color, and adding fun shapes like thought bubbles etc.

Figure 7.11

Chapter 7 - WhatsApp

Figure 7.12 shows how my photo looks after it has been sent as a message. If you take a look at the bottom right corner of the photo, you will see a time of 2:57 PM and a single checkmark. That is the time that I sent the photo to Regina.

Figure 7.12

When the single checkmark turns into a double checkmark (figure 7.13), that tells you that the other person read your message.

Chapter 7 - WhatsApp

Figure 7.13

When I get a reply to my message it will look like figure 7.14. It will also have the time that the message was received.

Chapter 7 - WhatsApp

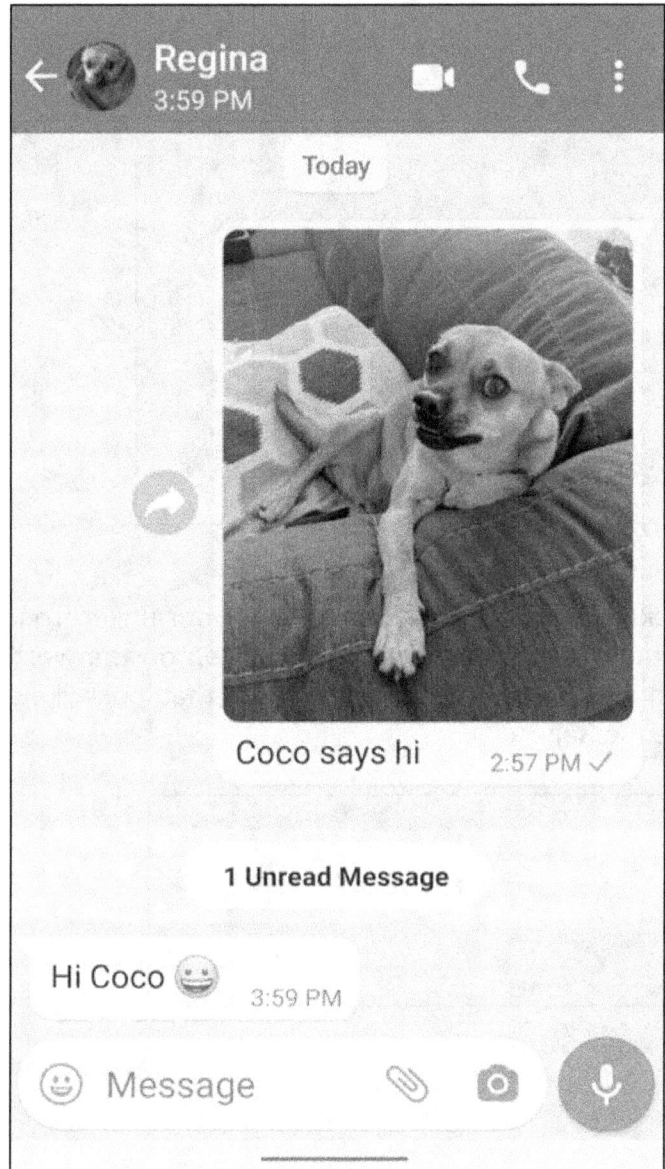

Figure 7.14

Now if typing isn't your thing, you might want to try and send a voice message instead. If you look at the lower right corner of figure 7.14, you will see a microphone icon. To send a voice message simply press the icon and hold down and speak into your phone or tablet and when you are done with your message, release the "button".

If you change your mind while recording, you can slide your finger to the left to cancel the recording, and then you can start over if needed.

Figure 7.15

Sliding your finger up to the lock icon will allow you to remove your finger from the screen while your device still records your voice. You can tap on the word *cancel* to stop the recording and delete it or tap the send button that looks like a paper airplane to send the voice message.

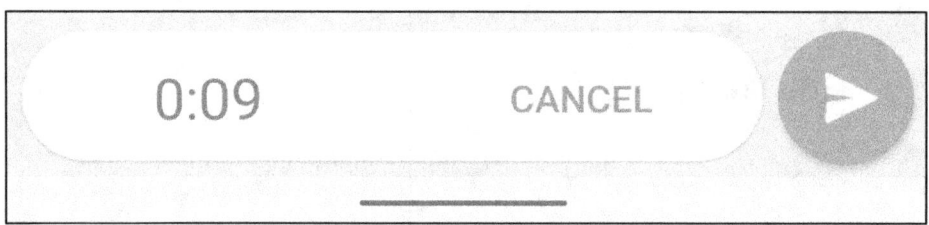
Figure 7.16

Making Voice and Video Calls
WhatsApp is not just a messaging app but can also be used as a method to make voice and video calls as well. Many times, if you want to talk to someone in a different country, you will need to change your phone plan to allow international access for an additional monthly fee or you might even be charged by the minute!

With WhatsApp, you can make phone calls to your friends and family overseas for free assuming they have the app installed and a decent internet connection. To make these calls you will need to go to the *Calls* tab in the app and select the contact you wish to call. As you can see in figure 7.17, you have the option to make a phone call or video call depending on which icon you tap next to the contact you plan to call.

Chapter 7 - WhatsApp

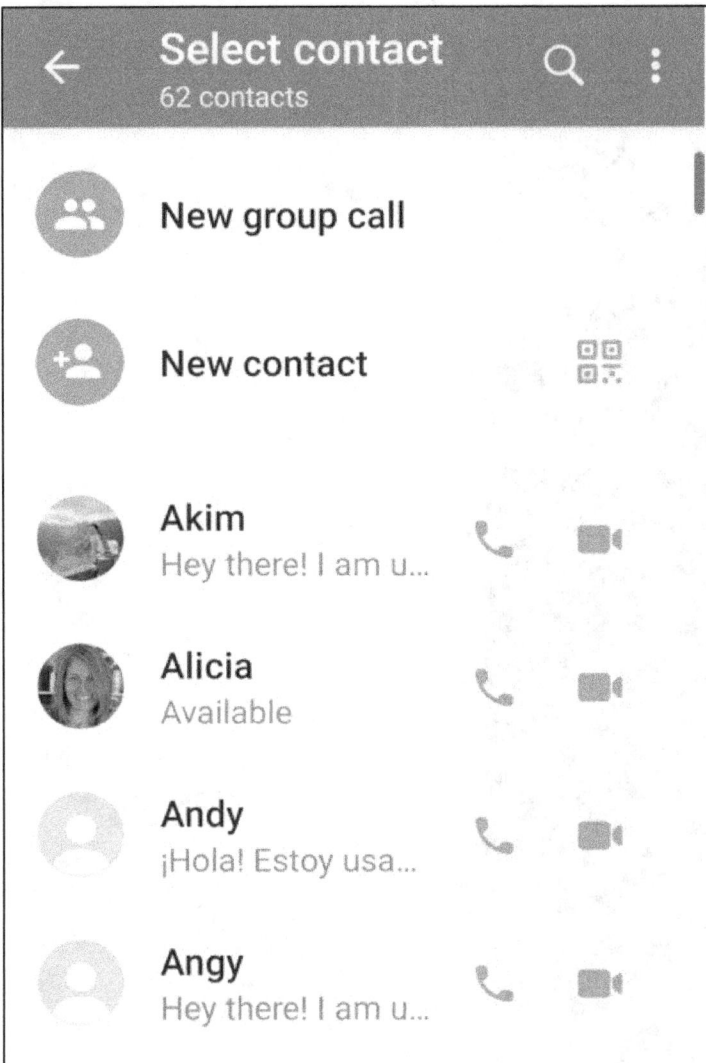

Figure 7.17

 You don't always have to go to the call tab to make voice or video calls. While you are in the Chats tab having a text message conversation with someone, you will see that you have the option to start a voice or video call right from the chat itself.

When you make a voice call, you will see the other user's profile picture on your screen and have some buttons on the bottom that you can use to do things such as adjust the volume, start a video call, mute your microphone or hang up (figure 7.18).

Chapter 7 - WhatsApp

Figure 7.18

Using WhatsApp on Your Computer
If you are the type that prefers to use your computer for most tasks rather than your smartphone, you can install the WhatsApp desktop software on your computer. They have software that will work for both Windows PCs and Apple computers (Macs). To download and install the free software you can go to the WhatsApp website at:
https://www.whatsapp.com/download

Chapter 7 - WhatsApp

Since I am using a Windows PC, I only get the option to download the Windows software and I have two options. I can download the program installation file and install it (download for Windows button), or I can go to the Microsoft Store and install it (Get it from Microsoft button).

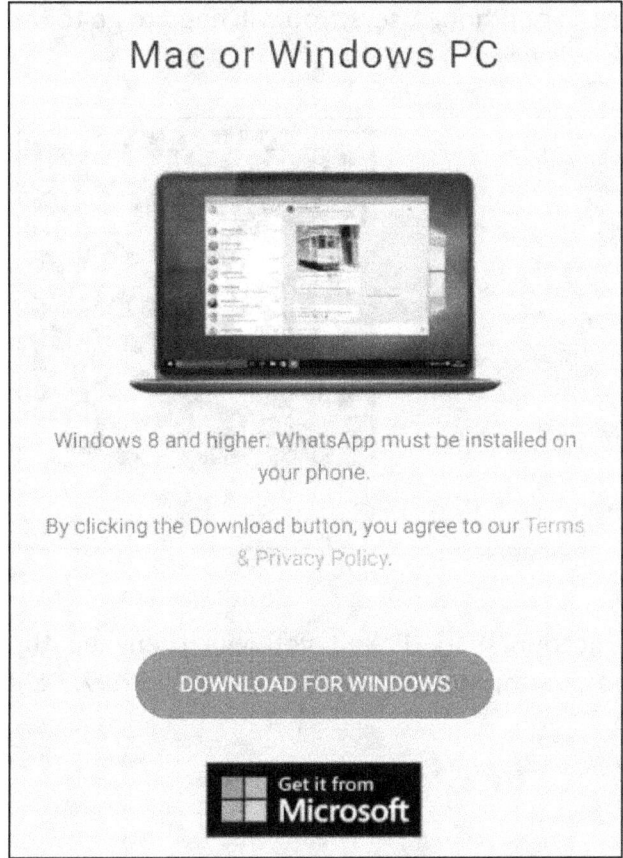

Figure 7.19

If I download the installation file, I will have to find the file on my computer and then run the installer. If I choose the Microsoft Store option, then I can just click the Get button to have it installed for me (figure 7.20).

Figure 7.20

Chapter 7 - WhatsApp

Either method will install the same software\app on your computer, and you need to then scan a QR code with your phone in the WhatsApp app to link your account to the software on your computer (figure 7.21.). Getting your phone to read this code can be a little cumbersome so be patient when trying to get this to work. For Android users, you will need to go to the Chats tab, then tap on the ellipsis at the upper right and choose *Linked devices*. For iPhone users, you will need to go to the WhatsApp settings and choose *Link a device*.

Figure 7.21

Once your phone and computer accounts are linked you will then see the WhatsApp computer interface on your computer. As you can see in figure 7.22, it looks very similar to the phone app.

Chapter 7 - WhatsApp

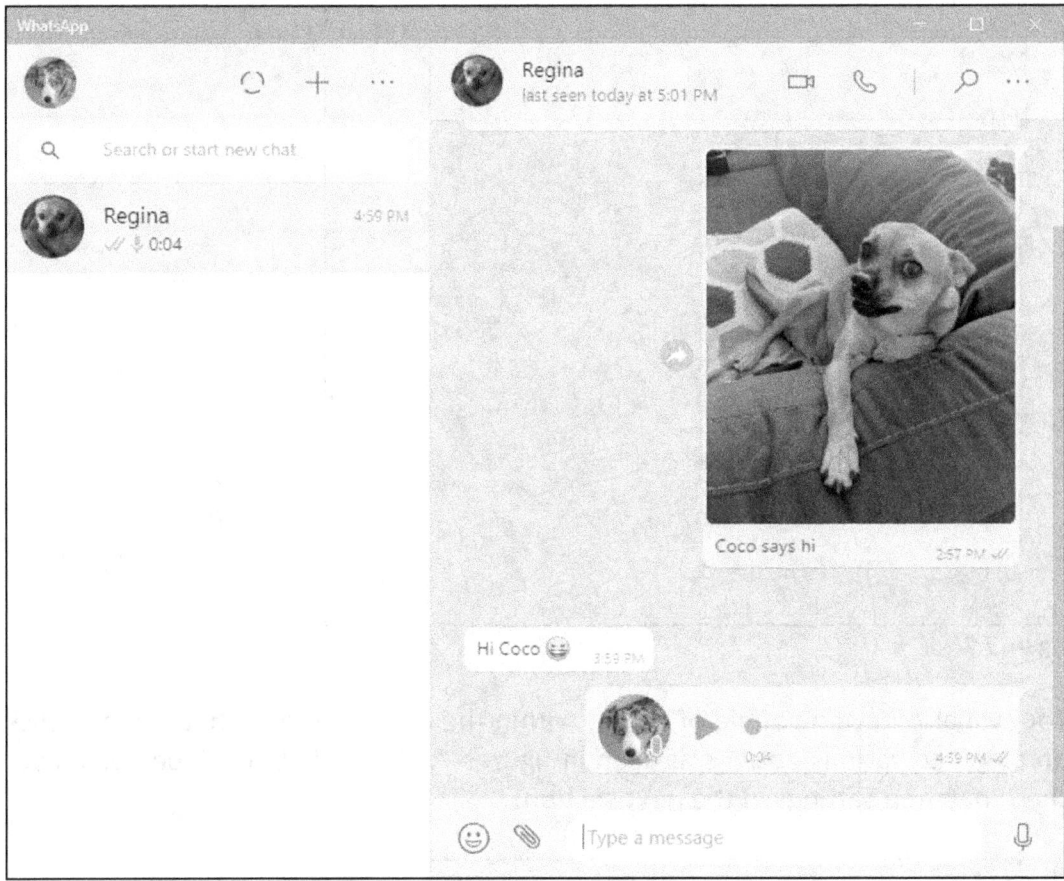

Figure 7.22

You will have some different options when it comes to attachments. Rather than the six options you have from the phone app, you will only have four which include contacts, documents, camera and photos & videos. You will still have the same emoji option as you do with the smartphone app.

Chapter 7 - WhatsApp

Figure 7.23

You will also have a couple of places within the computer app that you can click on to get to various options as seen in figures 7.24 and 7.25. I will be going over the WhatsApp settings in the next section.

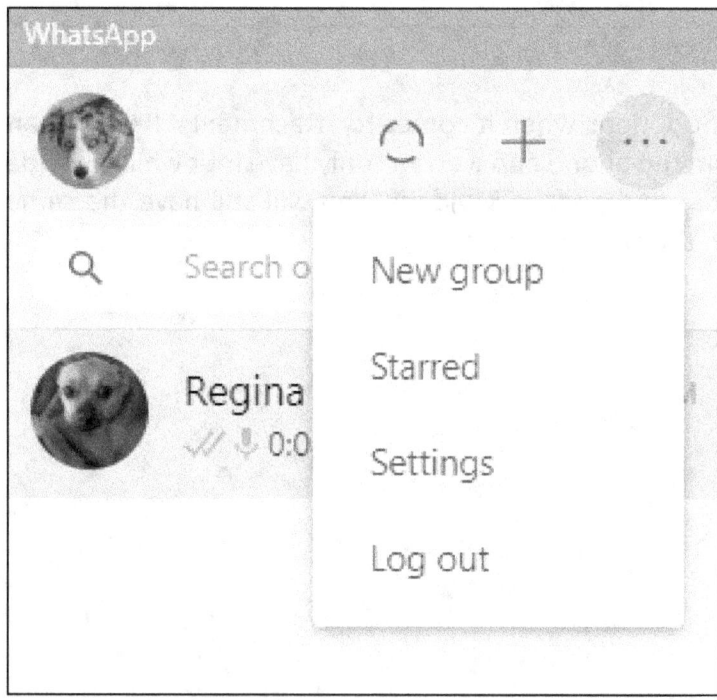

Figure 7.24

Chapter 7 - WhatsApp

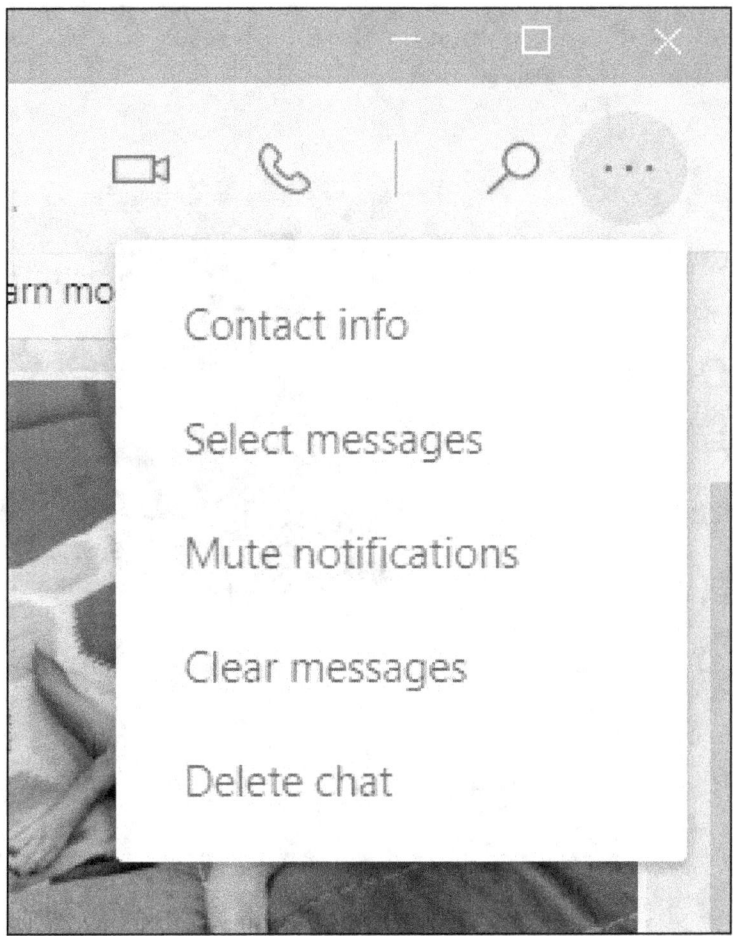

Figure 7.25

In order to make phone calls from the desktop version, you will need a microphone attached to your computer. And if you want to make video calls, you will need a camera\webcam installed on your computer that has a microphone.

Clicking on the + button at the top of the screen will allow you to start a new conversation with other WhatsApp users from your contacts (figure 7.26).

Chapter 7 - WhatsApp

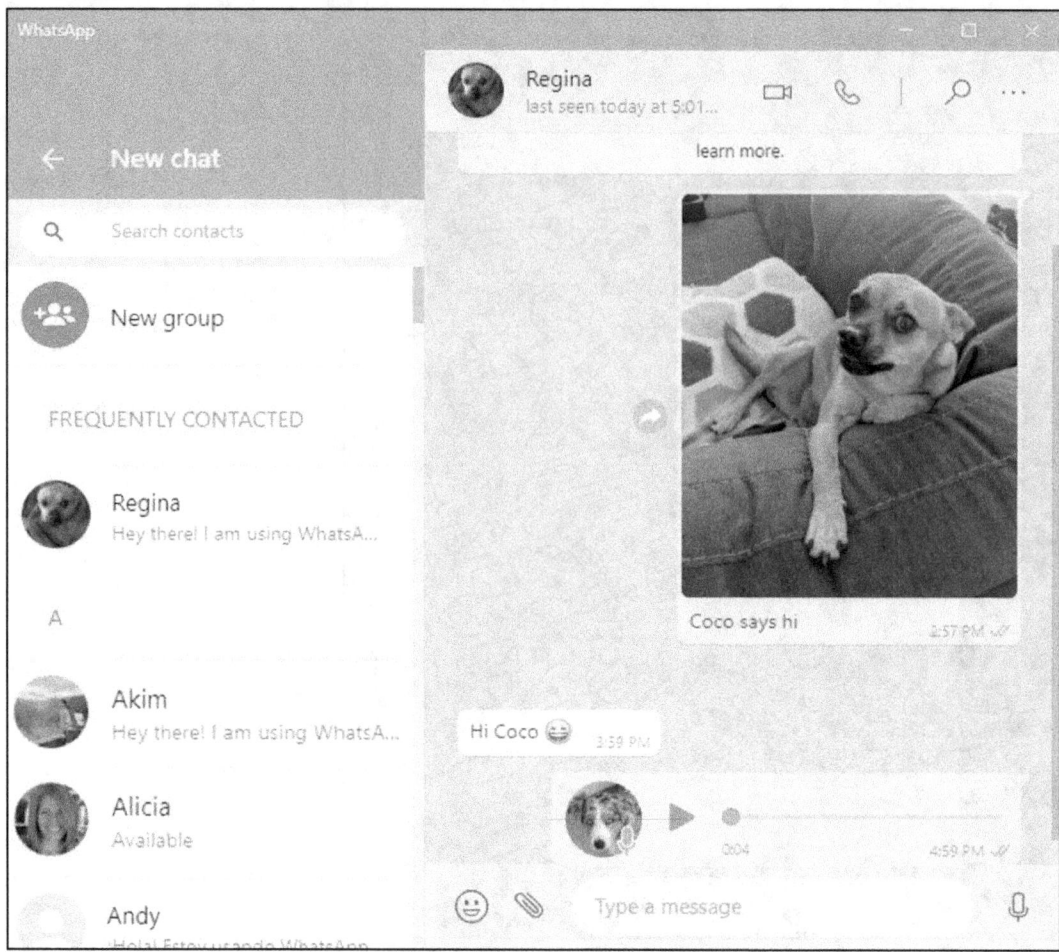

Figure 7.26

Settings
WhatsApp has quite a few settings that you can adjust to change the way the app looks and functions and I would now like to go over some of these settings so you know what they do and where to find them.

To get to the WhatsApp settings, tap on the three vertical dots at the top right of the app and choose *Settings*. You will then see the various settings categories as seen in figure 7.27.

Chapter 7 - WhatsApp

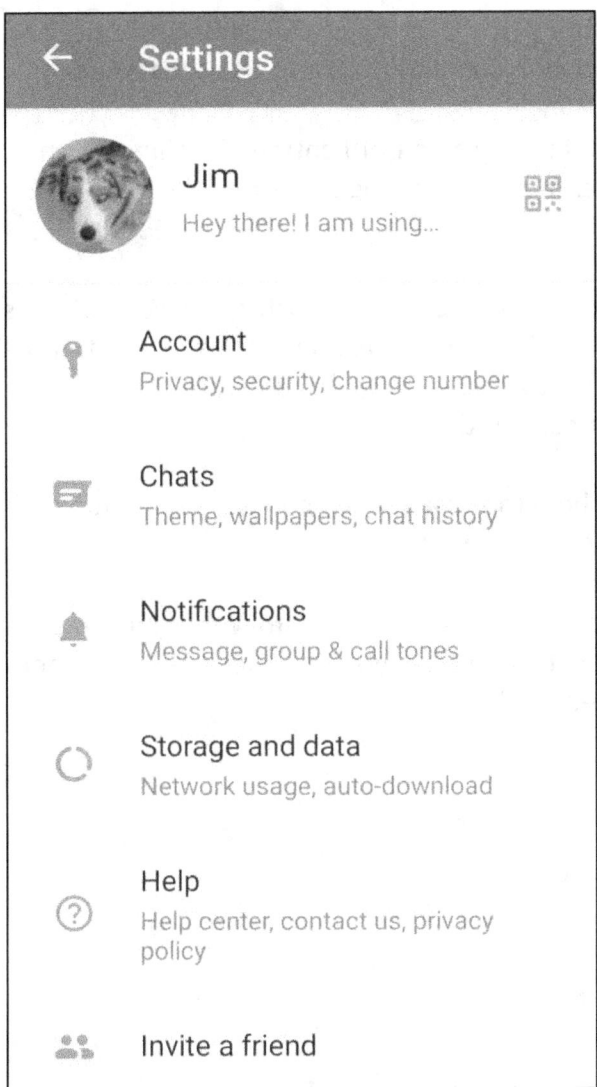

Figure 7.27

I will now go over what each of these settings categories does.

- **Profile** – Here you can do things such as change your name, profile picture and edit your phone number if needed. You can also change the default *Hey there! I am using WhatsApp* status that appears by your name when others view you in their contacts.

- **Account** – This section has options to do things such as change your privacy settings in regard to who can see what about your account. You can also enable additional security measures for protecting your account from getting compromised. It also offers another place to change your phone number and even delete your account if you decide you don't want to use WhatsApp.

- **Notifications** – Here you can enable or disable notifications for things such as incoming and outgoing messages and also change the default notification sound and call ringtone.

- **Storage and data** – If you are concerned about how much space WhatsApp is using on your device, you can check it here. You can also tell the app to only download certain types of files such as videos only when you are connected to your Wi-Fi rather than using your cellular data.

- **Help** – Here you can find various help topics and even contact WhatsApp with a specific question.

- **Invite a friend** – If you would like to invite a friend or family member to start using WhatsApp then you can select them from your contacts and send them a link to download the app on their device.

Chapter 8 - Staying Safe Online

For this final chapter, I will be discussing things you can do to protect yourself and your personal information while online. It will not apply to any one specific social media platform or app but is rather just some useful information I feel you should know about when using your computer on the internet.

There are many ways that hackers and scammers try to steal your information but if you know what to look for, it's not too difficult to avoid their tricks. Just remember, if something looks too good to be true, it probably is!

Email Scams
Let's begin by talking about email scams since they seem to be the most popular type of scam these days and almost everyone uses email at home, at work, or both. One commonly used method by scammers is for them to spoof a name or an email address of someone you know so it looks like the email is coming from them, hoping you won't notice that it's not. Then they will include malicious files or links to sites that will attempt to steal your personal information or install some spyware on your computer.

If you ever get an email from someone you know, and it just has a link with no explanation or says something like "check this out!" then you need to be wary of it and check the email address to make sure it belongs to the person who sent it. Sometimes you can click on the name of the sender in the email to reveal the actual email address that was used to send the message. Another common practice is for cybercriminals to hack the passwords of real email accounts and use them to send out spam emails looking for someone to fall for their trick. Also, be sure to double-check links before clicking on them if you are unsure if they are safe or not. Many times, you can hover the mouse arrow over a link to find its real address in case it's been masked to look like something else.

Another thing they will do is send you emails that look like they are from your banking site and actually use the bank's logo etc. to make it look like the real thing. If you ever get one of these and they say there is a problem with your account or you need to do something like reset your password, call your bank rather than click on any links. And if the email includes any phone numbers for you to call, you can assume that they are not actually the numbers that belong to your bank but rather their own call center.

Figure 8.1 shows what looks like an email from amazon.com but if you look at the sender's email address it says *amazon@**support.com***. If this were real, it would say something like *support@amazon.com* so it's important to look at what comes after the @ symbol to make sure everything matches up.

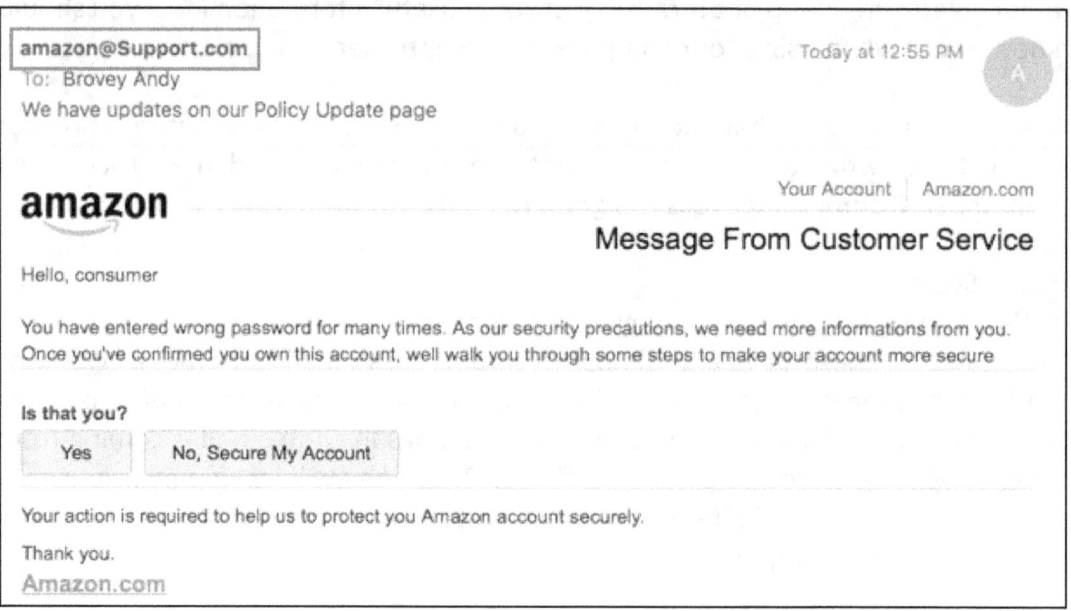

Figure 8.1

Phone Scams

Another tactic that is used to try and trick people into giving up personal information is the use of phone calls. What will happen is that these criminals will make calls and say that things like you owe the IRS or some bill collector money and if you don't pay, they will be sending the authorities after you. Or they will claim to be from Microsoft or another similar company and say that your computer is infected with a virus, or your copy of Windows is illegal and that you need to pay up to get things straightened out.

Sometimes they will try and convince you that they need to get on your computer to fix a problem that doesn't exist and will want to be paid for it. Then they will charge your credit card a couple of hundred dollars or so and have you give them remote access to your computer. Next, they will pretend to be fixing something while at the same time either stealing whatever information they can or planting some malicious software on your computer to do more harm after they are done. The bottom line is that nobody will ever call you to tell you that there is a problem with your computer because they have no way of knowing.

Chapter 8 - Staying Safe Online

You should also look out for phone calls that have the same area code as you do. The scammers do this to trick you into thinking it's a local call or maybe someone you know but it is most likely coming from another part of the country or even a different country.

Website Popups

Popup ads are a way of life when it comes to surfing the Internet, so we either get used to them or employ some sort of popup blocker to keep them in check for us. The problem is that it's possible to get around these popup blockers or overpower them, if you will, with multiple pop-up ads.

Normally these ads are more of a nuisance than anything else, but the craftier ones can freeze up your computer with alarming sounds and scary messages, causing the uninformed to panic. Many times, they will say things like your computer is infected and you need to click here or call this number to get it fixed. You will also see messages saying you are doing something illegal and your files will be deleted unless you call a specific number. If you call that number, you will then have to deal with the same scams I talked about in the last section on phone scams.

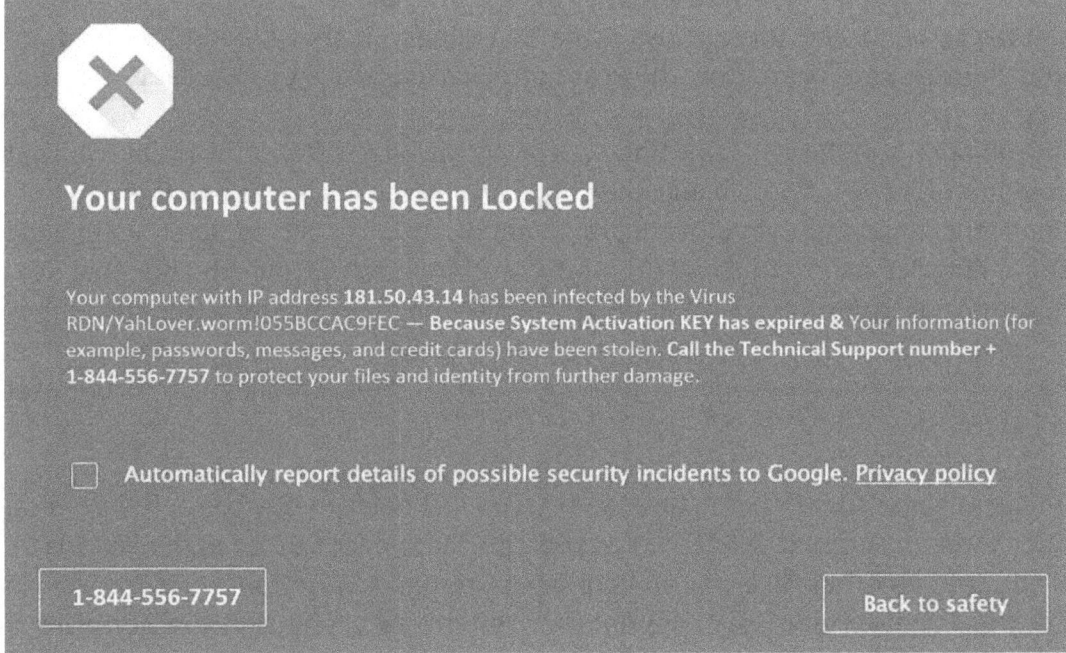

Figure 8.2

If this happens to you and you can't close out the ads, then try pressing *Ctrl-Alt-Delete* to bring up *Task Manager* to see if you can force your web browser closed by right clicking on it in the list and choosing *End Task*. If not, see if the Start button is working and try to shut down your computer, or at least save anything you need to save and close whatever programs you can before manually shutting down the computer by holding down the power button. Then restart your computer, see how things are looking, and run a manual virus and\or spyware scan.

 It's never a good idea to simply turn off your computer without properly shutting it down because you risk file corruption and data loss that may make your computer not want to start back up again. This applies to computers running Windows as well as Macs.

Fake Antivirus Software
We tend to trust our antivirus software and assume that it is looking out for our best interests. With that in mind, another scam is to silently install fake antivirus software on your computer without you knowing it. This can happen when you go to non-trustworthy websites and many times the fake software gets installed in the background and then shows up later telling you that it found all kinds of infections on your computer. These are often called "drive by installations".

If you notice that there is some antivirus or antispyware software installed on your computer that you didn't install, then you can assume it's bogus and there to hurt you rather than help you. There are some exceptions such as when you install something like an Adobe Reader update and forget to uncheck the box that says it will install some free virus scanner along with the update. After this bogus software gets installed, it will pop up notifications saying your computer is compromised and show you all the issues it found before asking you if you want them fixed.

The problem is that in order to fix them, you will need to buy the software first. Then after you do so it will "fix" the problems that never existed in the first place. If you see something like this on your computer, go to *Programs and Features* in Control Panel or *Apps* in the Windows settings and uninstall the software if possible or get some assistance from someone to help you. If it's not an option, then you will need to run your scanners to see if they can remove the software for you.

File Encryption Scams (Ransomware)
One of the worst kinds of threats currently out there involves getting a virus on your computer that encrypts all of your files and makes them inaccessible to you. When you encrypt a file, it takes that file and "scrambles it", for lack of a better term, so that nobody can read the file unless you have the encryption key to decrypt it. If you have any USB drives attached to your computer those files will most likely get encrypted as well. Plus, if you use a service like Dropbox there is a chance your remote files will become encrypted also.

This type of attack is often called ransomware because in order to get your files decrypted and put back to normal, you will have to pay a lot of money to get the key to decrypt them. This can often be $1000 or more. Even if you pay the ransom, there is still a chance you won't ever get the decryption key and just be out a lot of money. These attacks commonly come from different countries, so it's hard to prevent them or bring the criminals to justice. These types of attacks can come from something as simple as opening an infected PDF file from an email.

If you do get attacked by a ransomware virus then there is not much you can do except restore your files from a backup assuming you have one after you get your computer cleaned up. Your antivirus or antispyware software will most likely not be able to help you get your files unlocked.

Fake Websites
Another common way for cybercriminals to get your personal information is to create fake websites that copy legitimate websites in order to trick you into giving up your personal information such as passwords, credit card numbers, social security numbers, and so on.

They do this by duplicating an existing website, and many of them look so much like the real website that it's hard to tell the difference unless you know what you are looking for. Some things that will give away the fraudulent sites are spelling and grammar errors as well as low quality graphics and odd-looking text.

The way to distinguish the real site from the fake site is by its URL (address). Many times these sites will have a similar address, but just be off by one letter hoping you won't be looking or notice the difference. For example, if your banking site address is **http://www.safebank.com**, then they might make a fake site with an address of **http://saferbank.com** and count on you not noticing the difference. Then they would send you a fake or spoofed email with a link to the fake site saying something like there is a problem with your account and hope that you go there and log in, which will give them your name and password to the real site that they can use for their own evil purposes. Thankfully, you can't have two websites with the exact same address, otherwise we would all be in a load of trouble!

Secure vs. Unsecure Websites
By now you should have realized that the Internet is not a 100% safe place to be and that there are risks involved when going online. Thankfully, there are some methods that are used to help keep you safe when surfing the Internet. One of these methods involves securing websites in order to assure you that you are going to the site you want to be going to. To make a website secure, the administrator needs to purchase a security certificate from a trusted certificate authority and install it on the website to prove that they are who they say they are, and that all information passed back and forth between your computer or device and the website is over a secure connection. Most modern web browsers will let you know when your connection is secure or unsecure, but still let you access the site either way.

Just because a website is not secure doesn't mean that it can't be trusted and that you should avoid going to it. Many websites don't have any need to be secured because they are just for informational purposes and there is no need for you to input any personal information while on that site.

You might have noticed that website addresses begin with http even though many browsers hide the http and even the www in the address bar. When a site begins with http, that means it's not secure, and your browser should display a warning like the one seen in figure 8.3 (which is actually my mountain bike website).

Chapter 8 - Staying Safe Online

Figure 8.3

On my computer website, I do have a certificate installed, and many websites are going with certificates even if they really don't need them just so they can assure you of their security. Notice in figure 8.4 that the address begins with http**s**, and the S at the end stands for secure. There is also a lock icon next to the address indicating that it's a secure website.

Figure 8.4

Not all web browsers will show secure and unsecure websites the same, but it should be easy to figure out if the site is secure or not. For example, figures 8.5

217

Chapter 8 - Staying Safe Online

and 8.6 show two other browsers, and you can see how they both use the same lock icon to indicate a secure website.

Figure 8.5

Figure 8.6

If you are going to a website where you will be logging in with a username and password or entering any kind of personal information into a form, then you need to make sure that it is a secure website, otherwise you risk getting your information stolen. If it's a banking website or shopping website, then you *really* need to make sure that it is secure otherwise you are asking for trouble. Any banking or shopping website that is not secure should not be up and running and might even be a fake site to begin with.

If you get to your commonly accessed websites from your bookmarks, then you should be okay because they don't change unless you manually change them. (Just be sure your bookmark addresses are correct to begin with!) But if you do a search for a website such as your banking site, then make sure the link you are clicking on from the search results is the right one.

Figure 8.7 shows the results I get when searching for *Peoples Bank*. As you can see, there are several results, and they all have different addresses, so it's important to know the right address of the site you are trying to go to when it has to do with security, or a site where you might have to enter your personal information.

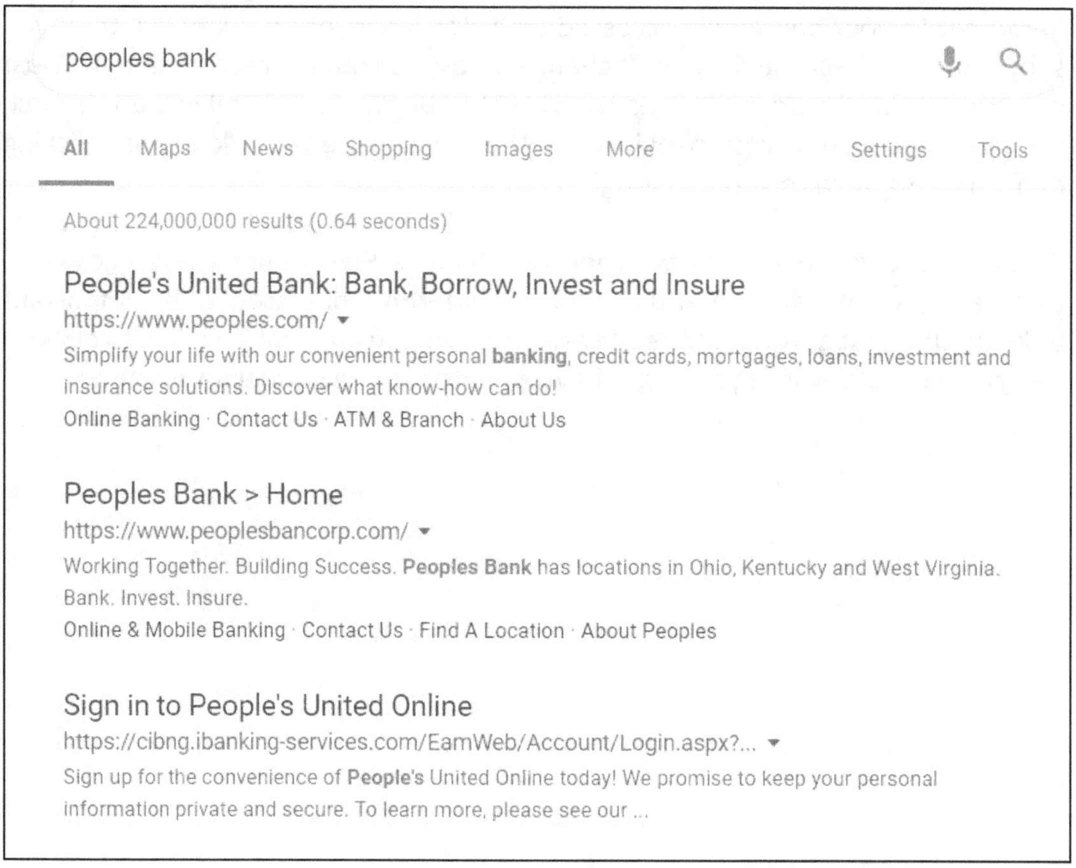
peoples bank
All
Maps
News
Shopping
Images
More
Settings
Tools
About 224,000,000 results (0.64 seconds)
People's United Bank: Bank, Borrow, Invest and Insure
https://www.peoples.com/
Simplify your life with our convenient personal banking, credit cards, mortgages, loans, investment and insurance solutions. Discover what know-how can do!
Online Banking · Contact Us · ATM & Branch · About Us
Peoples Bank > Home
https://www.peoplesbancorp.com/
Working Together. Building Success. Peoples Bank has locations in Ohio, Kentucky and West Virginia. Bank. Invest. Insure.
Online & Mobile Banking · Contact Us · Find A Location · About Peoples
Sign in to People's United Online
https://cibng.ibanking-services.com/EamWeb/Account/Login.aspx?...
Sign up for the convenience of People's United Online today! We promise to keep your personal information private and secure. To learn more, please see our ...
Figure 8.7

TIP

If you look closely at all the search results in figure 8.7, you will see that all the addresses start with http**s**, meaning they are secure websites, which is critical for banking sites to be. Try and get in the habit of noticing this in your search results for your own safety.

This also applies when people email or text website addresses to you. Before you click or tap on the link, give it a once over to make sure that everything looks okay so you can have an idea of what website it will be taking you to rather than just blindly clicking and hoping for the best.

Chapter 8 - Staying Safe Online

Providing Personal Information

When you do things like shop or bank online, you are expected to provide certain types of information such as your address, phone number, account number, and so on. But this doesn't mean you should just give any site the information they ask for. If you are on a site that does not require you to give out any information, then there is really no reason to do so. For example, you might go to a website and it will give you a popup to sign up for its mailing list. If you don't plan on using this site again or want to get emails from them, then don't feel obligated to provide them with your email address.

Many times you will go to a website such as a shopping site and it will want to know your location to show you their local stores, or maybe estimate shipping costs. When this happens, you may get a popup similar to what is shown in figure 8.8.

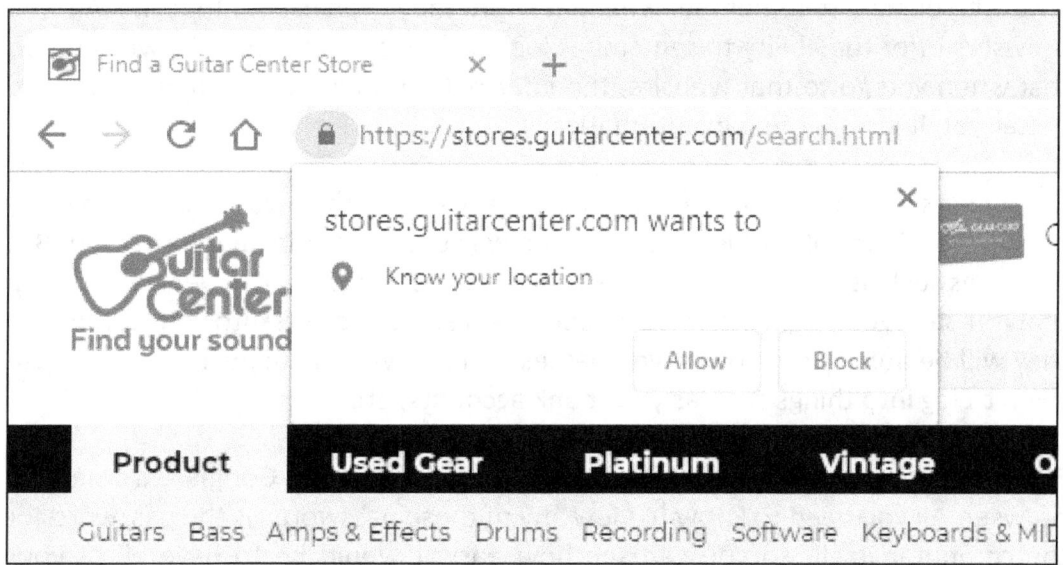

Figure 8.8

If you are okay with providing the site with your location, then you can click on *Allow* and it will tailor its results based on where you are. For the most part, there is no harm in doing this, but if you really don't have a need to give them your location, you might as well click on *Block*.

When shopping online you will often get asked if you want to save information such as your shipping address or credit card number. This is completely up to you because that way you won't need to type in the information each time you buy something from that site. I'm usually okay with saving my address on sites that I use often, but for the most part I don't let them keep my credit card information. (I do make one exception for Amazon.com because of how often I use their site.)

You should *never* give out your social security number unless you are absolutely sure the site is secure and it's actually a site that requires it. When typing it in you should see that what you are typing is hidden as you type. If it's not, then that might be an indication that you shouldn't be entering it in there.

Saving Your Login Information
Since technology has made our lives easier, it has unfortunately made us lazier as well. Nobody likes to type in their username and password every time they go to a website or have to remember what password they even use for that site. All web browsers offer the ability to remember login information for specific websites so that when you go to that website, the information is already filled in for you or, better yet, it just logs you in automatically.

For many sites this is okay as long as it's a website that won't cause you any personal or financial problems if someone was to get your login information. But for things such as banking, tax, or medical websites, you should *never* let your web browser save your login information because if someone gets into your computer, they will be able to get your saved names and passwords and will be able to use them to log into things such as your bank accounts, etc.

Figure 8.9 shows some of the saved passwords kept in the Google Chrome web browser. All you need to know to view any of these passwords is the password for the computer itself, so you can see how easy it would be to have all of your usernames and passwords compromised.

Chapter 8 - Staying Safe Online

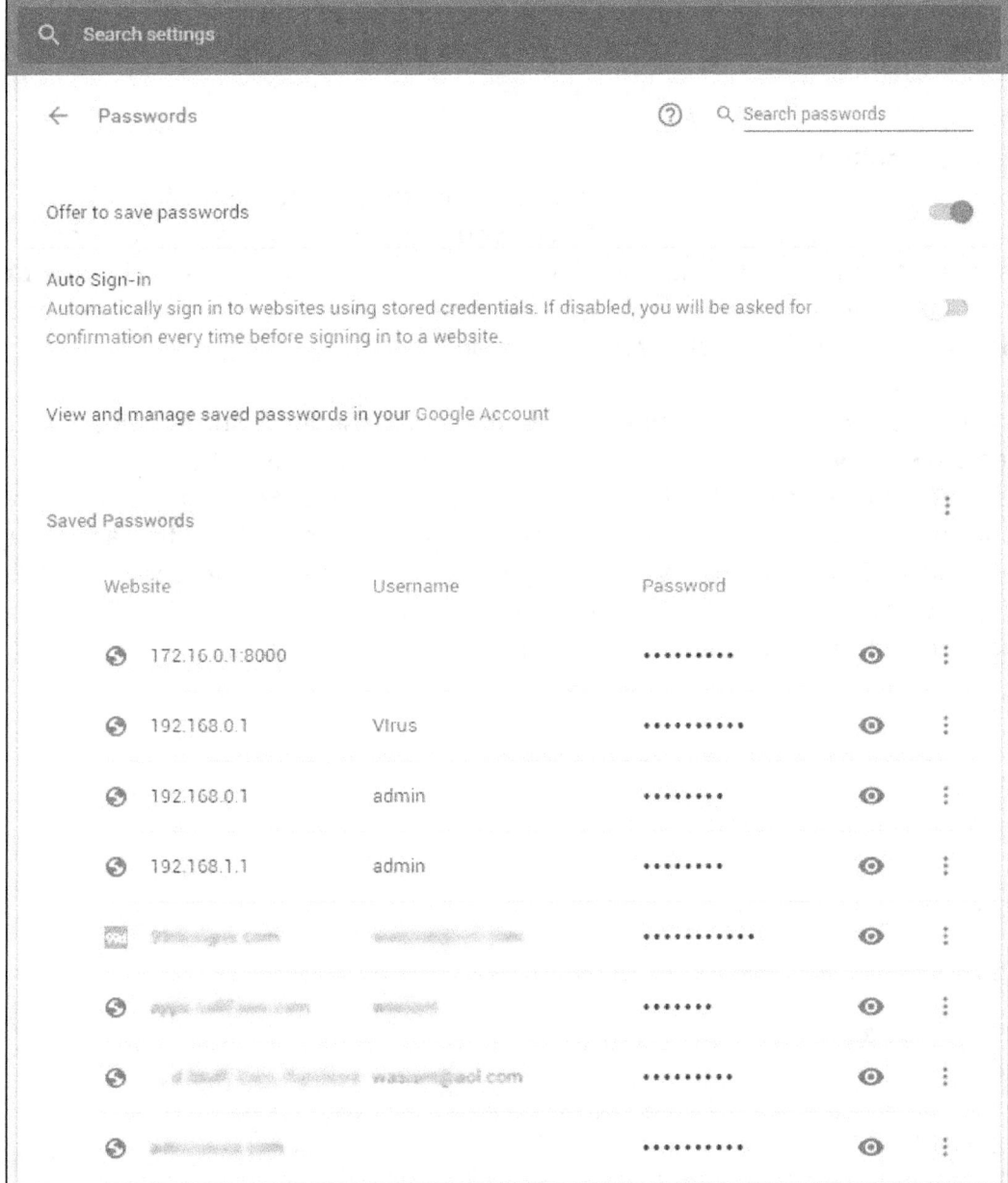

Figure 8.9

If you look closely, you can see the options to turn off the offer to save passwords feature, and also the automatic sign-in feature. These settings will vary from browser to browser and device to device.

If you have a saved login that you want to get rid of, you should be able to just remove the saved information for that site rather than have to remove all of them

Chapter 8 - Staying Safe Online

or disable the ability for your web browser to save logins\passwords altogether. (How you do this will vary on your browser and device, of course.)

Browser Toolbars

Browser toolbars are another one of those things that can be legitimate, or caused by malicious software getting installed on your computer. Toolbars are add-ons to browsers that add additional functionality such as buttons to easily check your email, the weather, or do specific types of searches. Not all toolbars are bad, and some people actually install them on purpose.

Figure 8.10 shows some examples of toolbars that can get installed within your web browser. Many times when this happens you will notice that your homepage also gets changed to match the toolbar that got installed. For example, let's say your homepage was Bing.com and all of a sudden you noticed you had a toolbar called *Social Search* and now your homepage was changed to *Social Search* as well. (FYI, your homepage is the website that loads when you first open your web browser and also what gets loaded when you click the home button in your browser.)

Chapter 8 - Staying Safe Online

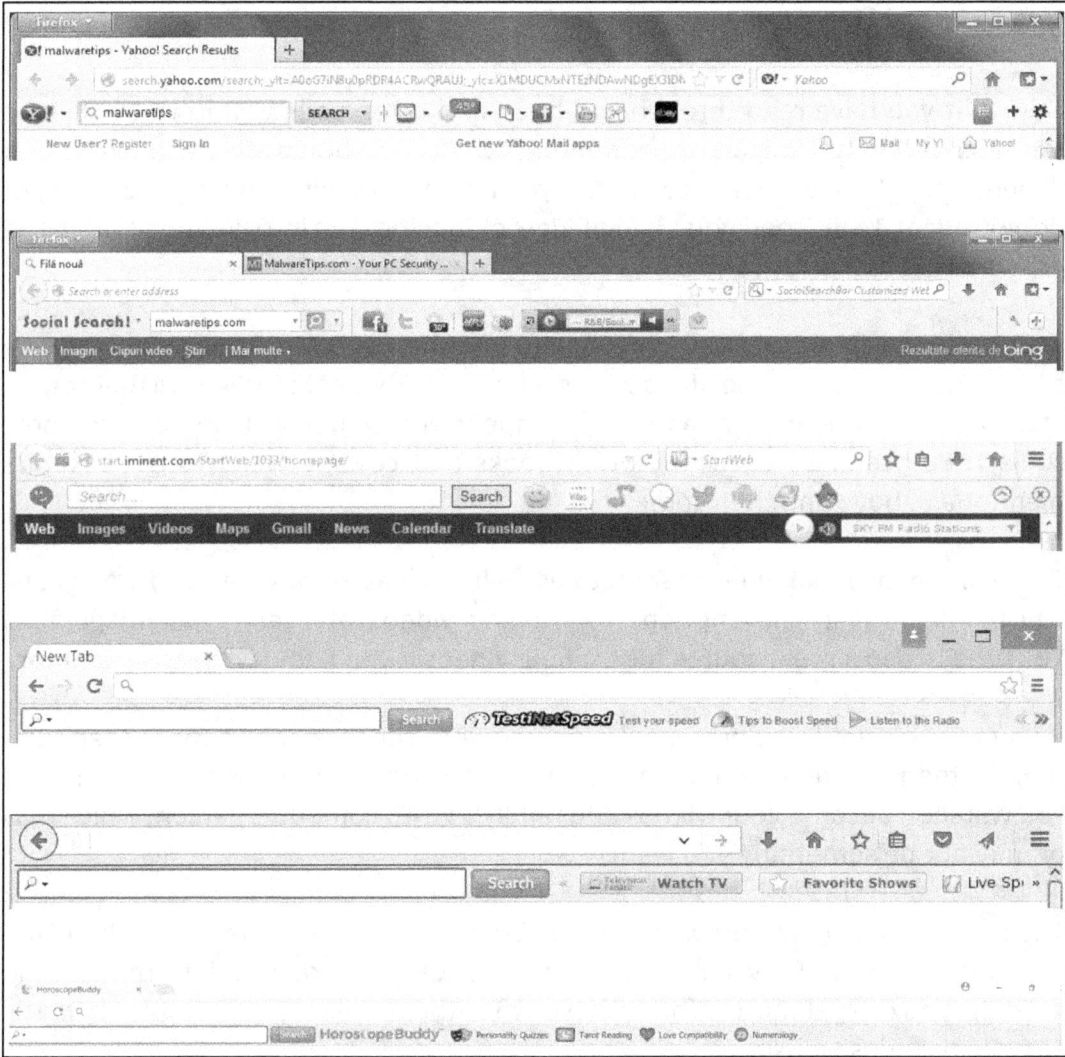

Figure 8.10

Many times all you need to do to get rid of these toolbars is uninstall them from your computer the same way you would uninstall any other type of software. (You may also have to use antispyware software to get rid of them if that doesn't work.) You might also be able to remove them from your browser add-ons, which is a little more advanced procedure.

What's Next?

Now that you have read through this book and taken your Windows 11 skills to the next level, you might be wondering what you should do next. Well, that depends on where you want to go. Are you happy with what you have learned, or do you want to further your knowledge or maybe get into a career in the IT (information technology) field?

If you do want to expand your knowledge on other computer-related topics, you should look at subject-specific books such as networking, storage, virtualization, etc. Focus on one subject at a time, then apply what you have learned to the next subject. You can also check my other books that cover a wider range of topics mentioned above and then some.

There are many great video resources as well, such as Pluralsight or CBT Nuggets, which offer online subscriptions to training videos of every type imaginable. YouTube is also a great source for training videos if you know what to search for.

If you are content in being a standalone power user that knows more than your friends, then just keep on reading up on the technologies you want to learn, and you will soon become your friends and family's go-to computer person, which may or may not be something you want!

Thanks for reading **Windows 11 Made Easy**. You can also check out the other books in the Made Easy series for additional computer related information and training. You can get more information on my other books on my Computers Made Easy Book Series website.

https://www.madeeasybookseries.com/

What's Next?

You should also check out my computer tips website, as well as follow it on Facebook to find more information on all kinds of computer topics.

www.onlinecomputertips.com
https://www.facebook.com/OnlineComputerTips/

About the Author

About the Author

James Bernstein has been working with various companies in the IT field since 2000, managing technologies such as SAN and NAS storage, VMware, backups, Windows Servers, Active Directory, DNS, DHCP, Networking, Microsoft Office, Exchange, and more.

He has obtained certifications from Microsoft, VMware, CompTIA, ShoreTel, and SNIA, and continues to strive to learn new technologies to further his knowledge on a variety of subjects.

He is also the founder of the website onlinecomputertips.com, which offers its readers valuable information on topics such as Windows, networking, hardware, software, and troubleshooting. Jim writes much of the content himself and adds new content on a regular basis. The site was started in 2005 and is still going strong today.

www.ingramcontent.com/pod-product-compliance
Lightning Source LLC
Chambersburg PA
CBHW080454220526
45465CB00006B/2263